CRITICAL TEACHING
AND
EVERYDAY LIFE

CRITICAL TEACHING AND EVERYDAY LIFE

Ira Shor

THE UNIVERSITY OF CHICAGO PRESS

Chicago and London

The University of Chicago Press, Chicago 60637
The University of Chicago Press, Ltd., London

96 95 94 93 92   5 4

Library of Congress Cataloging in Publication Data

Shor, Ira, 1945–
   Critical teaching and everyday life.

   Reprint. Originally published: Boston : South End
Press, 1980.
   Includes bibliographical references.
   1. College teaching—United States.   2. Labor and
laboring classes—Education (Higher)—United States.
3. Discussion.   4. Creative thinking (Education)
5. United States—Social conditions.   6. Education—
United States—Aims and objectives.   I. Title.
[LB2331.S49   1987]   378'.125   86–24986
ISBN 0–226–75358–1 (pbk.)

CONTENTS

PREFACE

Since this book first appeared in 1980, a lot of water has passed under the bridge. I reread these pages for the new printing and was relieved to feel that they had stood the passage of time well. I hope this book continues to help teachers as an introduction and guide to critical pedagogy.

I've been grateful to hear from many teachers that *Critical Teaching* was useful to them. Letters arrived from unexpected places, and I met many teachers on the road and in New York, all experimenting with liberatory education. Most of us work in isolation or in small groups, in schools, colleges, community organizations, church and trade union programs, and political projects. Our paths don't cross often enough, so it's hard to learn from one another's experiences. This book, my travels, and my correspondence enabled me to meet and learn from many teachers testing liberatory methods. *Critical Teaching*, then, became a network supporting my morale through the long conservative 80s. I also think of this book as a surprise magic carpet that took me to places and people I didn't know I'd visit. This helped to balance the long-term solitude many writers live with when we sit down to write.

I tell myself a few things about the passing of time: You can't escape your past, but neither will it desert you. Our experiences are cushions to fall back on when the going gets tough, as well as sources of energy that help us push ahead. They can also limit how far we can go and control what we choose to do. It's indispensable to know the past with a fearless intimacy and a critical detachment, but it's a great mistake to rewrite it. So, I don't want to revise this book. Not only does it continue to help teachers to transform their classroom practice, but it captures what I thought, felt, and did at a crucial moment in my life, in my teaching, and in a fateful episode of cultural democracy.

In subsequent writings, I tried to answer some questions raised by *Critical Teaching*. For one thing, I wanted to know why cultural democracy retreated after its blossoming in the 60s. Why did experimental and egalitarian programs such as Open Admissions fall in the political battles of the 70s and 80s? *Critical Teaching* helped me to articulate a dialogic pedagogy set against the political interference of mass culture, traditional teaching, and state education policy. In battles *outside* the classroom, we lost the conditions needed to pursue cultural democracy *inside* the classroom. This was very evident at the City University of New York, where a key national conflict was fought over Open Admissions while I taught the classes recorded in this book. A wonderfully creative frontier for cultural democracy was decimated at the City University in the retrenchment after 1976. I needed to study the political forces which invaded and dominated our classrooms. So, in *Culture Wars*, I analyzed the "conservative restoration" from Nixon through Reagan, in order to understand the reactionary transition from the egalitarian movements of the 60s.

Next, in *A Pedagogy for Liberation*, with Paulo Freire, I wanted to pursue some questions teachers themselves had been asking year after year, about the relation of liberating methods to social change; the role of lectures and texts in a dialogic course; the language differences between teachers and students; student resistance; the application of liberating methods to courses other than literacy; and the fate of liberating theory in the affluent culture here in the U.S. My dialogues with Freire confirmed the lessons of the Open Admissions battle—that the classroom cannot be defended from *inside* the classroom, and that teaching cannot work if it is controlled from *outside*. Political opposition on campus, in schools, and in society is needed to protect the right of teachers and students to invent the critical pedagogy we need. Lastly, many other teachers are carrying forward the work of dialogic education. In *Freire for the Classroom* I gathered some of their work as another guide for teachers, and as another indication of the creative breadth of liberating pedagogy.

No one book can possibly cover all the ground in a field like this, so it makes sense to tour the liberatory terrain book by book. Still, in this preface, which I think of as a letter to all the people I've met and have yet to meet who choose to study and practice liberating education, I want to say a few things that came to my attention when I reexamined *Critical Teaching*.

Fortunately, I discovered that I still agreed with the book. My opening analysis of why the corporate state invented the community college system and why the elite set up a debased and manipulative form of mass higher education for working people is still valid. The need to absorb surplus labor and commodities in the education sector of the economy is only more functional now in a period of underemployment and ultra-automation. The need to dangle a dying American Dream of upward mobility through college careers is only more necessary now in a period of long-term low-growth economics. This monumental decision to absorb the working class into vocational higher education still troubles curriculum planners and policymakers, while imposing severe pedagogical demands on classroom teachers. For one thing, the collegiate conflict between vo-tech careerism and the liberal arts is unsolved. The pendulum has begun to shift back to traditional humanities after the dismal performance of careerism and back-to-basics in American education in the 70s and 80s. But the old-fashioned liberal arts are not the "liberatory humanities" I suggested in *Critical Teaching*. The establishment's new "core curriculum" in traditional academic subjects is primarily a rote, passive pedagogy devoted to the transfer of skills and facts, not to participatory learning and critical empowerment.

Further, the conflict between higher education and the job market continues, with the flow of graduates still creating unstable surplus labor in the economy. Masses of people are getting more and more education while unemployment is high, entry level wages are low, and part-time work increases. Lastly, cutbacks in the public sector are generating more inequality, as the condition of public schools and colleges deteriorates while the private sector does well. Degraded public schools only produce more anti-intellectualism (the "discipline problem"), weakening the ability of mass education to integrate people into the American Dream. Students and teachers have gone on what I call a "performance strike," refusing to work their hardest under the austerity conditions of school and society. This strike has been misnamed "mediocrity" by the official commissions which have studied education in recent years. Thus, the social contradictions discussed in *Critical Teaching* are still operating, still undermining education.

Also fully operative are the social "interferences to critical thought" which I wrote about in one of my favorite chapters of *Critical Teaching*. Regarding interference, I might now discuss "mystification" in the Reagan Administration, which practiced information control and news management more aggressively than previous White Houses did. The Reagan drive for a conservative consensus in the U.S. included promoting a false consciousness about many key issues—inequality, hunger, the arms race, pedagogy, cutbacks, the Cold War, apartheid. The Reagan years were times of grand mystification. We were told that ketchup is a vegetable (when Washington wanted to cut school lunch budgets), that we'd survive nuclear war if only enough shovels were passed around, that people are hungry because they don't know where to go for food, and that the "contras" in Nicaragua were "freedom fighters," although many of their commanders were holdovers from the former Somoza dictatorship. The images of Reagan as very popular, as "the Great Communicator," were also carefully-managed myths flung about a leader used to performing with a spectacle behind him and a script in front of him.

In addition to this new intensity of mystification, I'd also discuss further the nonpractice of democracy in everyday life. My analysis of "the absence of democratic experience" is correct but can benefit from considering the differences between "democracy" and "permissiveness," to focus on the absence of formal political means to assert popular will. In our culture, the lack of independent organizations and mass parties leaves people without formal vehicles to remake society and to practice democracy. A corporate elite takes turns ruling through its two-party system. About 20 percent of the work force maintains membership in unions which can offer some protection for its standard of living and its work conditions. Voluntary associations (like ethnic or block organizations) occasionally offer group influence on politicians. For the largely unorganized people, instead of electoral and extraparliamentary democracy, "liberty" is experienced through consumerism, through feisty "bitching" on the job and in private life, and through the lack of traditional restrictions on behavior. "Freedom" is not the practice of democracy but rather the practice of shopping, casual complaining, and individualism, in a society which offers wide license for individualism. This recognition of "cultural permissiveness" as a substitute for political democracy could help develop critical learning inside the myths and experiences of everyday life. In my chapter on Utopia, I offer a conceptual study of "freedom" in experience, which can be expanded to include "liberty," "democracy," and "license" in a permissive society.

In the chapters on the theory and practice of pedagogy, I still find helpful the concepts and cognitive techniques for developing critical literacy in the classroom. These methods have been useful for literacy classes as well as in some other disciplines, notably philosophy, sociology, social work, and psychology. We can benefit now from teachers in other social sciences, natural sciences, and in elementary grades developing more applications for those settings. Let's have a hundred books on how to practice critical dialogics in every corner of school and society. In terms of the societal impact of this pedagogy, what I would want to point out is the difference between raising consciousness in the critical classroom and transforming society through political action. The two relate, and some of that relation is discussed in the coming pages. But, I would want now to define the classroom as a place where knowledge, perception, ideology, and socialization are challenged, not where the social structure of society itself is changed.

My interest in emphasizing this distinction grew out of questions that Paulo Freire raised to me in long discussions for our book *A Pedagogy for Liberation*. Another issue emerging from these dialogues was the teacher's "democratic directiveness" in a liberating classroom. Paulo's remarks on the responsibility of the teacher made me rethink my metaphor of the "withering away of the teacher." By the withering or "dissolution" of the educator, I meant a teacher-created "vacuum" which would open classroom space for the emergence of the students. As a Utopian goal, the self-regulating class represents a highly-developed group which requires less and less teacher-intervention. I named this goal "withering away" to help desocialize teachers from our previous training. We have little opportunity to study or take part in dialogic programs. We begin our teaching careers with little or no background in liberating theory and practice. Therefore, our most likely method will be a passive transfer of skills and information from ourselves to the students, what Paulo calls "banking education." I point to "withering away" to alert us to the habits of our own training, which was authoritarian, not dialogic.

The "withering" metaphor can help in our movement away from our authoritarian training. But "withering" does not mean a passive teacher or a permissive classroom. Teachers have a long-term responsibility to initiate and direct the liberating class. The teaching chapters in this book demonstrate the assertive role I take in the classroom. Teacher-direction must be democratically coconstructed *with* students, not *for* students, so that they codetermine the study. To invite students into a participatory, dialogic course, we must balance our strong interventions with restraint, so that the class is genuinely open to their voices. "Withering away" is a metaphor for the teacher's balance between saying too much and saying too little; enough withdrawal to create a vacuum for student assertion, enough direction to structure a critical inquiry. The teacher has to be careful not to substitute his or her own words or activity for the students' activity. The transfer-of-information lecture is a constant trap waiting for us with wide-open jaws. It's very easy for the verbal density of overtrained intellectuals to inhibit the verbal expression of students.

When we practice dialogue, what withers or dissolves is not exactly the "teacher," but rather the authority-dependence of the students, the authoritarian training of the teacher, and the ideology of a corporate society which socialized us into the myths and values needed to support inequality and a war economy. What replaces these conditioned habits is a camaraderie not yet of equals but moving in that democratic direction, in which the intellectual development of the teacher focuses inquiry without suffocating the creativity of the students. Thus, liberating education is not a *lecture* on freedom, democracy or domination. It is an educational *practice* which disconfirms the unequal social relations dominant in society and in the class-room.

In 1980, I wrote in *Critical Teaching* that "every major institu-tion of American life is in worse shape now than ten years ago—school, family, work, health care, housing, mass transit, the two-party system, welfare." Now the situation is only worse. The crises of American life are boiling just beneath the surface celebrations. Few crises received the attention devoted to the troubled school system in the 1980s. The parade of alarm-ing reports since *A Nation at Risk* appeared in 1983 has been truly stunning. But, the major commissions which defined the school crisis did not come up with workable answers. Authoritarian solutions can only worsen the predicament in the classroom. Liberatory pedagogy, slowly maturing for two decades in the U.S., remains one hopeful alternative to traditional schooling.

For liberatory learning to help in remaking society, we can consider being more than the very best critical teachers every day in our classrooms. We can also try to be the very best teachers and citizens outside of the school, in the community, the profession, the society at large; in groups, movements, and political arenas which influence social policy. In *Critical Teaching*, I wrote that "the consciousness developed in a liberatory course lays a base for transcendent change which will have to be fought for and won in multiple social arenas." Far from our heroic efforts in the classroom, far from our daily commitments to the students, lie the centers of power where the fate of education is ultimately decided.

I. S.

New York City, 1987

PART ONE

PROBLEMATIC SCHOOLING

Imagination is held in low esteem in the state schools and community colleges, where training replaces education....The importance of the socializing institutions is that they make unnecessary the open use of force.

Stanley Aronowitz, *False Promises*

...most employers simply raised educational requirements without changing the nature of the jobs....for a large number of jobs, education and job performance appear to be inversely related.

Work in America: Report to HEW

Because so many have been to college, a college education is now a necessary but no longer sufficient condition for social mobility. Not having a degree may block opportunities, but having it will not ensure them.

National Policy and Higher Education: The Second Newman Report

Very few of my 32 students will learn an awful lot this term about English, social studies, science or math. Mostly, they will learn what they can and cannot get away with...

Marc Bloom, "No Matter What," *New York Times*

CHAPTER ONE

THE WORKING CLASS
GOES TO COLLEGE

The Many Layers of School: an Orderly Disorder

Not long ago, most Americans never went to school. Then, primary education began spreading around the time of the Civil War. Soon after, junior and senior highs emerged, with compulsory school laws that helped end a long tradition of child labor in the nation's mines, mills, and shops. In the years after World War I, universal schooling through grade twelve was generally available and free, but still, many kids dropped out and few entered college. Now, a two-year college network grids America, placing a campus within commuting distance of almost every household. The school enterprise is vast and still growing.

School is such a routine part of life, that it's easy to assume it's always been here. Yet, it grew gradually in layers, one on top of the next, through periods of severe crisis and successive reform.[1] As it grew into being an institutional leviathan, it remained a scene of constant problems. Ironically, education has been demanded by so many and has wound up pleasing so few. Its current notoriety makes it one of the crankiest parts of American life. Something so big has gone wrong, that a parade of public and private commissions have issued studies. Some forty years ago, John Dewey was troubled by the failure of school to promote democratic literacy, a full century after Horace Mann had laid the foundations of mass education.[2] The old problems appear to be worsening. As schooling grows in size, so do its crises.

1

The rich vein of school issues has been mined vigorously in the past decade by scholars of many persuasions. One school of thought, known as "Revisionism," has attempted to revise the official image of American education as "the great equalizer."[3] The Revisionists' research strikingly demystifies the democratic aura of the schools. At the most schematic level, they argue that schooling is a device through which a corporate society reproduces its class-based order. The evidence for school inequality uncovered by Jencks and others fuels an awesome simplicity— school recreates a stratified society by socializing each new generation into its place in the established order.[4] This linear functionalism exposes the orderly surface of the vast school machine. Beneath the surface truth is a host of complex reversals. Both school and society cannot escape the contradictions of their own development. Besides being functional to preserving the social order, schools are also dysfunctional. They disturb social life as much as they stabilize it. The school saga needs to be both linear and paradoxical, because school often does the opposite of what it's supposed to. Like a psychotic patient, school is systematic and unpredictable. How come? How did a school system designed as a solution to social problems become a major social problem in itself?

Public schooling was driven forward by the force and cycles of industrial growth. A wildly growing and uncontrollable machine-economy rushed across the land transforming everything it touched, overwhelming the old things standing in its way and creating the new things it needed. In such a milieu, the early school reformers had every reason to be hopeful and every need to push ahead boldly. Confronting them was a scene of national disorder: periods of boom and bust, massive unemployment alternating with sudden demands for labor, ragamuffin gangs of unschooled children wandering the streets, great wealth and over-production side by side with abject poverty, a peasant-based immigrant workforce fresh from feudal countries of Europe, which needed conversion to urban life, English, machine culture, and republican institutions.[5] In a vast American frontier dotted with cities, New World Utopianism emerged from cheap land, no kings, an expanding economy, and the possiblities of a public school system.[6] Great expectations were applied to education: to democratize, equalize and stabilize an unsettled society. Yet, each form of schooling proved inadequate to the task. More layers were needed on top of the ones in place, spawning an immense education bureaucracy and the planting of another professional interest group in American life. It was surely in the interest of educators to propose more layers of schooling to increase their purview, while it was the search for a disciplined workforce which made school attractive to the men of wealth.[7] Working people and progressives, who hoped that school would educate and equalize, had their own humane agenda for the mass education system which grew spasmodically phase by phase. Now late in its development, it's not clear that school has satisfied anyone's expectations. Still, it spreads, with a new concept of "life-long learning" that can make school a cradle-to-grave feature of life.[8] More adults are finding themselves legally required to take continuing education courses.[9] All this may indeed be water for a drowning man. With upwards of a hundred million Americans involved in some form of schooling, the great national debate is over the decline of literacy, the breakdown of discipline, and the eclipse of reason.[10] As Illich has suggested, the spread of school endangers learning.[11] Mann and Dewey rest uneasy in their graves.

A New Layer: the Budget College

In the expansion of school, an unprecendented new layer emerged following World War II. With great velocity in the late 50s and 60s, workers started enrolling en masse into special campuses, the community colleges. The budget campuses represented a great leap forward. The new mass higher education quickly overshadowed earlier popularized layers of college, such as the land-grant institutions, night-school degree programs, and even the GI Bill which brought a million veterans to elite campuses after 1945. The new initiative called for massive state investment in community college construction. The strategy took over twenty years to fulfill, and now at its zenith, brings four million worker-students to campus each year. For the first time in American life, a whole generation of working people can take up college study on budget campuses built just for them.

There was a gold-rush quality to this scene of social development. In the 60s, two-year campuses sprouted like boom towns, at the rate of one every ten days. Junior college enrollment increased ten-fold in the decades following 1957. Virtually overnight, a headlong rushing economy created and peopled an educational frontier. This new line of growth became known as the "community college movement"; it was set up especially for working students. Now, with the early frontier turned into a middle-aged empire, we can ask who built it for what reason. Why has college suddenly become available to American workers? What's the meaning of this meteor which blinds as well as illuminates?

Community Colleges Absorb Surpluses

One way of understanding the spectacular rise of two-year colleges lies in education being a growth sector of the economy. School is a business activity. It not only trains people for their role in the world of business, but it exists as a huge market through which money, labor and goods interact. The enormous expansion of the education market after World War II helped stimulate the nation's recovery from the Great Depression. After 1945, the new American economy advanced through permanent war expenditure, through automation and computerization, through relating automobilization to suburban growth, and through expansion of the service and public sectors of the workforce. Internationally, dollars have been leaving America as multinational corporations seek high-yield and cheap-labor scenes abroad. A highly mechanized economy like ours produces great wealth. It can send its extra dollars overseas, to make more dollars than it can earn in America. However, it has severe problems disposing of its domestic over-production and its domestic pile-up of unemployed workers. Over-production and under-employment are the twin nemeses of American development. If you don't move the goods, then productive power only causes stagnation. Traditionally, wars and market-expansion have helped keep unemployment and inventories low. The worldwide depression of the 30s showed just how desperate things can get in an economy irrationally designed to produce more than people can afford to buy. Since that traumatic time for workers and capitalists alike, when nothing short of a world war could exorcise world depression, education has been mobilized as a surplus-absorbing mechanism. Large parts of surplus commodities and surplus labor have been absorbed by taking workers out of the labor pool and into higher education.

The building phase of community colleges employed countless thousands of construction workers who otherwise might have been without work. When the colleges opened their doors, they turned workers into students, reducing the labor pool. All the people who work for wages on campus are performing service labor, which produces no material goods, thus creating a locus of employment without creating more surplus commodities. All those who build, operate or attend community college are drawn away from the mechanized arenas of industry and agriculture, which now can overproduce with less and less labor. Further, the new campuses absorb enormous amounts of materials produced in other sectors. Junior colleges are activities which not only engage millions of people every day, but as waste consumption they devour commodities such as paper, furniture, brick, plumbing, bulbs, glass, office equipment, food, etc., and such services as computer grading and registration, banking, laundry, food delivery and preparation, gas, electricity, telephone, etc. Mass higher education is thus a unique device for handling the glut of unsellable goods and unemployable people. It develops the economy which developed it.

This arrangement is almost ideal. Mass higher education is a creative response to the ineradicable problem of surplus under capitalism. College is an attractive instrument through which to mediate human and material surpluses. Yet, the decision to build a massive infrastructure of two-year campuses has placed a permanent fiscal burden on the state. Here we have the spectacle of an irrationally productive economy which can move ahead only by creating gigantic non-productive parasites on itself. The vast school system joins the defense budget and welfare as ironic monuments to American enterprise. The sheer cost of sustaining these institutions is problematic enough; their day-to-day administration is equally stress-creating, leading to corruption, inefficiency, and alienation. What is even more fateful is that in their present advanced shape they resist reform and rationalization; they simply can't be deconstructed at this point. They can only be superseded by a more complex and more contradiction-riddled layer on top. In this scenario, the public schools promise to cost more each year even though they can't promise to produce more literacy or discipline. The colleges have the option of passing on some of their costs to their students, in the form of raised tuition. But the state will still have to drain capital from the economy to pay large parts of the bills. Besides, even if students are required to pay more, that will only create problems for other sectors of the economy. The money comes from the same pot. If students use more of their income for college, they will spend less in the private marketplace, causing stagnation in the consumer businesses. Because of all the capital already invested in two-year colleges and all the people involved, there is no simple way out of this. The fiscal drain is a large contradiction of the community college movement, but it is only one of many.

Warehousing Labor in College: Work and Worklessness

As a parasitic catalyst, or catalytic parasite, in the surplus-ridden economy, the two-year college network had built into it from the outset a divided character. A prolonged economic stagnation in society-at-large has now served to unbalance the network's role and identity. It has become more of a drag than a propellant; its parasitic side has become another institutional frankenstein in American life. It's tempting to moralize on how such an enterprise was doomed to writhe in its own contradictions, but hindsight is not foresight, and those who laid the community college foundation a few decades ago did not think of themselves as gravediggers. They saw economic and human development wrapped up in their work.[12] To a large extent they were right: the economy grew, people learned. Yet, like Oedipus, it's what they didn't acknowledge that caused the most problems.

One of these unacknowledged realities is that mass higher education is the largest warehouse in America. Surplus labor is stored there and regimented. The strength of this operation is the action it gives to inaction. Mass colleges are busy and noisy places. They project themselves as a necessary period of non-work which prepares students for their future earning of wages. Worklessness is thus neither empty nor permanent. Your removal from the labor pool prepares you for entry into it. Everyone knows how hard it is to find a good job, so it is entirely reasonable to be busily enrolled in college, as preparation for joining the quickly changing work-world.

The changing occupational structure especially affects young workers, women, minorities, older adults, recent immigrants and downwardly mobile children of the middle and upper classes.[13] The career curricula of the two year colleges is a paper replica of the job market, and thus habituates students to the shape of their future occupations. The essential narrowing of career options is re-presented as a legitimized field of choice, which you have to spend years studying. One of the sad realities of life in a monopolized economy is the stifling of ambitions of would-be self-made men and women. The closing of chances for self-employment coincides historically with the rise of community colleges, as twin phenomena mediated by the economy's growing concentration. The irony is that the dehumanizing impact of being warehoused helps discredit the same job market which the collegiate curriculum tries to legitimize.

While the warehouse idea is an accurate metaphor in the mass college story, at least two realities contradict the storage effect. The first has already been alluded to—the dizzying pace of the two-year campuses. They are very busy sites. The second goes beyond the colleges being the noisiest and costliest warehouses in the United States. While they attend college, a majority of worker-students are employed off-campus.[14] They comprise a low-paid, unorganized pool of temporary and part-time labor. Torn between family life, school-work and wage-earning, they live days of wild commuting from job to college to home and back again. They put in staggered hours for small businesses, banks, national chains, as helpers to tradesmen or assistants in hospitals. Supermarkets, discount emporiums, burger bins and gas stations depend heavily on this manipulable, unprotected source of employees. College attendance keeps students dependent on piece-meal, non-union jobs because they can't accept full-time work and easily stay in school. Many do work a full week, their eyes struggling to stay open in class. Thoroughly absent is the leisured repose familiar in the greenhouse college towns.

Worker-students have been warehoused in school largely as a result of the absence of full-time work for them outside. While preparing for your future work, what choice do you have but to support yourself in the meantime? The economy can wait to offer you full-time work, but you can't wait to eat or pay the rent. So, while in storage, you work where you can earn some money. These part-time jobs are an interim solution. They feel as temporary as college itself. What this situation amounts to is a simultaneous experience of work and worklessness. You wind up inside and outside the work-world at the same time. Community college is the non-work feature of a part-time work-life, while part-time employment is the wage-earning feature of community college attendance. This neat formula of being under-employed while you get under-educated sets terms most favorable to business. The cost-effective and anti-union dimensions of using part-time labor are obvious to management. The recent rise in the use of part-time workers is one of the more dynamic sides of the business world.[15]

Community colleges not only make demands on the time of workers which impede their ability to handle full-time work, but they also leave the students feeling as if it is the students themselves and not the economy which has chosen this arrangement. College is widely accessible; it's become almost obligatory in the job market. It has meant so much in the work-world to have a degree, that it's hard to pass up your chance. So, while you take up the newly available option for higher learning, the price you pay is being able to work only before, in-between, or after classes. After all, no one forced you to go to college; no one held a gun to your head. You walked in the open door under your own steam. So, part of the deal is part-time work and periods of worklessness.

Community colleges assume responsibility for the custodial care of all those students caught between part and full-time job lives. For a good portion of their non-employment and non-family hours, worker-students are kept off the streets, supervised on campus by professional, state-employed authorities. This collegiate warehousing amounts to the cultural occupation of life by public institutions. What school, family and job cannot invade, the mass culture industry then covers. The result is the liquidation of autonomous time and space. This is an issue of systemic importance. The continued hegemony of corporate life in America rests on its ability to crowd out alternatives. The successive layering of the school system fits in here, in the system's need to supervise potentially free time. As private enterprise employs fewer people for fewer hours, the number of workers un-regimented by work increases. As the work-world supervises workers less, school has been arbitrarily prolonged to supervise them more. It appears that the extension of school through college is still not enough. The invasion of unorganized time in daily life will be completed through the concept of "life-long learning." This contradiction between the actual and the apparent functions of schooling serves to discredit the whole enterprise. Because the artificial elongation of school makes it into a warehouse instead of a learning center, it is an illegitimate imposition on people's freedom and time. Students wind up being pulled in opposite directions by this. On the one hand, they need real education and school credentials for the job market; on the other hand, their time is being wasted. The result is a lot of anger, destruction of school property, and attacks on teachers.[16] After years of regimentation, students know how to sabotage classes at any level of schooling. How can schools be effective agents of social control when they are themselves barely under control? An elaborate exercise in order has produced alienation and disorder.

At this stage of social development, the die is cast, and the ironic search for order only deepens. Thus, the community colleges emerge and offer the business world its deepest penetration of higher education, through the career curriculum modeled on the job market, and through the marshaling of a vast part-time labor pool. The use of worker-students as cheap labor *while* they are in school, and the function of a campus to monitor them *during* non-working hours, rival the use of the two-year colleges as training centers for the *future* use of labor. The trivialization of work-skills through mechanization raises serious question about how necessary several years of college are to work performance.[17] What sense does it make to escalate the training of the workforce while decreasing the skill-requirements on the job? Business has always sought trained labor, but it used to do a lot of it at its own expense, on the job. The state has socialized business' training costs by building schools and colleges with tax funds. The college warehouses are maintained by worker-tuition as well as by their taxes. At the end of the road, an over-supply of worker-graduates floods the saturated job market, facilitating the practice of "credentialism" by employers. The credentials demanded for a job can be raised in a market where so many credentials exist, while the pay for the job is not raised, because so many aspiring graduates compete for the same positions. This is a perfect arrangement to depress wage levels, but the business world pays a price for it, in other more ominous ways. The whole transaction of work and worklessness is so alienating, that the labor arriving from college, fresh from the costly national infrastructure of higher education, is very unproductive.[18] Seeking some concrete economic gains, business has wound up with one of the worst productivity crises in the Western world.

The American Dream: New Colleges, New Careerism

The economic functions of mass higher education—surplus absorption, job-market promotion, unemployed warehousing and cheap labor channeling—are matched by ideological functions as well. A grand historical irony frames the whole enterprise. No plans exist to develop jobs equal to the training and education of the workforce. The creation of an over-trained and over-aspiring workforce is a tense social contradiction. With the paradoxes of warehousing versus educating, and work versus worklessness, the process of being-trained-for-jobs-that-don't-need-training actively undermines credibility in the system. A system which educates people for more than it can deliver is dangerously de-legitimizing itself.[19] By encouraging people to deserve what they can never have, the society and its colleges are educating their own gravediggers. Two ideological mechanisms have been mobilized by the mass colleges in their effort to navigate this contradiction: the American Dream and the process of "cooling out."

A disintegration of social life has made the invigoration of the American Dream urgent. Everyday pathology includes more than low productivity at work and in school. The rise of alcoholism, absenteeism, theft, sabotage, fights, lateness, and drug use on the job signify the depth of worker alienation.[20] In this context, the rise of mass higher education is an effort in civil restoration. The many new budget colleges are a unique form of ideological discipline. They serve to resurrect the American Dream as part of daily life, by offering a new way of "making it." In the new age of automation, and giant institutions, the Dream re-appears as an immediate promise of higher education leading onward to a career. The new collegiate layer of mass education borrows the "great school legend" which supported school and society in earlier times, namely, that education is "the great equalizer."[21] Until the community college movement was launched, the American Dream and the academy had never been brought together on such scale for an exercise in mass thought and management. Never before could the system afford, or did it need, such an advanced service from schooling.

In times past, white European colonialists found the American Dream in cheap land, jobs and the absence of an aristocracy. Later, in the nineteenth century, the Dream's legendary emblem of "Go West, young man," helped extend the borders of our settler state. As coastal and interior frontiers closed, the Dream for working people converted to a small-business vision. Since then, the absorption of family farms and family businesses by monopoly enterprise has made small-scale ventures a disappearing Dream. Today, instead of "working for yourself," a new goal is promoted in the culture—the career. The road to a career begins in the layered school system, where you gain the preparatory credentials for the work-world. In the 40s and 50s, it was customary to begin the career right out of high school. Now, college is virtually mandatory.

Pursuing success through the Dream, working people took to the land when it was cheap. They work when jobs can be found. They buy homes when mortgages are available. They go through school as each new layer appears. A theme of rising expectations has been the ideological force of their lives in America. Side by side with chasing rainbows, they have a cynical appraisal of life's real limits which contradicts their illusions. There is a tawdry dimension to the need to strike it rich: playing the ponies, dealing drugs, hitting a number, following the lotteries, sitting through poker and crap games, etc. In ideal or debased form, the Dream represents freedom from poverty, the dull routine of work, the arbitrary whims of bosses, and the intrusion of government authority. Freedom is not conceptualized as a new social order. As part of an individualized Dream, mass higher education entered on the ideal side. The community colleges appeared as opportunities for personal advancement, blending academic growth now and a career later on. This was an exciting turn of events. Only the rich used to send their kids to college; now, almost every family could do it, and then, mom and dad could enroll as well. The new colleges legitimized themselves by drawing on the old Dream, while the old Dream of rising opportunities restored itself through the new colleges. This marriage of the central American myth to the community college propelled the two-year network forward on a wave of dynamic values. In the social evolution of America and the schools, a myth found a new mechanism and a mechanism drew on a myth to invigorate the culture, ideologically and economically. Like the socially glueing effects of music, movies, fashions, sports and cars, the community colleges distributed their promises everywhere—a common experience for a widely dispersed population.

The convergence of a new form for college and a new locus for the Dream could not be achieved overnight, however. To facilitate the general entry of workers into college, a national infrastructure of budget campuses had to be built, thousands of new teachers had to be recruited, pedagogical and curricular issues had to be debated. Nothing less than a whole new college network was needed because the established campuses had costs, residency requirements and academic policies beyond worker resources. Besides, the new schools were to be low-budget phenomena. They were not to be designed in a style appropriate for the elite. The state's heavy investments had to go as far as possible if a national infrastructure was going to be built. Wood paneling, rugs, drapes, indirect lighting, upholstered chairs or quiet lounges were common on elite campuses but were inappropriate to the mass mission of the community colleges. Thus, an unprecedented building program culminating in the 70s filled the land with monuments to class bias and imperial bad taste. Using functional architecture and cheap materials, deploying hard surfaces and dull colors, the state inaugurated hundreds of non-residential, low-tuition community colleges near worker homes. After more than two decades of development, by the 70s, the mass higher education campaign had established beachheads in worker consciousness and neighborhoods. Developed especially for a non-elite constituency, the new schools assumed the contours of institutional life: giant parking lots surrounding drab buildings, computer registration and mass counseling, fiberglass furniture jammed against cinderblock walls, classes crowded into tight block-scheduling to maximize use of time, space and personnel, and the inevitable flourescent-formica cafeteria sporting food machines side by side with steam tables serving grey tuna fish and greasy fries. Mass colleges were not to be Ivory Towers or "the best years of your life" or homecoming parades on crisp autumn afternoons. They were from the start shaped outside the elite traditions of the academy, by the state for the masses, in the genre of public housing and the welfare bureaucracy. They were college and not-college at the same time, inside and outside the academy which had never seen such things before. The stark aesthetic functionalism was merely the product of the network's stark economic functionalism. The forces of work, job-market and surplus-absorption were modeling the mass college audaciously. This latest layer of schooling, aesthetically and pedagogically inferior to the rest of academe, appeared as a model of inequality announcing itself as another "great equalizer."

Such was the collegiate face of the American Dream turned to working people when the doors of higher education were finally flung open to them. They stormed in by the millions. Enrollments rose for twenty-five years, until 1976, without a break. After having been tracked away from college throughout American history, worker-students were now tracked in. They found themselves with the opportunity, the need and the desire to get advanced learning. Through national television, radio and magazine campaigns, and through high-school counseling, word was passed on the new college opportunities. Workers were seduced into the new career palaces by the mass media's reiteration of something they always knew—how much more life-earnings college graduates can expect. How could they pass up a chance for more income for the rest of your life? They also came looking for the learning that meant dignity, which brought respect, which restored them from the low self-image imposed by school and culture. Besides, the job market was fast filling up with college graduates, so they each needed their own sheepskins to compete on equal terms in a society where it's every man (and woman) for himself (and herself).

In popular life, the Dream had changed its shape once again. It used to be cheap land in a wild frontier where you risked your life to make it on your own. It used to be your own small shop, keeping nose above water in a cut-throat market-world, to make it on your own. Now, it's a college campus with a catalogue full of new careers, a new frontier where you need to go to make it on your own.

Shaping the Frontier

A frontier is an undeveloped piece of reality. It gets developed by settlers who use tools and ideas from old sectors of society. Their material and ideological resources create the character of what emerges, which is simply a way of saying that the new community colleges stand on the shoulders of the previously elaborated layers of school, and the previously developed state of the economy. Of course, the old schooling and the economy also stand on the shoulders of the new college network, by setting its agenda, by directing its course of development. The same forces which propel development also limit it.

A simple example of this relationship can be found in the way many community colleges began in high school buildings. Many of the early mass colleges opened their doors in local public schools, offering degree-programs there before state funding capitalized them into their own campuses. Neighborhood schools housed the new college movement before the movement itself was given its own home. Late afternoon and evening classes could thus be offered without delay, without the need for a whole separate educational plant. These early programs were close enough to workers' homes for them to attend after work, before dinner, or after the family was fed. The practice of chartering a community college on paper, before they actually settled in their own space, strangely mimicked the way royal charters were issued to New World conquistadors prior to their empire-building in the Americas. The charter-before-campus mode of community college development persisted into the 70s. It was a convenient *modus operandi* which acknowledged the fiscal limits of even the richest society in the world. The economy needed a mass higher education network before it could fully finance the operation. Community college planners were resourceful; if no high school was available, then they would headquarter the new two-year unit in an old office building, an abandoned army barrack, or a remodeled warehouse. Compared to Harvard, there was a certain lack of elegance. But compared to the narrowness of mass college opportunities before, it was a major breakthrough. Even with the sparest of planning, the implementation of this national curricular frontier was expensive, contributing to a 500% increase in general outlays for education from 1960-1975.[22]

Many community colleges not only began in high schools, but they often employed former high school teachers as the foundational instructional corps. In the dawn of its growth, the two-year network thus reached down to the lower grades for both its physical base and for its labor. The older layers of school were a primitively accumulated source of facilities and cadre for a new mass line in higher education. The secondary teachers who got the MAs and PhDs required to work part- and full-time in the new junior colleges gained higher pay and prestige. The college ambience, time off, salary and amenities made their move to the new layer a distinct step up from their former work. In this regard, the new American Dream on campus quickly went into action. Those teaches hired before the end of the 60s, when teaching jobs were still plentiful, experienced upward mobility, a clear example to their newly matriculated students. Driven out of the family farm and the family business, the American Dream reappeared in college drag, to legitimize the system once again. Worker-students who could no longer hope to go West, move to their own land, or be their own boss, were presented with a credible alternative: higher education.

Because the curriculum evolved as a careerist mirror of the job market, the college programs were vocationally weighted and regionally oriented to meet the needs of local business and government. Financed by worker taxes, the colleges responded flexibly to business conditions. Skills needed by nearby shops, hospitals, plants and offices took shape as one-year certificate and two-year Associate degree programs. For the most aspiring students, a transfer-track existed apart from the vocational-technical ("vo-tech") courses, enabling the scholastic fraction of each class to go on to a four-year degree. The campus challenge came at workers personally and immediately: improve yourself to get ahead, learn a new career. Opportunity is close by; your community college is near; you can live cheaply at home; you can support yourself with a part-time job; fees and tuition are low; your friends go there; local businesses are looking for trained people. On top of this appeal, the curriculum has been legible and even refreshing, promising a break from the old routine. You can become an orthopedic assistant, a legal secretary, a medical technologist, an X-ray technician, a dental hygienist, a child-care worker, or a computer programmer. You can choose among media electronics, mechanical, civil or electrical engineering, environmental science, auto dynamics, nursing or accounting. Skills once taught in vocational high schools or on-the-job were upgraded into paper credential programs, and re-named "para-professions," a linguistic hocus-pocus needed to promote career-ism and to integrate the Dream.

The attractiveness of this college menu is obvious. Worker-students took to it *en masse.* It sounded great. High school tracking and media messages made it sound even better. The social prestige of college, in the American folkway, added to the appeal. And then, to top it all off, the job market made it mandatory to have a degree. A career through college was the dynamic new ballgame, and if you didn't play, then you faced some rougher choices—unemployment, welfare, crime, the Army, struggling with self-employment or marrying money. There's only one job market out there, and you owe it to yourself to be fully armed in dealing with it. The open door of college, the new campus chance, offered worker-students another weapon in dealing with the work-world. Ironically, as a warehouse for surplus labor, the new colleges were also weapons of the corporate economy against the workers. The mass colleges which strengthen the hand of business over labor also strengthen the hand of labor over business. More worker-students have graduated than the job market can reward, putting social and ideological pressure on a strained private economy. Further, workers whose aspirations have been stirred by college study are proving to be the most alienated and least efficient employees.[23] Alluded to earlier in terms of the work and worklessness contradiction, this irony is compelling: the Western economy with the most advanced school system produces one of the least productive workforces. This speaks to the grave legitimation crisis in the United States. The land of opportunity had to locate its central myth of rising expectations in a new two-year college network, promising more than the system had to offer. Working people heard the news, learned the rules, and played the game too well.

Cooling-Out

The job market used to reward college graduates with the best work, prior to the mass arrival of working people into higher education. The occupational hierarchy simply cannot now accomodate the demands of all those who successfully complete college. So, along with college's offer of success there is included its denial. The elaborate process of lowering expectations, called "cooling-out," is where the mass higher education system makes its ideological stand.[24] Strong psychological prophylaxis is needed to prevent worker-students from expecting college to do for them what it has traditionally done for the elite. The Dream must be tangible and inaccessible at the same time.

The process of "cooling-out" is sophisticated thought-control. It transfers the locus of failure from the institution to the individual. At issue is the student's setting of goals and the student's perception of who is responsible for the place he or she reaches in society. As it functions in the schools for worker-students, "cooling-out" is depressant tracking. It is the ironic counter-point in a schizoid system which stands you up only to knock you down, which needs you to believe in a Dream that won't come true. When "cooling-out" works, the student feels that she or he blew the chance to make it, and what choice is there but to settle for less. The ideological trick is to change thought from "my unmet needs" to "my unrealistic aspirations." Because any system can only sustain itself by promising more, American society has itself provoked the high aspirations which it must quell to survive. To depress what it has released is no simple task. The giant school enterprise includes batteries of scientific tests, elaborate tracking schemes, and an army of counseling specialists, to facilitate mass "cooling-out." Sights have to be lowered because unmet needs and frustrated aspirations generate alienation and rebellion.

The importance of "cooling-out" in the community colleges is underscored by how soon it took shape in the evolution of the two-year network. By 1959, the "cooling-out" function was so systematic that Burton Clark was able to detail its operation, from his vantage point in the California system.[25] In the junior college, computer transcripts and apologetic counselors serve notice: It is your own dullness, your own thickness with book learning, that caused your failure and destined you for the lesser programs, the vo-tech track, the lesser career. The successful conversion to failure can be seen in the numbers who lower their aspirations. While some 70% of community college freshmen and freshwomen plan to get a BA when they enter college, only 30% go on to a four-year program.[26] Despite this appalling rate of attrition, the two-year system and the society take credit for being generous, blameless, and even democratic. As shocking as the high drop-out rate of the community colleges is the fact that some 85% of the newly educated workers must take jobs that used to be done by workers with less credentials.[27] Even success leads to failure. The irony of these motions is painfully obvious. Society offers a mass higher education system which does not lead its drop-outs or its graduates higher up. Economically, your motion is lateral, after spending years moving up through the school layers.

Despite "cooling-out," the millions of workers pouring into junior colleges do get the best formal education ever made available to them. Their desire to learn competes with the disguises and contradictions of a system structured for failure and built on a hyped myth of success. Because people in college do learn, even in the face of depressant tracking, the demand for open access to higher education is a progressive one. However, the growth of worker-students on campus is hardly straight-forward or uniform. There is a pedagogical crisis in the two-year network, as well as a fundamental curricular split, which frame a gallery of dysfunctions in the mass higher education strategy.

Functions and Dysfunctions

Prior to the mass arrival of worker-students, the academy had articulated for itself comfortable standards. There was wide-spread concordance on canons, methods, appropriate research, the proper place for women, blacks, and politics, the acceptable conventions of discourse, styles of interaction, reading lists and requirements. While the radical movements of the 60s shook things up at the top, the channeling of non-elite students into mass colleges shook things up at the bottom. A conservative restoration is now underway at all levels of the academy to reverse the political effects of both these influences. It has been necessary and convenient for an automated economy to warehouse excess labor on campus, and thus confuse the authentic role of college as a center of intellectual life. This development, however, has been most inconvenient to elite academics, who resent a plebeian disruption of their house of thought. Professorial resistance to democratic access has helped narrow the open door to college, under the slogan of "keeping standards high." Yet, the permanence of mass higher education has become a fact of American life, so the rollback will be partial and the crisis will need further resolution. To address the pedagogical confusion, a prodigious number of publications appear on how to teach the new learners. Commercial presses spew forth no end of tonics and cure-alls for bewildered teachers. Pedagogy has become problematic at the college level because working class language, thought, culture and experience are antagonistic to the genteel ambience of academe. Conversely, the elite training of community college teachers, in universities where few worker-students are enrolled, intensifies the cultural clash of the classroom. This kind of class conflict in the academy has spilled over from the lower grades, where it has been underway for a long time. With the rise of mass higher education, the institutional skyline of America now includes one more gigantic operation where clients and professionals struggle it out day after day. Between worker-students and professors, the stark difference in needs and styles is most often painful and destructive, sometimes productive, and even comic. In the disruption of institutional decorum, there is a real chance for supportive teachers and students to evolve an empowering worker pedagogy. Such a pedagogy can make the new colleges active generators of critical thought, an eventuality rich in possibilities because of the mass constituency served by these campuses. The dysfunctional potential here is exciting.

Day to day on campus, the process of mass higher education proceeds grindingly because the academy never had to "cool-out" or track workers en masse. Sincere teachers often find themselves caught doing imitations of Harvard or repeats of high school. Neither pedagogy works, leaving teachers at a loss to know what to do from any point of view. Worker-students sense the confusion, and the con. They rightfully refuse to perform in arenas which insult their intelligences or are rigged against them. They have already experienced twelve years of mass education, so they know what's going on, and carry over from high school much resentment and defensive hostility. Their "reactive stupidity"[28] includes passive and active resistance to dummy education. Non-attendance, non-performance and blank agreement with the teacher are the limits of their pacifism. Vandalism, fights, con games, drugs and alcohol, theft, and challenges to the teacher's lectures and methods comprise their active sabotage.

This disturbance of academic repose is an unavoidable consequence of a higher education strategy launched to solve economic surplus problems and to head off worse social crises. It is far easier for the state to supervise unemployed workers in a classroom than in the streets. However, as a dynamic and problematic sector of education, the community colleges pose a broad range of politicizing questions to the teaching profession. Dysfunctional debates around literacy methods, open access and cultural democracy, levels of tuition, equal opportunity for women and minorities, designing effective compensatory programs, and lack of parity in tax support for elite and worker campuses, create an atmosphere of consciousness-raising crisis. The democratic mystique of the community college movement gets exposed in such an arena of issues.

Women Rising

Another dysfunction of mass higher education is that in socializing women into the workforce it also de-socializes them by propelling feminism. The two-year network has made it easier for women to enter college.[29] College experience and defining career goals help worker-women develop assertiveness and autonomy. For women who would have been tied to the home, or to periods of part-time labor to supplement the family income, or to full-time clerical, domestic or service jobs with low-pay and no career ladder, the community college may prove more developing than it is for working-class men. Advanced study strengthens their self-images. A degree encourages women's as-

pirations and makes them more mobile, within the larger con-
straints facing all workers in the job market. The relative improvement of their subordinate positions is an aid to their emergence from shadow lives.

While community colleges will not equalize working people
with the upper classes, they can help equalize female and
minority workers with their white male peers.[30] This is a
significant dysfunction in a network designed to reproduce
stratification. For both women and minorities, community
colleges can play a role contradictory to their historically lesser
place in their class and in the economy. As college degrees get
broadly distributed, women and minorities will be assisted in
doing within their class what workers will do generally within
the economy: increase their demands. By gaining credentials
equal to male whites, the female and non-white sectors of the
workforce will de-legitimize their own cheap-labor status. In this
way, community colleges not only function to ease a divided
working class into its lesser place in a stratified job market, but
they also begin discrediting stratification. The equalization of
female and non-white labor with white workers will produce a
disequilibration on the occupational structure. Besides the
economic destabilization, there will be an ideologically unsettling
effect as well. The two most divisive forces in working class life—
sexism and racism—will be aggressively examined as women and
minorities assert their equality. An economically and ideologically homogenous workforce will cost business more in wages and
in political resistance.

The long-range homogenization of the divided workforce is
a potential built into the contradictions of a college network
which continues to absorb millions of workers year after year.
The equalizing effect will be gradual and relative. Its latent
disruption of the old order will be held back by sexist and racist
features of depressant tracking, in school and in society. Non-
whites continue to collect in the lower channels, while women
are pushed into the "helping" careers like nursing and secretarial
science. Meanwhile, the technology courses are over-repre-
sented by white men. Liberal arts is where the most advanced
women go to further develop themselves. Many male students
readily admit to taking liberal arts courses to meet interesting
women. The humanities curriculum is thus a curious and very

educational mating ground, a social mix quite unlike the macho encounters elsewhere. Worker-women can finally meet the men of their class on equal or superior terms. There is space in the collegiate milieu for an assertive intellectual life, which can mediate an egalitarian encounter between the sexes and races of the working class. The community colleges provide non-violent forums in which the internally divisive issues of sex and race can be discussed. These consciousness-raising arenas are a rare addition to everyday life; few exist elsewhere. They directly contradict the cultural divisions based on sex and color. Ironically, while the college-warehouse crowds the free time and space of daily life, it also opens up critical spaces not available in other spheres.

The opportunity to break with the divisive past is an exciting eventuality of the two-year network. Ideologically, it is hard to measure consciousness growth. Economically, it is easier to note the large numbers of women and non-whites entering college and getting degrees. Of course, ideology and economics interact, so the growth in one will relate to growth in the other. The mass distribution of degrees to females and minorities will undermine their subordinate wage status in the workforce. This will make the workforce as a whole less susceptible to its own cheap-labor segmentation. In this process, the case for women is most striking. The full-time increase of female students at community colleges from 1974-1976 was more than triple the rate for men.[31] Still, ideological change is not a mechanical derivative of economic change, so the community college as an arena for consciousness-raising dialogue is important in itself.

The de-socialization of women, minorities and the workforce has further consequences. While the two-year network has been especially accessible to females and non-whites, college as a whole has been affected by affirmative action in the 70s. Programs and courses for these constituencies widely emerged and are now under attack. In the 60s, higher education responded to questions of sexism and racism primarily at the elite campuses, where the New Left was then based. Now, with the mass absorption of workers into two-year schools, these issues have a political base in a mass worker institution. On the one hand, there is a politicizing effect when women and non-whites raise feminist and racist problems regularly in a class. On the other hand, there is a long-range and systemic dysfunction. We now have a permanent infrastructure of two-year campuses. Mass higher education affords women and minorities mobilizing territories they could not have built on their own. The two-year warehouses are ironic gifts from the state which matured simultaneously with the women's and civil rights movements. The colleges offer those forces a national structure through which to make concrete demands, in a decade when progressive space has generally narrowed. In addition to the consciousness raising which can go on in a single course, there is an invitation to agitate around micro-systems: enrollment and tuition policies, curriculum, hiring and firing of teachers, new construction plans, etc. Thus, a national mechanism to ease social stress and to disguise inequality winds up enlarging the terrain for political confrontation and for resistance to inequality. Such latent dysfunctions are significant as the base of contradictions from which a new period of insurgency takes off. They are manifested now only erratically, in a troubled pocket like the City Univeristy of New York. Yet, they remain as fertile fields of operation for the next societal return of mass militancy.

Humanities and Inhumanities: The Vo-Tech/Liberal Arts Split

All students face the most fundamental curricular split in the community colleges: humanities versus vocationalism. This basic incompatibility of liberal arts and careerism miniaturizes the contradictions of the two-year network. The vocational bias of the two-year network is as inegalitarian as the prefab architecture. By setting vocations against philosophy, the new colleges reaffirm the dead hand of school's narrow past.

Elite students expect and receive broad liberal education in art, history, science, etc. Contrarily, worker-students learn that liberal arts is a frill, society really can't afford it for them, and maybe they don't deserve it anyway. Besides, everyone knows that liberal arts don't get you a job. Stick to skill-training and you'll learn a career. This pragmatic advice, in a society with rising expectations, encourages worker-students to commit intellectual suicide. The school curriculum is structured so that they have to make exclusive choices between earning a living and learning how to think, between a narrow skill and a spacious encounter with reality. This bias against creative and critical courses in the mass college is fitting preparation for an occupational structure which will require no creativity or analysis or independent thought. Herein lies the triumph of a class-based job market over freely developing minds. The anti-humanities of the community colleges anticipate future work relations. The work-world can tolerate neither the economic demands of worker-graduates nor the development of their critical faculties. Career training is a way of keeping workers materially and ideologically in their place. Vocationalism economically reproduces stratification and politically retards alternative thought. The curriculum enforces the rules of working life. Employers do not want workers who think for themselves or who demand and deserve raises and advancement.

Vocationalism dominates a wide variety of mass educational facilities, not only the two-year network. There are vocational high schools and vocational tracks in comprehensive high schools, into which worker-students, especially men, are channeled. There are post-secondary technical institutes, trade union apprentice programs, government jobs projects, military training centers, proprietary schools, private company programs, and on-the-job training. Through this vast vocational matrix, the great majority of working people pass, getting a narrow skills-training which is identified as "education." From these bottom tracks of the school universe, worker-students get sent into the bottom levels of the job market.

The "cream" of the working class has two upper tracks set aside for it in the lower grades and in the high schools. One identifies mid-level personnel (public school teachers, accountants, grey and white collar supervisors, etc.), while the other selects a handful of worker-students for enriched and accelerated classes leading to university education. The university-bound fraction is segregated from its peers, into special classes in the regular schools and into special schools within the entire system. This extremely white group is removed from working class life by the state's meritocratic testing, and then trained to join the children of the elite, who get to the best schools not by merit but by their upper-class background. While state and teachers colleges receive the mid-level cream, the most elite part goes on to the best universities, where lavish resources prepare a literary/scientific cadre, an oligarchy of managers and thinkers. In this brave new world, the higher the school track, the larger the liberal arts component. The lower the track, the larger the vocational orientation. Career-training for the many and liberal education for the few corresponds macrocosmically to the different constituencies for mass and high culture. The small elite is afforded a broad liberal program of study in school because it must be literate and conceptual to handle its ruling function. It is exposed early to critical and creative learning environments because it is the decision-making, command-giving, problem-solving, and rule-writing fragment of society. Conversely, the vocationalized mass is prepared to take orders, follow rules, obey the decisions of superiors and look to the knowledge of experts. The restriction of thought and autonomy is the law of the bottom tracks of school and the occupational hierarchy. This regimented denial of mind is so dehumanizing that it provokes widespread resistance, commonly referred to as the "discipline problem" in school. On the job or in school, people of every age continue to resist depressant channeling. Their rejections are often morbid, self-destructive, or anti-social, a sign of how confusing the contradictions of late capitalism have become.

As the highest contradiction in the layering of mass educa- tion, the two-year network has both strengthened and weak- ened the state's power to vocationalize the population. The mere existence of such a vast network of junior colleges extends institutionally the long arm of careerism reaching out from the lower grades. On the other hand, in college, the state is now warehousing and supervising older people, whose maturation strengthens their ability to see through it all.[32] Older students are as big as their teachers and more worldly-wise, so they are more difficult to manage. Physically and ideologically, disci- plining them requires more elaborate security measures, and more intricate counseling, testing, and myth-making. While colleges have had their own police forces long before such things were needed in the lower grades, some routine violence of the working class high-school has made its way into the open-door network.[33] There are good reasons for these tensions. Through vocationalism, the state challenges the self-education/mutual-socialization that workers (who think for themselves) can engage in. Historically, the rise of vocational schools during World War I came at a time of radical labor agitation; state-controlled labor-training was a way of supplanting union apprentice programs and self-development by rank-and-filers.[34] Vocationalism thus speaks to a chronic generational power struggle between the state and the people, over who will control the use and possession of knowledge, thought, skill and training. The weaponry of the state in this battle over mind and memory is formidable; yet, it includes a self-sabotaging element: liberal arts.

Liberatory Humanities

The collegiate development of vocationalism is caught in the trap of its own advance. Mass higher education shrouds its inegalitarianism with a democratic mystique, but to support the mystique, it must present some authentic signs and substance of progress. To sell the two-year network as a new and genuine breakthrough for workers, the campuses had to emerge as real *colleges*, that is, a distinct step beyond the prior levels of schooling. This sets a broad agenda for change, administratively, physically, and pedagogically. The school principal is now called a president; the school grounds are now designated as a campus. The curriculum presents a more formal array of requirements and electives. In the pedagogical domain, the need to construct an authentic advance into the echelon of higher education compelled the community college movement to offer something mass schooling had dwarfed in its earlier layers: a humanities component. Without what is known as liberal arts, the new mass colleges would be ideologically weakened in their offer of progress, of something new and better than before. There is a price to be paid for the unavoidable inclusion of humanities in a mass school system devoted to vocationalism.

The luxury of liberal arts legitimizes marketing the two-year college as part of the American Dream, as an immediate delivery on rising expectations. After all, before the 50s, possession of a liberal education, a distinct stamp of status, was the virtual monopoly of the elite. Providing college and liberal arts to almost everyone is a great democratic coup for any system to manage. However, the trap in this process is that, in using an elite form for a mass mission, education planners had to develop for worker-students a humanities dimension which contradicts the evolution and effects of vocational tracking. There was really no way out of this. The shape of *college* has a strong presence in the popular imagination. This presence generates contempt, envy, and anger at the people allowed to get advanced learning. *College* in the American folkway includes liberal arts, the leisured, open studies where you grow into a *complete human being*. Who would accept the new two-year campuses as real colleges, if they offered only career training and remedial writing? Weren't the high schools set up to do just that? For mass education at the college level to distinguish itself as something new and better than the prior layers of school, more had to be offered. That more took shape as stylized vocationalism modeled on the job market, and as formal liberal arts derived from the elite units of the academy. The release of humanities into popular life was an inescapable concession. If the Dream, the academy, and the erstwhile vocational school machine were to be brought together for a new development, public education could no longer quarantine liberal arts from the working class. Thus, the two-year schools had to present non-careerist courses reflecting the evolution of Western thought: literature, sociology, psychology, history, political science, philosophy, economics, anthropology, art. And these rather non-utilitarian, unvocational subjects were to be offered to worker-students at their most adult moment of growth. Because liberal arts operate as much more than a mating ground in the two-year college, the transcendent possibilities are promising.

To see how community colleges enforce vocationalism is not nearly as promising as uncovering their contradictory and dysfunctional offer of humanities. Yet, nothing can be taken for granted. The de-socializing impact of a liberal arts class is hardly automatic. The historic flinging together of careerism and humanities guarantees nothing except an ongoing curricular confusion in the community colleges, carried on by a corps of exasperated teachers standing before an army of bewildered students. It is a social exercise only rich in potential. The possibilities can stay latent indefinitely or get realized only partially because many variables impact their development. They are conditioned by a number of factors inside and outside the college. The social matrix which influences the liberatory impact of mass higher education will be discussed systematically in the next chapter, but some elements of the problem can be sketched here.

The first item on the agenda should be no surprise: the job market. Forces in the economy are the prime movers in creating both the occupational structure and state policy vis a vis education. The job market is not only the model for the community college curriculum but it is the fundamental problem for worker-students during and after their college years. Confronted by the need to earn a living, they find basic literacy and some technical skills helpful in getting hired. They discover that connections are the most helpful thing of all. A command of the humanities is hardly ever needed in the jobs they apply for. Further, if the employer suspects you got too fancy an education, he or she will worry about hiring you. You might do too much gabbing, or talking back, or agitating, or reading on the job, or daydreaming, or thinking of moving on if you don't get a raise soon. Now, you don't have to go to college to be guilty of any of these things, but recent studies sympathetic to private enterprise demonstrate how higher education contributes to worker dissatisfaction on the job.[35] Scholarly inquiries have only documented what bosses and workers know in daily life—the more you can think and the more you can do, the less you can stand the work you're doing. Workers are alienated enough when their technical skills exceed what the job asks them to do; they get even more resistant when they feel as bright as the elite. In work-life, bosses and supervisors pick out the most critical and articulate workers for special discipline or for promotions that can buy off their exemplary resistance. Liberal arts education offers workers the verbal and philosophical practice to become leading factors of dissent. The employers know this, as do some union leaders fearful of their own rank-and-file.[36] Thus, liberal arts is viewed contradictorily by worker-students because their humanities education has *less* than no value in the marketplace; they can have their intellectual development held *against* them. Here we have a society which economically and ideologically needs a two-year network, but which opens colleges that promote (and a job market that rejects) the political development of worker-students. It is commonplace for workers to come to campus looking to be *complete human beings.* (Some use those transcendent words themselves when asked why they are in college.) They already know that liberal studies facilitate self-growth. How can you balance the desire for growth with the narrow demands of the job world?

The other side of denying what you do know and can do is asserting aggressively what the employer needs you to know and do. So, to get a job, a raise, a transfer or a promotion, workers shrewdly zero in on the technical and informational skills which impress the boss or supervisor. It's fair to say that a critical knowledge of modern poetry or the French Revolution will not help you make it through the job market. Politically and economically pressed, worker-students need to get in and out of college fast, into a full-time wage-earning position. How much time can you have for leisured looks at art and history, when the landlord, boss and banker are leaning over your shoulder?

Several other problems need attention in considering the liberatory influence of liberal arts. The humanities' potential for critical thought is matched by its potential for non-thought, on a number of grounds. An obvious issue in liberal studies is the elite, white and male character of its canon and teacher corps. The "great tradition" of any discipline, or what is sometimes referred to as its "architectural elegance of thought," is based in a tradition which largely ignores the achievements of women, minorities, and working people. It is habitual for humanities courses to have over-loaded reading lists enshrining texts by upper-class white men. A critical study of the "great tradition" has to proceed hand-in-hand with a revision of the canon. The growth potential of the humanities is enhanced by presenting more than the cultural works of one sex, one race, one class.

This obvious issue of liberal studies based narrowly in white, male texts exists side-by-side with a not-so-obvious problem: the politics of discourse. Seen from another angle, the humanities question is one of linguistic compatibility between teacher and students. Liberal arts teachers are viewed by their students as nicer and more visionary than the vo-tech instructors, but the humanities professors are also seen as snobbish, condescending, and economically protected from having to deal with the nitty-gritty problems of working-class life. Students are suspicious of intellectuals who hold forth on the nature of society, life and reality, when those same people don't inhabit the student world they analyze. There will be no simple answer to the cultural-economic differences between liberal arts teachers and their worker-students. The problem can be addressed, however, by examining how language either assists or impedes what Paulo Freire calls the "communion" between teacher and student.[37]

The opening issue is to determine how far the humanities have been vocationalized. Both tech and liberal studies can lend themselves to the regimentation of intellect. When teachers speak like imposing authorities who pour monopolized knowledge into students, then the students are turned into inactive objects of somebody else's process. Fortressed behind a lectern, professors can machine-gun lectures in ways which crowd out heretical challenges from less articulate students. An undemocratic politics of discourse allows the professor to dominate the process through words. Acceptable and unacceptable knowledge is decided by the teacher's responses and by the books the teacher assigns. Every teacher knows how to manipulate language to control the classroom, or at least attempt to control it in the face of student sabotage. Weapons available to the teacher include the special terminology of the discipline, the use of obscurely conceptual language, and the sophisticated wording based in ridicule, sarcasm, irony, parody, and innuendo. The classroom gestalt itself encourages the teacher's offensive via words, because both students and teachers have already been conditioned to accept certain rules of discourse: the teacher is allowed to speak whenever she or he wants to, the teacher asks the questions and the student answers, etc. A humanities teacher's linguistic style can retard student thought as effectively as the de-politicized vo-tech courses, unless the teacher presents her or his expertise in democratic discourse to students, critically questioning each other, as well as the orthodoxy, for mutually evolving awareness, or "conscientization," in Freirian terminology.

Besides the issue of language, there is a further complexity in the transcendent potential of humanities. It involves the differing mystiques attached to vocational and to liberal studies. Technical training does not claim to be liberatory or personally illuminating. It only claims to be the route to a job. Now, as the job market tightens, the career potential of the vo-tech curriculum gets harder to sustain. Yet, it's still a surer bet to lean on a tech skill than on liberal arts when you hope to land a job. On the other hand, the humanities component of the community college has to justify its self-promoting mystique of opening new worlds of experience. It is precisely this promise which makes liberal arts courses so marketable in the expanding adult education world. The humanities offer a place to grow, to change yourself, to examine things in new ways. All sides of the political spectrum believe that there is foundation to this transcendent fancy, because the right opposes liberal arts as strongly as the left supports it. Humanities courses suffer in periods of conservative resurgence, when regressive forces push a broad agenda that includes more testing, stiffer requirements,and fewer electives in college for liberal studies.[38] Why is the right uncomfortable with liberal arts? It's not a coincidence. There is an unpredictable quality to a thoughtful reflection on history, experience and ideas. A key to transcendent consciousness-change lies in critically studying the shape and motions of life. Electrical tech and computer courses do not ask for or allow moments of detached reflection. An encounter with the larger issues of human history can be devilishly and unexpectedly developmental. To the dismay of vocationalists and the delight of humanists, this growth potential is a rich possession of liberal studies. The question remains whether or not humanists can take advantage of the opportunity dumped in their laps, to promote spacious development at the mass colleges.

Every liberal discipline has a role to play in the transcendent potential of cultural reflection. Humanities teachers can be aided by a critical revaluation of our classroom practice as well as our own educations, to see what moments held us back or propelled us forward. Negative examples abound. When I studied American history in college, I never heard about the IWW or the Socialist Party or Mother Jones, Emma Goldman or Sojourner Truth, but I did learn that the Great Depression involved a lot of New Deal legislation sponsored by Roosevelt. My literature courses had many shrines for me to worship— Spenser's *Faerie Queene*, Wordsworth's countless walks in the forest, Tennyson's lifetime laments for his lost friend Hallam, Arnold ready to join his Empedocles leaping into Aetna. Fortunately, I had enough exposure to a few critical teachers, whose example helped distance me from worshipping monuments, even though these male pro-

fessors never mentioned such words as marxism, socialism, revolution, capitalism, feminism, etc. Who can tell what the mere
presence of these words would have meant, in an educational
process that was primarily stacked against my own developing
thought. Schooling was not rooted in the reality around me. College was not about my practice of freedom, my exercise of
democracy, my thinking critically. An appeal to critical thought
and a strategic relation to daily life can help existentialize academic study while intellectualizing experience. These values are
weapons in the war of humanities against vocationalized
thought. The need is urgent where vocationalism is strongest:
community colleges.

The task will not be easy but it will give to the community
colleges the most meaningful education they can offer. The
Freirian emphasis on dialogue instead of lectures is one critical
touchstone, but other values for implementation include rigor
and comedy. A democratic, entertaining and penetrating dialogue can be a dynamically developing way to present the
invisible histories of social movements, to set about bringing art
and philosophy into the mainstream of life. These are some of
the values and modes which can fully exploit the liberatory
potential of humanities education. These goals, and others
discussed in the pedagogical sections following, justify the
transcendent mystique of liberal studies.

If liberatory humanities sink deep roots, the system will
have a high political price to pay for warehousing adult workers
in college. The delayed arrival of workers into fixed jobhood can
ease an economic problem only by propelling an ideological one.
The seeds of a long-range conflict are being sown here, in the
potential emergence of a grass-roots intelligentsia and in the
forging of an empowering worker pedagogy. Some contradictions in the economy will serve to promote liberal arts, despite
the general conservative reaction against them, so humanities
teachers may be called upon to teach larger numbers of students.
A tight job market will force workers to spend more time in
college, getting more credentials demanded by employers, and
simply as a result of there being no full-time labor out there to
occupy their time. The two-year Associate degree will not be
enough of a weapon in the work-world, so more students will be
forced to get the next degree. The longer students are in college,

the more liberal arts they wind up taking. They may not choose to become liberal arts majors, because the tech courses will still have stronger clout in the job market, but they will spend more semesters taking humanities courses. Each year they are compelled to stay in school by the lack of jobs, they will be studying at a more mature moment of their own development, and will get more out of their humanities courses thanks to the prior years of college time which habituate them to intellectual life. Further, as the fiscal crisis of the state remains, there will be some pressures to freeze school budgets. Because liberal arts education costs about half as much as vo-tech, the system will just find it cost-efficient to pack students into humanities classes, which require no special machinery or equipment besides the brain and voice of the teacher. As hundreds of worker-students get pushed into large liberal arts courses, there will be tremendous force on the teacher to lecture her or his way out of the madness. An arena-room jammed with fifty or a hundred students will put the greatest strain on a humanist's ability to invent dialogic education. As a brake on these eventualities, the forces of "cooling-out" have been accelerating. The rise in tuition levels, the imposition of entry and exit testing, the reduction in sources of financial aid and compensatory tutoring, all work to stop the rushing growth of the two-year network, and keep its student population leveled at four million.[39] In this push and pull, the system is truly caught between Scylla and Charybdis. If students are not warehoused on campus, they will loiter the streets and create police problems, social stress, etc. If students are warehoused in college, they will take more liberal arts and cost the strained public sector monies in support. If liberal arts are closed down, then the costly vo-tech courses have to be expanded. If the expensive tech courses are limited, then the students will have to go into unpredictable liberal arts. If students are cooled-out of college, there won't be work for them outside. If they are kept in college, they will expect even better jobs later on. The labyrinth only deepens.

Minds in a Maze: Limits and Transcendence

Before college even begins, students have already spent nearly 13,000 hours in the school maze. Each layer relentlessly circles you on to the next. The pervasive repetition of material year after year encourages students to fade out. Their *refusal* to perform is generally interpreted by teachers as their *inability* to perform. In truth, we know little of how much working people can do, in school, or in other arenas of regimented life. So much of their energy is guarded, that on the job or in class we see only a fragment of their abilities. The most concrete meaning of their alienation is that they will not break their backs to make a boss rich or a teacher happy. What's in it for them?

At the community colleges, workers easily see that they are higher education's third-class citizens. The cheap facilities, bad food, and bureaucratic rigmarole signal that college is one more impersonal institution set up for them by someone else. So, they hold back, withdraw, resist. A succession of experiences through the institutions of American life has left them with "institutional" personalities. They have accumulated injured pride, fear of failure, need for recognition, self-doubt, cagey watchfulness, and unpurged anger. This psychology of defensive withdrawal develops over a long period of time through their institutional transactions. No wonder, then, that the non-institutional streets around schools and the unsupervised hallways around classrooms are so noisy, while the classes themselves are so lifeless. On the job, the noisy non-custodial space includes bathrooms, lunchrooms, diners, parking lots and bars. Worker-students entering school's doors walk through a membrane that triggers their institutional behavior. Their action in this setting is marked by silence, submission or sabotage. In this pathological complex, the community colleges play an equivocal role. By simultaneously promoting and cooling-out aspirations, they cause more confusion.

Because of so much regimentation and so little chance to practice freedom in daily life, worker-students react to college and other official moments of society with a highly armored, self-protective suspicion. Wary of teachers, even benign or radical ones, they may simply choose not to cooperate with democratic pedagogy. Many will not be able to notice or respond to an egalitarian mode in class. This will discourage teachers as well as those students ready for an empowering classroom. Teachers invest so much ego-energy into their courses that they get easily hurt when students refuse to participate. Discouraged, they may simply blame the students and find themselves drifting back to the pedagogy of the talking teacher. The widespread non-cooperation of worker-students with even the best-meaning teachers is not personally directed at the lone teacher in the room, but he or she will most likely take it personally. It helps to remember that student-teacher conflicts are social problems. Students resist because daily life has made them justifiably mistrustful. Why should they risk more humiliation in a game rigged against them? The big lesson of everyday experience is that you have to make it on your own. Class solidarity is very low; students can mistrust each other as much as they mistrust their teachers. They have trouble believing that people who are not relatives or close friends will be honest with each other or will take risks for someone else. Being cagey is a survival skill, useful in school and every place else.

This sad but inevitable individualism is strengthened by a dual quality in their social lives. Their potential for collective life is distorted not only by sexism and racism, but also by the presence of too much and too little order at the same time. Sometimes they have to live by the law of the jungle and sometimes they must submit to impervious bureaucracies. The rules governing daily life swing from feudal rigidity to threatening lawlessness. Either they are surrounded with too many rules, too many laws, too much red tape, or too many responsibilities (school, work, union, family, church, motor vehicle bureau, internal revenue service, credit payment plans) or they are thrown into a dog-eat-dog world (the un-secure streets, the rushing highways, the changing job market, the consumer frauds of businesses and of "fences" selling hot goods on the sly). These polarities of daily life create the simultaneous experience of too much and too little structure. This schizoid contradiction evokes defensive mistrust on a mass scale. The routine paranoia you get from everyday life does more than isolate you socially; it also atomizes or disintegrates your perception. It is hard to gain a structural knowledge of the whole, a conceptual or systemic appreciation of society, when you are always dealing with pieces and fragments making big demands on you. Knowledge of reality is as divided as humanity, into confused and conflicting parts instead of a meaningful whole.

A liberatory classroom which stimulates conceptual thought can surely address the need for systematic knowledge. However, this need for structural perception is hardly acknowledged by the worker-students who come to college. They have other means to deal with the social contradictions of life. They try to identify an affinity group of relatives, friends or co-workers who agree to cover for each other, who make a commitment to go down or up together. While they wind up choosing members of their own class for this voluntary grouping, it is a tribal rather than a class-based survival mechanism. Sometimes you turn to an aid society based in a union, a church or an ethnic association for help. You can call on the priest, the rabbi, or the local don, when other forms of assistance fail. But you start with your family or your best friend. This rather ordinary means of defensive networking does not exist side by side with an extraordinary vision of social change.

Defensive individualism leads worker-students to sit tight in class, checking things out to learn the score. To them, liberated classrooms will be unfamiliar and threatening, at first. As their defenses lower, they will pour out complaints about bosses, cops, teachers, parents, judges, shopkeepers, landlords, corporations, etc., even as they remain convinced that they live in the best country in the world. If the learning process of critical awareness sinks root, they become ecstatic to discover how smart they are, even though they begin thinking that knowledge is only what the teacher and the library have. This critical self re-appraisal is one foundation on which social vision is built. A class in the politics of imagination stimulates their imagination of politics.

There are further contours to the strengths remaining in worker-students despite a fragmented social life and their institutional ordeals. They pride themselves on their toughness. They don't whine, ask for pity, or feel sorry for themselves. Their need to show the world that they can take it leads them to reject help, even when they want it. This is their way of preserving their autonomy. They express a rebellious independence in the face of giant institutions which have tried to make them obedient. The thumbs of authority have left them neither docile nor defeated. When it comes to getting something they really want, like a car or a camera or tickets to a concert or cheap car insurance, they marshal enormous energy. Surrounded by hostile street life, disapproving authorities, and a competitive job market, they still value friendliness and fair play. Contradicting their commitment to fairness is the way the men trade in violence against each other, against women and children, and against minorities. They do this to gain respect in a society that denigrates them and to feel power in a culture that sinks them to the bottom. The sexist and racist powermongering of some white male workers serves as a restorative to their damaged egos, in the absence of other means to feel good about themselves. Engaged in no unifying and organized reconstruction of themselves and society, the men are most susceptible to divisive aggression against other sectors of their class. They are riddled by feelings of inadequacy in a society that glamorizes the rich and powerful. Their sexist and racist feelings are difficult to transcend in class, but it can be done. The men are especially sentimental about everybody getting along with each other. They want social harmony among the races, love between the sexes, tolerance for differences, and golden childhoods for the kids. So, they contain within themselves a nascent critique of their own violent potentials. Further, they have a deep distrust of bosses, superiors, politicians and the rich. Most encouraging is that years of depressant socialization in and out of school has not erased their abilities to learn to think critically and creatively.

These cultural skills are not easy to gain. My own experience of being lifted out of the working class and sent on to the university has shown me how long it takes. Critical education can be an empowering support for social emergence. Reading closely, writing clearly, thinking critically, conceptualizing and verbalizing, are some means to penetrate the maze of reality. These are foundations for becoming a conscious re-maker of social life. The chance to gain this consciousness is available now at a wider variety of colleges than when I became a freshman in the 60s.

Open Doors and Closing Ones

The open door to community colleges has been closing. Tuition increases and restrictive academic policies have served to level off the burgeoning enrollments of the two-year schools. The monumental expansion of the nation's junior campuses has completed its line of development in American life. When a growing, war-based economy in the 50s and 60s fueled college growth, the growth of the colleges fueled economic expansion by absorbing surplus goods and labor. Now, stagnation in the economy compels the system to offer less of everything while charging more. High levels of unemployment and cutbacks in public sector funds require limiting the costs and the job-market saturation of the two-year colleges.

As community colleges get settled onto a plateau, two dynamic policies are emerging to deal with education in the economy. These plans involve curriculum conversions at all levels of mass education. The first strategy is for "career education" in the lower grades, while the second is to expand "adult education" in place of full-time college study. Career-educationists appear to have the final solution for the problem of the public schools. They propose the complete vocationalization of schooling. According to their plans, school children will be tracked into narrow clusters like health employment and secretarial science.[40] This kind of gambit intends to restore discipline and legitimacy to the ailing schools by bringing the imposing work-world completely into education. The effect will be to depress the economic and collegiate aspirations of worker-youth as early in life as possible. Adolescents will be prepared through junior and senior high to go to work right after secondary school, instead of going on to college. In fact, school kids will begin cheap-labor apprenticeships while in high school, lured by spending money and time away from stuffy classrooms. Overall, it's an accelerated form of "cooling out," which tells us that the cost of combining college and the American Dream has gotten out of hand.

A second development, "adult education," is also a contradictory phenomenon. While adult ed has been around for decades, its recent efflorescence represents a new mass line in higher education.[41] It serves to replace *full-time, degree-bearing* study with *part-time, non-degree* coursework. This conversion of college in popular life will help reduce the numbers of graduates in the job market and will also reduce the cost of education on the state. Community colleges will recede as career-ladders for worker-students as adult ed advances. Carried on by night and on weekends, this familiar but newly booming form of part-time college is structured piecemeal to go on and on in a student's life. The formula is so cost-effective because part-time students wind up paying by the credit, on a full-time pro-rated tuition scale. Further, it is easy to assign part-time teachers to adult ed courses, where the instructors are paid less than half what full-time professors teaching full-time students get. Not only does adult ed make colleges more self-supporting and less in need of state subsidies, but it also promises students no pot of gold at the end of the rainbow. The new adult ed does not forbid anyone from trying to get a better career out of college study, but it makes it harder. The "cooling-out" from economic advancement is softly structured in the prolonged nature of part-time college work. At the same time that career-ladders are pulled out from under worker-students, the blow is softened because they are offered something new and good. Adult ed is a less costly and more adventurous form of study. It cannot sell itself without personalizing and humanizing its learning milieu. The colorful array of adult ed courses promotes a mystique of creative self-growth. The impressive offerings invite you to study playwriting or basic Russian, Egypt or photography, ceramics or the modern novel, wine-making or existentialism, small-business accounting or social life in Cuba. Confronted by this exciting menu, adults have taken the ball and run. Like all those who come to the community colleges, they continue to pursue educational chances in any form offered.

As a phenomenon of vigorous development in the midst of economic decline, adult education is a short-term measure with built-in contradictions. Because more adults will receive cheaper doses of college, larger numbers of worker-students will be brought to campus than are now there. Many working adults who could not afford the time or money for full time attendance will now find themselves able to add academic study space to their lives. This can lead to unpredictable critical and creative growth on an even larger scale than facilitated through full-time matriculation on a two-year campus. Because schooling through adult ed makes smaller demands on your time and money, and because it is a form of study less ruled by careerism, you can get into the work with less anxiety, less vocational interference to thought, and more voluntary enthusiasm. It's the kind of solution that costs you and the system less money, but only by allowing you more choice and more free space to learn. The immediate reduction in state costs and in the production of graduates sows the seeds of future conflict, by providing more opportunities for intellectual growth. Adult ed is a finger in the dike, against which waves of educated workers will be pounding in the years to come.

The story of the working class in college is one of the unacknowledged epics of American history. It shows how vulnerable workers are to changes in the economy, and how vulnerable the economy is to its irrational and unresolvable contradictions. All the conflicts of American life converge in school, turning education into what the other giant institutions of America are—battlefields for the conflicting interests of the state and the people. The successive layering of mass education is one key feature of this chronic irresolution. Business and government keep acting to stabilize social life, yet it remains in constant need of new adjustment. Initiative in this flow of forces still eludes working people. They are captives of the institutions which they sabotage by getting all they can. Labor reaction sets the parameters for the action of corporate and state policy. This tug and pull drives American society backward and forward at the same time. Workers finally enter college *en masse* in an historic opening up of the academy, only to find they are offered a debased and manipulative campus to call their own. Undaunted, once inside they get up and go to the many places intended for them, but also to levels of thought and aspiration not meant for them. Millions have passed through college and millions more want in. Other generations could only long for the higher education massively taken up by this one. Their experience of college will continue to affect the temper and direction of American life.

Notes

1. Two substantial histories of crisis and reform in the public schools are Lawrence Cremin's *The Transformation of the School* (Vintage, New York, 1964) and Diane Ravitch's *The Great School Wars* (Harper, New York, 1974).

2. John Dewey, *Philosophy of Education,* (Littlefield, Adams, New Jersey, 1975).

3. The failure of the public schools to deliver on both Horace

Mann's and John Dewey's democratic expectations has been studied by a number of Revisionist scholars: Samuel Bowles and Herbert Gintis, *Schooling in Capitalist America* (Basic Books, New York, 1976); Colin Greer, *The Great School Legend* (Penguin, New York, 1976); Michael Katz, *The Irony of Early School Reform* (Beacon, Boston, 1968), and *Class, Bureaucracy and Schools* (Praeger, New York, 1975); Joel Spring, *Education and the Rise of the Corporate State* (Beacon, Boston, 1972) and *A Primer on Libertarian Education* (Free Life, New York, 1975); Martin Carnoy, *Education as Cultural Imperialism* (McKay, New York, 1974).

4. Christopher Jencks, et. al., *Inequality,* (Basic Books, New York, 1972.) On structured failure and built-in inegalitarianism in public schooling see also Annie Stein, "Strategies for Failure," *Harvard Education Review*, Vol. 41, No. 2, May 1971, and Jerome Karabel, "Community Colleges and Social Stratification," *Harvard Education Review*, Vol. 42, No. 4, Nov. 1972.

5. See Katz, *Class, Bureaucracy and Schools,* and Stanley Aronowitz, *False Promises,* (McGraw-Hill, New York, 1973), pps. 69-74, for a picture of the early industrial era vis à vis disorder and the need for mass schooling.

6. William Appleman Williams, *The Contours of American History,* (Quadrangle, Chicago, 1966), offers a larger social analysis for the emergence of the public school as a "great equalizer." Williams sets school side by side with other special interest demands for compensatory help in gaining equality in the emergent industrial order.

7. Williams, *ibid.,* pps. 237-238; Aronowitz, *op. cit.,* 69ff; and Bowles and Gintis, *op. cit.,* pps. 164-179.

8. While the former Commissioner of Education Ernest Boyer had embraced "life-long learning" as federal policy, the concept itself has been critically studied by Ronald Gross in *The Life-Long Learner* (Simon and Schuster, Garden City, 1978).

9. On the issue of compulsory continuing education for adults, see *Second Thoughts,* Vol. 1, No. 1 (newsletter of a network questioning mandatory continuing education, published by Basic Choices, Madison, Wisconsin), and John Ohliger and David Lisman, "Must We All Go Back to School?", *The Progressive,* Vol. 42, No. 10, Oct. 1978, p. 35.

10. The figure of upwards of a hundred million Americans currently involved in some form of schooling is derived from *National Policy and Higher Education,* (MIT Press, Cambridge, 1973). In this second report, the Newman Commision estimates that 50-60 million adults are enrolled in post-secondary schooling alone.

11. Ivan Illich, *Deschooling Society,* (Harper, New York, 1972) and *Medical Nemesis,* (Bantam, New York, 1976).

12. For a positive eye-witness account of the making of a community college, by a founding president, see Thomas E. O'Connell, *Community Colleges, A President's View,* (University of Illinois Press, 1968).

13. On the impact of community colleges on the mobility of

minorities, women, and middle-class youth, see Bowles and Gintis, *op. cit.*, pps. 202ff, and Karabel, *op. cit.*

14. Sherry Gorelick in "Open Admissions: Design for Failure?" *Politics and Education*, Summer, 1978, reports that in the City University of New York 56.6% of full-time students had jobs during the semester, 14.4% were unemployed, and 29% were working more than 35 hours a week.

15. Jerry Flint, "Growing Part-Time Workforce Has Major Impact on the Economy," *New York Times*, April 12, 1977. See also David Deitch, "The New Capitalist Strategy," *The Nation*, November 12, 1973, p. 500.

16. See "Senate Report Finds Violence a Major Threat to Education," in *The American Teacher*, March 1977. This article concerns the Bayh Committee, which found vandalism costing the schools some $600 million dollars a year, while 70,000 serious attacks on teachers are registered annually.

17. Aronowitz's *False Promises* has a chapter on "trivialized work and colonized leisure," which focuses on the meaninglessness of daily labor. The long-range de-skilling of the workforce is a major preoccupation of Harry Braverman's *Labor and Monopoly Capital* (Monthly Review, New York, 1974). Braverman deeply analyzes the political economy behind the removal of skills from the workforce, seeing it as a long-evolving means to depress wage levels. He touches on the vacuous layering of mass education, as a response to the need to restrict the work-participation of youth, and the providing to employers of a tool for "credentialism" and job-applicant screening. The alienated impact of empty years of education is magnified by the ironic over-education of the workforce. In *Education and Jobs* (Praeger, New York, 1970), Ivar Berg discovered work performance to be inversely related to the years of higher education. Excess mental and skill-development in an economy with de-skilled jobs leads to alienation and non-productivity in dissatisfied workers.

18. In addition to Berg's study of education and worker productivity, the HEW report *Work in America* (MIT Press, Cambridge, 1973) found that workers operate at only 55% capacity. Lack of productivity and absenteeism (see "Auto Worker Absenteeism Still High Despite Layoffs," *New York Times*, February 6, 1976) are the twin nemeses of corporate enterprise. Some five years after the publication of the HEW report, the problem had not been resolved, necessitating the convening of a special labor-management high-level conclave, hosted by federal authorities in October, 1978, in Washington. See also "Productivity Rate Causes Worry," *New York Times*, May 7, 1979, D1, and "Stress Can Cause Work Epidemics," *New York Times*, May 29, 1979, C1, for more reportage on productivity problems.

19. See "Too Many Youths Found Aspiring to Too Few Jobs," *New York Times*, Nov. 8, 1976. This report by Gene Maeroff discusses a conference in Houston which brought together 6,000 educators. The issue was the "unrealistic" aspirations of worker-youth. "Career

education" was repeatedly brought up as a means by which the lower grades could adjust (depress) the economic expectations of school children. See also Deitch, *op. cit.*, p. 498, on the economic crisis and the new interest in child labor.

20. The pathology of everyday life is rather forthrightly observed in the HEW report, *Work in America*. It sees broad patterns of social disintegration circling outward from alienation at the workplace.

21. The great democratic legend of school, by which its role in educating, integrating and Americanizing the polyglot population is promoted, is confronted head-on in the work of Greer, Katz, Bowles and Gintis.

22. Baran and Sweezy, in *Monopoly Capital* (Monthly Review, New York, 1966), report that the national outlay from public and private sources for education was $23.1 billion in 1960. By the late 70s, this figure had increased five-fold.

23. Berg's research on education and productivity picked up where the Bright studies at Harvard (1966) left off. Both raised questions about training workers for jobs that don't exist, or for jobs that require less skill than the mass higher education system graduates you with. They point to a long-range crisis in the creation of a workforce permanently skilled and educated far beyond the ability of the job market to reward its achievements.

24. Burton Clark's essay "The Cooling-Out Function in Higher Education" (*American Journal of Sociology*, LXV, May 1960) was a seminal study on the process of depressant tracking in the academy. Since then, the political economy of vocationalism and tracking has attracted a good deal of attention. Scholars have awarded it a variety of linguistic motifs: "the integrative function" (Bowles and Gintis), "successful selection of losers" (Greer), "the sorting machine" (Spring), "the illusion of equality" (Milner), "social stratification" (Karabel), "strategies for failure" (Stein), "internalizing failure" (Aronowitz), "the appearance of fairness" (Jencks and Riesman). At issue is the artificial lowering of expectations built into the mass experience of schooling. Frank Ryan's motif of "blaming the victim" appropriately describes how the process of cooling-out transfers responsibility for failure from the institution to the individual.

25. Burton Clark's full-length study of the triple-tiered, mass university system (*The Open-Door College*) appeared in print in the same year as his influential article on "cooling-out."

26. Bowles and Gintis cite studies by the American Council on Education (1970) and by Jaffe and Adams (1972) which document the community college drop-out rate to be nearly 3/4 of those who intend to go on for a four-year degree.

27. On the effects of "credentialism," see the HEW report *Work in America*, the chapter on "Education."

28. Paul Goodman was one sane voice against blaming the victims

of the school machine. In *Compulsory Mis-Education* (Vintage, New York, 1966) he understood the "reactive stupidity" of students as a defensive behavior, conditioned by the imposition of negative schooling.

29. See college enrollment statistics in *The Chronicle of Higher Education Yearbook* (Editorial Projects for Education, Washington, 1977), p. 185.

30. Jerome Karabel's 1972 study in the *Harvard Education Review* is the best documentation against the democratic mystique of the two-year network.

31. *The Chronicle of Higher Education Yearbook,* 1977, p. 185.

32. Ellen Kay Trimberger's article in the *Insurgent Sociologist* (1973), "Open Admissions: A New Form of Tracking?" was one of the first studies of how the economic and ideological functions of mass higher education were in contradiction. Trimberger touched on the potential for dysfunctional consciousness-growth, when workers at an adult moment of their lives are offered advanced learning. From the point of view of liberal arts education, Bowles and Gintis also assert that it's impossible to offer humanities courses without passing on some of the critical faculties with which students can demystify the system (*Schooling in Capitalist America,* p. 206). Trimberger speaks more to the situation of the mass college, where the contradiction between elevating and depressing the students' aspirations is most intense, while Bowles and Gintis address the emergence of consciousness on the more elite campuses.

33. For a senior faculty reaction to violence at an Open Admissions college, see Geoffrey Wagner's letter-response in the January 1978 *College English.*

34. The role of vocational schooling in removing a self-socializing power of labor is discussed in Spring's *Education and the Rise of the Corporate State.* Vocational schools emerged in the radical labor period of World War I, and served to challenge the formal trade union apprentice programs and informal means through which co-workers broke in new employees.

35. See Berg's study on education, training and jobs, as well as the HEW report *Work in America.*

36. Nat Hentoff's two-part article "The Irrepressible Rank and File" (*Village Voice,* October 9-16, 1978) affords a lively account of the fortunes of a dissident rank-and-file steward in the communication workers union. The story of a worker-activist being disciplined for publishing a newsletter critical of union and management policy offers background to rank-and-file activity in a number of America's largest unions. The role of higher education in promoting labor militancy was acknowledged by the vice-president of a large United Mineworker local, Cecil Roberts, who estimated that some 8,000 young miners had gotten college training ("New Breed of Coal Miners Showing Defiance," *New York Times,* September 1, 1977).

37. See Paolo Freire's *Pedagogy of the Oppressed* (Seabury, New York, 1970), *Education for Critical Consciousness* (Seabury, New York, 1973) and *Cultural Action for Freedom* (Penguin, Baltimore, 1972). Freire's theory of education as democratic dialogue has had an impact in the Cuban Literacy Campaign (see Jonathan Kozol's "A New Look at the Literacy Campaign in Cuba," *Harvard Education Review*, Vol. 48, No. 3, Aug. 1978) and in the emerging states of Africa (see Freire's *Pedagogy in Process*, Seabury, New York, 1978). Freirian modes of education are now beginning to be developed in America.

38. On the shaping of reactionary school policy during periods of conservative resurgence see Joel Spring's *The Sorting Machine* (McKay, New York, 1976), and Bowles and Gintis, *Schooling in Capitalist America*. Spring reports on conservatism in the 1950s, while Bowles and Gintis ("IQism," p. 114) relate the post-60s backlash against liberal reforms.

39. See the *Chronicle of Higher Education*, reports on the leveling of college enrollments after twenty-five years of unbroken growth, in the November 22, 1976 and February 22, 1977 issues.

40. The acknowledged "father of career education," Sidney Marland, launched the new careerism in school policy while serving as Nixon's Commissioner of Education, in 1972. In that year, his book on career education appeared, and he continues to be a voice for the further vocationalization of public schooling. The queasiness of trade-unions to career education can be found in the AFT testimony before the House Committee considering the Career Education Act of 1977 (February 9, 1977, by AFT representative Eugenia Kemble). AFT President Albert Shanker offered his mild critique in *The American Teacher* of that same month: "Career Education: Built on Fantasies." The AFT position is that channeling school kids out of school will create fewer teaching jobs for their members inside school, while career education unfortunately glamorizes the work-world outside the class-room. Like the AFL's final acceptance of vocational education through the Smith-Hughes Act of 1917, the bland position of the AFT on career education reads like an accomodation to corporate-federal policy rather than a resistance to it.

41. In the *New York Times'* "Spring 1977 Survey of Continuing Education," the panorama of adult education is phenomenal. New York University promotes itself as the place "Where Adults Go to Grow". Hofstra University says "You never outgrow your need to know." The sales pitch is to self-growth, while the courses themselves are creative. The new, large adult education market is rescuing colleges from their budget crises. This new growth area has been acknowledged in "New Routes to a College Degree" (*New York* magazine, Aug. 29, 1977), "Adult Students Breathe New Life into Education" (*US News and World Report*, March 28, 1977), "Students of the Subjective" (*Harpers*, June, 1977), and in an article in the *Chronicle of Higher Education* (April 25, 1977) which reports that ailing two-year colleges will have to fight with the more elite campuses for the new market in older students. A new gold-rush is on.

CHAPTER TWO

INTERFERENCES TO CRITICAL THOUGHT:

Consciousness in School and Daily Life

Reality as it is thought does not correspond to the reality being lived objectively, but rather to the reality in which alienated man imagines himself to be.

Paulo Freire, *Cultural Action for Freedom*

...hegemony is exercised not merely *by* a minority but *in the interests* of that minority...

Georg Lukács, *History and Class Consciousness*

...everything that creates or maintains a bond with the bourgeois order, that supports and reinforces it, is an impediment to class consciousness.

Wilhelm Reich, *Sex-Pol*

The noise, oh, it's tremendous. It don't stop. It just goes and goes and goes. I bet there's men who have lived and died out there, never seen the end of that line. And they never will because it's endless. It's like a serpent. It's just all body, no tail. It can do things to you...

auto worker, in *Working*, Studs Terkel

He had an awe of education, he regarded it as a open sesame that unlocked the gates to freedom and power; its secrets would deliver Antoine from the chains which he himself had to bear. How could a father hinder his son from escaping unhappiness?

Paul Nizan, *Antoine Bloyé*

Kidnapped Reason: Search at the Scene of the Crime

There is something both relentless and routine about the experience of time in everyday life. On the one hand, it seems to slip by quietly, and on the other, time sweeps you up into an irresistible rush. Monday becomes Tuesday, January turns into June, and before you know it, ten years have passed. It's hard to get a feel for what it all means. You know you are part of the big picture, but someone else is doing the painting.

The powerlessness and confusion in daily life can only be understood through critical thinking, yet most people are alienated from their own conceptual habits of mind. How come? Why don't masses of people engage in social reflection? Why isn't introspection an habitual feature of life? What prevents popular awareness of how the whole system operates, and which alternatives would best serve human needs? Why is political imagination driven from common experience? Confronted by an "eclipse of reason" in mass culture, what can liberatory pedagogy do?[1]

Because liberatory learning is an exercise in consciousness growth, the obstacles to critical awareness need investigation. Writing on the decline of reason in everyday life, Stanley Aronowitz stressed the consequences of irrationalism in mass culture: "The issue is the capacity for theoretical or conceptual thought itself. When people lack such competence, social action that transcends the struggle for justice within the empirically given rules of social organization and discourse is impossible... Since critical thinking is the fundamental precondition for an autonomous and self-motivated public or citizenry, its decline would threaten the future of democratic, social, cultural and political forms."[2] Faced with this threat, the designers of an empowering pedagogy have to study the shape of disempowering forces. As allies to the powerless, liberatory teachers need a working knowledge of the anti-critical field in which a critical pedagogy evolves. The systematic investigation of mass reality prepares the teacher for using daily life as subject matter. The teacher's own critical learning prefigures the knowledge the class as a whole will gain.

Critical Consciousness

"Critical consciousness" and "conscientization" are terms used by Freire to denote the product and process of liberatory learning.[3] The Freirian literacy teams do field-studies of their students' reality prior to teaching in an area. They begin the education of the teacher at the scene of the crime—the daily world where reason is denied.[4] Literacy and political awareness evolve simultaneously because reading and writing are the occasion for questioning social reality. For Freire,

> the literacy process, as cultural action for freedom, is an act of knowing in which the learner assumes the role of knowing subject in dialogue with the educator...a process through which men who had previously been submerged in reality begin to emerge in order to re-insert themselves with critical awareness...the right of self-expression and world-expression, of creating and re-creating, of deciding and choosing and ultimately participating in society's historical process.[5]

A pedagogy which empowers students to intervene in the making of history is more than a literacy campaign. Critical education prepares students to be their own agents for social change, their own creators of democratic culture. They gain skills of philosophical abstraction which enable them to separate themselves from manipulation and from the routine flow of time. Consequently, their literacy is a challenge to their control by corporate culture. Because critical literacy can detach people from mass domination, the existing social order has a stake in preventing the popular emergence of conceptual consciousness. Anti-critical mass culture is the first and largest learning problem of the general population. Thus, the interferences to critical thought must be conceived as social and pervasive, not as personal problems or as isolated pedagogical ones. A social matrix convenes against mass intellectualism because a class-based society cannot offer the full human development of its own people. A population richly critical and creative would be a risk to hierarchy and exploitation. Critical learning aids people in knowing what holds them back; it encourages them to envision a social order which supports their full humanity. By critically studying the lives they live uncritically and the culture which eclipses reason, students begin changing their powerless places in society.

Thought-Control

The mass denial of reason is achieved through a network of cultural instruments. There is no single mode through which critical thought is denied. It takes complex machinery to effect thought-control. The variety of anti-critical forces in American life include vocational culture in school and on the job, several forms of false consciousness (reification, acceleration, mystification, and pre-scientific thought), the absence of democratic experience, the demands of private life, and the aesthetics and social relations of school in general and the community colleges in particular. Each of these forces will be detailed in the coming pages. It is useful to begin by seeing them as over-lapping and mutually supportive interferences to critical thought. They are cultural over-kill operating simultaneously in daily life, at both the ideological and institutional levels. For example, vocationalism is a concrete curriculum in school, but it is also a form of consciousness. It is an institutional course of study which imposes a class-based, hierarchical thinking on students, conditioning them to accept their lesser place in society, distancing them from philosophy. The aesthetics of the community colleges are similarly dualistic—a drab physical reality communicating a depressing ideological message. The architecture of worker-campuses signals to four million non-elite students how unimportant they are. The "budget" campus supports inequality in life and thought. In some instances, a single cultural interference serves several thought-denying functions. The electronic mass media demonstrate this. They not only convey carefully managed information about reality, but they are also a form of speeded and debased communication which inhibits the mass practice of careful scrutiny.

Concrete and psychological, the interferences are routine ways of life developing manipulated thought and feeling. While the machinery of thought-control is large, it is not 1984. It is not that thorough, that complete or that grotesque. Its strength lies in its everyday shape—school, family life, shopping, TV, the clichés of conversation. By hegemonizing the routines of existence, the interferences crowd out autonomous thought, feeling, and action, the base on which an alternative society could grow. In this way, the control of present consciousness amounts to a control over the future. Because the future of critical thought involves the future of society, the comprehensive obstacles to liberatory thinking are politically understandable. A great deal is at stake in the emergence or suppression of critical learning.

Both the consequences and the operation of the interferences are complex, so only a working survey will be presented in this chapter. This report on thought-denial will explore the social field in which my experiments in liberatory process evolved. Part of the matrix of interferences is applicable to the culture as a whole and to students from all classes; part is rooted in the experience of teaching for primarily white urban worker-students. The whole involves an enormous question of human development which critical educators must address. One good place to start the inquiry is the familiar nemesis of mass schooling—vocationalism.

Vocational Culture: The Machinification of Character

Vocational culture is a root interference to critical thought. It is a school practice with grave social consequences. A group of self-educated Italian workers reflected on the issue like this:

> On the one side you have liberal arts, on the other manual arts. The former is conceived as the kingdom of the spirit, freedom and knowledge; the latter is the dark region of matter, slavery and ignorance.[6]

Freire reaches a similar conclusion, that the skills-training offered by capitalist schooling "implies the suffocation of the workers' political consciousness."[7] School vocationalism begins the stifling of human potential, towards the creation of a non-critical, divided adult workforce. The routine disgrace of being relegated to the bottom strata of the job world promotes widespread depression and self-doubt. In his worker-interviews, Studs Terkel heard this from a college woman turned receptionist:

> I changed my opinion of receptionists because now I'm one. It wasn't the dumb broad at the front desk who

took telephone messages. She had to be something else because I was something else. I was fine until there was a press party. We were having a fairly intelligent conversation. Then they asked me what I did. When I told them, they turned around to find other people with name tags. I wasn't worth bothering with. I wasn't being rejected because of what I had said or the way I talked, but simply because of my function.[8]

She was victimized by the same vocational prejudice she believed in, and despite her elite college training, her education was less important than the menial work she performed in a stratified workforce. Most working people don't experience her shock of downward mobility, so they move laterally and routinely from vocational schooling into menial jobs. The banality of this dehumanization is achieved by bureaucratic testing in school and work-classification on the job. At the end, a divided humanity is delivered to more than dead-end labor. Accompanying vocational culture is socialization against intellectual life, against feeling, and against autonomy.

Vocationalism narrows human development. People channeled through vocational culture are denied spacious growth. They emerge as the laboring "hands" of society. The "hands" that do the work of society are not supposed to think or feel. Dismembered and disintegrated, the workforce becomes dishabituated to its own critical, creative, and emotional potentials, which atrophy from lack of exercise. One consequence of not being allowed to think, to govern, to create, or to express deep feeling, is a defensive rigidity when confronted with the forbidden. The self-discipline and mutual dialogue of a liberatory classroom will be as threatening as they are empowering to students who have been conditioned to await orders. While nominally only a skills-training curriculum, vocationalism thus creates a whole authority-dependent personality. It is a social-psychology for a dominated character.

The vocational dismemberment of human workers into "trained hands" is a fitting product of alienated labor in a corporate state. The appalling logic behind the metaphor of "trained hands" involves the machinification of character. The vocational process tries to wed human labor so closely to the machine that people become machines. The mechanical model for human character greatly disturbed Wilhelm Reich, who wrote that for the worker "The machine became, is, and will continue to be his most dangerous destroyer, if he does not differentiate himself from it."[9] The fear of being completely dominated by machine culture, to the point that we will be made into robots, reappears as a major theme of the interviews Terkel recorded with workers.[10] In my classes, this fear and this reality is frequently manifested. At the same time that students hold back their feelings, and fear expressing their thoughts, they also complain about how unimportant they are at work, in school, in society at large. They feel depersonalized, treated like dirt. In social and sexual life, no less than at work and in school, they act bottled-up, their emotions and intellects filed down by the constant pressure of machine-training.

The vocationalization of character rests on a sturdy reality of corporate society: machines are the most reliable part of the production process. The "human factor" has emerged as a synonym for error and unpredictability. Humans are emotional and demanding. They resent their dehumanization. They react to alienated work by going on strike, stealing and sabotaging, drinking and fighting, working slowly and staying home sick. Machines don't act like this. Machines don't expect vacations, sick leave, lunch hours or raises. With machines as the exemplary workers, corporate planners automate as much human labor as they can, while supporting a vocational culture which tries to turn workers into machines. The dialectics of corporate automation are thus clear: machines replace humans and humans are machinified. Called upon to surrender critical thought and creative feeling, playfulness and natural eroticism, vocationalized people live with a cultural motif of robots, a nightmare vision of being turned into metallic computeroids. The combination of technology and class hierarchy has created such a negative experience with mass production and institutions that little popular imagination is devoted to the controlled, cooperative use of science, as in Skinner's *Walden II*. Corporate culture and popular reaction are inverse mirrors: while vocationalism exalts the machine, the victims of industrial life reject technology. Critical learning is crucial here, as a means to evolve ways to control the machine force which now controls human life. Political imagination needs stimulation to invent alternatives to technocracy.

Fortunately, the vocational machinification of character remains incomplete. In some of my teaching experiments, we were able to critically examine and then reconstruct the mechanical nature of our work and institutional lives. These projects will be reported in detail in the next section of the book. For now, it's encouraging to observe that the monumental spread of vocationalism has failed to liquidate dysfunctional thought and feeling. Beneath the hesitancy, the doubt, and the rigidity of my students, there remain stores of intellect, emotion, comedy, and Utopian needs, waiting to happen. They have fought the robotizing of their characters to a kind of stand-off. In class or on the job, they know how to sabotage any process which alienates them. They have ways to set limits on their own dehumanization. They can be unproductive while looking busy, they can be clever while playing dumb, they can scheme against the boss while looking honest. Their protective ploys stop vocational ideology from totally penetrating them. Still, they have been invaded and distorted by machine culture. This can be seen in the rough way they treat each other and in the insecure way they feel about themselves. Further, they may have defensive reactions to being dehumanized—like drinking on the job, being absent, covering for each other, etc.—but, while they limit their cooperation with the corporate order, they don't have a vision of alternatives. They don't assert or fight for their own order. They learn how to break the rules and get away with it, but they don't yet assume the responsibility of being the makers of the rules, together. If individuals move up the hierarchy, they become like their despised superiors, mimicking an authoritarian model of power.

The liberatory class can be helpful here by provoking critical reflection on models of authority. So few people will be allowed to move up into positions of command that most of the students in class will have a stake in democratic management. The liberatory process can speak to this need by forcing wider the crack between undemocratic machine culture and the popular desire for power. People chafe under the limits of vocationalism, which C. Wright Mills dubbed "a routine training of nationalist loyalties."[11] Mills understood the result of socialization-against-thought in terms which preview the upcoming discussion of "false consciousness":

> The citizen cannot see the roots of his own biases or frustrations, nor think clearly about himself, nor for that matter about anything else. He does not see the frustration of idea, of intellect, by the present organization of society, and he is not able to meet the tasks now confronting "the intelligent citizen."[12]

The machine modeling of mass character leads to resignation, confusion and haphazard rebellion, in the absence of a systematic appreciation of reality. Both the process and product of liberatory learning de-condition this behavior, because they promote conceptual inquiry. They restore critical intelligence through examination and re-invention of daily life, giving concrete shape to negative and positive social models. This begins a reconstructive vision which can reverse anti-critical vocationalism.

False Consciousness: Wrong Answers, Right Questions

Automation and vocationalism are the meat and potatoes of monopoly culture. Their one-two punch is a great lesson in social control. On one side, mechanization reduces the amount of labor needed for production, while lowering the skill-requirements called for at any job, so that lower wages result as well.[13] Automated processes magically increase productivity while decreasing the workforce in numbers, in skills, and in pay scales. On another side, vocational culture assumes the preparation of people for life under hostile and diminished conditions. The easing of humanity into degraded worklives demands a trivialization of thought and feeling to match the trivialization of work skills, wage rewards and social relations at the point of production. Automation needs vocationalism as its force for mass socialization, while vocationalism is the base for a culture-wide denial of reason and emotion. The corporate-machine offensive forces dysfunctional sensibilities into marginal sanctuaries. Generosity, honesty, affection, cooperation, become quaint idiosyncracies of romantics and the "good-natured."

In the mass retardation of critical, political and affective life, vocationalism is a potent weapon. Its effect is to limit the capacity for transcendent thinking as well as to shape the quality of thought. Still, despite the vocational parameters of mass life, there remains in the popular character a residue of undominated resources. To contain these residual possibilities, a whole battery of cultural instruments are at work to produce "false consciousness," that is, manipulated action and reflection which lead people to support their own oppression. The symbiosis between vocationalism and false consciousness strengthens each: the first lowers the mass ability for critical thought and spacious feeling while the second distorts the rational and emotional qualities which remain.

False consciousness is an irrationalizing force. It conditions people to police themselves by internalizing the ideas of the ruling elite. The great power of dominated thought is that people deny the means of their own liberation while taking responsibility for acting in ways which reproduce their powerlessness. Freire finds this kind of consciousness to be a fundamental interference to critical learning. He describes a few simple examples of it:

> Submerged in reality, the oppressed cannot perceive clearly the "order" which serves the interests of the oppressors whose image they have internalized. Chafing under the restricitons of this order, they often manifest a type of horizontal violence, striking out at their own comrades for the pettiest reasons...the oppressed feel an irresistible attraction towards the oppressor and his way of life. Sharing this way of life becomes an overpowering aspiration. In their alienation, the oppressed want at any cost to resemble the oppressor, to imitate him, to follow him. This phenomenon is especially prevalent in the middle-class oppressed, who yearn to be equal to the "eminent" men of the upper class...Self-depreciation is another characteristic of the oppressed, which derives from their internalization of the opinion the oppressors hold of them. So often do they hear that they are good for nothing, know nothing and are incapable of learning anything—that they are sick, lazy and unproductive— that in the end they become convinced of their own unfitness...They call themselves ignorant and say the "professor" is the one who has knowledge and to whom they should listen.[14]

These suggestive remarks speak to several destructive features of false consciousness in American life: sexism, racism, and worship of the rich and powerful. Divided "horizontally" against each other by race and sex, working people turn to "striking it rich" as the most lively fantasy of liberation. In such a cultural setting, any specific feature of false consciousness—like racism—is supported by deeper levels of irrational thought. The deepest dimensions of false consciousness can be abstracted into several major categories: reification, acceleration, mystification and pre-scientism.

Reification: A Piece of the Action

The process of popular thought, feeling and action known as reification has been discussed at length by Georg Lukács.[15] He traced the philosophy of reification from Hegel through Marx, and located it historically in the triumphant rise of commodity culture and the dramatic fragmentation of social life. In mass corporate society, the reproduction of daily life becomes mysterious. Who makes the commodities we buy or the rules we follow? With the system-as-a-whole so hard to grasp, thought and action lose their transcendent, political and systemic qualities.

Reified thought is static and contained. The parts of the social whole are changeable and related, but reified consciousness experiences life in stationary pieces. This mental narrowing originates from the isolated fragment of labor each person performs on the job. On one side, we have the detailed division of labor turning work-activity into dissociated, trivial and repetitive tasks. On another side, we have commodity markets delivering our material needs through invisible processes, an enormous chain of appropriation, production and distribution of which the single purchase by an anonymous consumer at the end is but the tip of a social iceberg. On still another side, we have the institutions of public life—such as the internal revenue service, the motor vehicle bureau, the schools—whose compulsory transactions appear independent of or beyond human intervention.

Simultaneously invisible and imposing, too present and too intangible, the system gains an aura of mysterious invulnerability. Popular powerlessness results from feeling overwhelmed

by an oppressive yet incomprehensible system. The contradictory presence and elusiveness of social control leads to
confusion about what freedom is or what are the means to be
free, happy and whole. Driven by such confused consciousness,
people act against their own interests, against their need for
power.[16] Lukács understood the disempowering effects of reification in this way:

> Neither objectively nor in his relation to his work does
> man appear as the authentic master of the process; on
> the contrary, he is a mechanical part incorporated into a
> mechanical system. He finds it already pre-existing and
> self-sufficient, it functions independently of him and he
> has to conform to its laws whether he likes it or not...his
> activity becomes less and less active and more and more
> *contemplative*...the personality can do no more than look
> on helplessly while its own existence is reduced to an
> isolated particle and fed into an alien system...It de-
> stroys those bonds that had bound individuals to a
> community in the days when production was still
> "organic."[17]

In this discussion of reification, Lukács uses the word *contemplative*
as a synonym for *spectative*, that is, watching without critical
reflection, action dominated by the process you are in. Reified
culture achieves this disempowerment through related aliena-
tions: people are alienated from their own holistic habits of mind;
people are alienated from their own class-peers, lacking the
solidarity needed to organize for power; people are alienated
from a grasp of the system's whole operation and the mediating
mechanisms which reproduce daily life. Alienated from power in
class society, labor is also alienated from *the power to think critically
about gaining power*. Demobilized, masses of people are channeled
into spectatorism: sports, television, movies, following the
glamorous lives of film stars and jet-setters, being activated by
experts, authorities and opinion-makers from the mass media.
One spectator activity, "window-shopping," registers the routine reification of everyday life, where the alluring given order
freezes transcendent action.

"Beating the System"

In reified culture, social life is full of strange paradoxes. Society feels fixed forever, yet it seems constantly changing. The rules, demands, commodities, and changes seem to come at you from everywhere and nowhere at the same time. Whatever the whole thing is about, fixed or changing, you are not in control of it. Life teaches you to settle into a small corner of existence, which amounts to the full-time preoccupation of "making ends meet." Stuck in such a corner, you learn how to minimize your victimization by small-scale manipulation of rules, markets, authorities, and institutions.

The survival skills needed in daily life expose yet another contradiction about consciousness in reified society. The words "static," "frozen," and "fixed" are appropriate to describe the loss of dynamic, critical and transcendent thought. Alienated labor, and atomized social relations, do result in modes of thought and feeling too fragmented to organize popular liberation. Now, while people dominated by reification do not think critically, or make social change, or experiment with spacious artistic and sexual lives, they are not zombies, automatons or robots. They are very active, very busy. There is a bustling quality to daily life. The culture keeps people as busy as possible. They are energetic, amusing, aspiring. They shrewdly learn the rules and how to break them for personal profit. They become highly skilled in surviving situations which oppress them. They con bosses for raises, teachers for grades, cops for no ticket. One of the most energetic and paradoxical things people do is the game called "beating the system."

In this social practice, you look to buy cheap. You search out connections who can get you a car or a camera wholesale. You develop a nose for leads into good apartments or reasonable car insurance. Several forces converge to propel the need for "beating the system": an affluent society with surplus goods piled everywhere, a consumerist culture manipulating high-levels of material needs, a national life built on a dream of rising expectations, a class society where workers are paid less than they need to buy "the good life," and where corporate managers can engineer price inflation much easier than labor can negotiate wage increases. Mass life in such a commodity culture involves a search for bargains, short-cuts, deals, hot goods, fire sales, close-outs, mark-downs, specials-of-the-day. This practice is a short-term answer to the economic rigors of capitalist society without solving the root problem. It keeps people busily chiseling a higher standard of living out of an order supported by just such consumer activity. In this contradictory way, "beating the system" is a very active way to stay frozen in the system. It is a means to outsmart capitalism by playing within the rules of the business world. In the end, you wind up devoting huge amounts of time learning the ropes of the system, and none to rejecting the social model. You can do all this knowing that the rich control everything, that big business has the government in its pocket. You can know that landlords write the property codes and that tax laws favor millionaires. These recognitions are not mobilized into combative class consciousness. The sense of powerlessness convinces you that the system can't be changed.

"Beating the system" is an act of reified false consciousness in which you experience illusory power—a deal, a rip-off, getting more for your money. The power is illusory because you may or may not have needed the commodity in the first place, most likely it's a debased product anyhow, and no sooner have you clinched one deal than you're back in motion needing another. This social game retards political resistance to the system, but it also preserves a mental agility, a shrewd watchfulness in people. It forces thought to be narrow, immediate, and practical, thus crowding out critical thinking, but it doesn't destroy the capacity for critical thought. This form of consumerism is, however, a monstrous distraction to liberatory reflection, in a consumer culture where critical scrutiny offers no *immediate* material gains. When you play "beating the system," the carrot held out in front of you is the promise of some direct acquisition. In contrast, the practice of social reconstruction is obviously a long-term solution to daily problems; reified consciousness can look to an immediate reward from consumer life which thus interferes with the futurity of critical thought.

In the absence of a mass liberatory offensive, the defensive maneuver of "beating the system" is one way to get more of what you need (and don't need) within the terms of the corporate order. A liberatory culture contending for the future could conceivably co-exist with short-run defenses, but that is not the

case now. Protecting your immediate self-interest involves sur-
rendering the future. Future-making or Utopian consciousness,
as features of critical thinking, have been emphasized by Freire
as fundamental to liberatory culture.[18] The mass dissociation
from a self-designed future is another definition for false
consciousness in general and for reification in particular. The
liquidation of Utopia from human thought will propel society
farther down the path to barbarism; a line of dystopic novels, of
which *1984* and *Brave New World* are the most prominent, offer
visions of the triumph of domination over liberation. Critical
learning is one front in this war for the future. It has a part to
play in unfreezing popular consciousness for its Utopian possibilities.

In regard to reification, the critical classroom can promote a
democratic future in a number of ways. It can address future-
denial in mass culture by focusing Utopian thought on immediate
reality; it can make ordinary routines the subject of transcendent
inquiry. Further, the class can investigate the economic laws and
mediations which are responsible for the making of everyday
life. Such a study can deal with the sense of powerlessness by
showing just how society is made. Also, besides tracing the
routes of production and decision-making, the class can question
the apparent invulnerability of the system. It can problematize
the seeming power of the old order and the weakness of the
people. The long history of victories through resistance to
oppression are invisible in daily life. These historical and sociological approaches to the making of everyday life can stimulate
the kind of systemic reasoning which is by itself a holistic and
dynamic reversal of reified consciousness. In fact, a conceptual
examination of a familiar feature of culture such as "beating the
system" can provoke the critical detachment on social life out of
which reconstructive thinking grows. This educational attack on
reified thought can deal with one serious interference to critical
thinking, but mass culture is hydra-headed, and other obstacles
remain.

Return to Galileo: Science versus Mysticism

Pre-scientific thinking is a deep support for irrational behavior. It is a retreat from comprehending cause and effect in reality.

Instead, mystical causations reign, as unverifiable explanations for the phenomena of everyday life. The mass disposition against rational inquiry has the strength of vocationalism and reification behind it, leveling the popular practice of critical thought. For consciousness already conditioned against systematic analysis of culture, pre-scientific modes of thought are familiar and comforting. Science is rational and demanding; it expects that truths can be tested. Pre-scientism is magical; it is emotionally reassuring to minds which have been socialized to fear the use of their critical intelligence. For people raised with doubts about their ability to think, the big, quick, untestable truths of prescientism have the authority of being simple and certain.

"Blind faith" and "blind obedience" are two familiar phrases which denote the practice of pre-scientific thought in mass culture. A common example of this interference to critical thought is the popular belief in "human nature" as a fixed, damaged and limiting fact. This simple way to consider human life is an easy answer to many troubling issues. Why do people fight, rob and kill? Why is there so much poverty and degradation? Why are people greedy? Why are there wars? A single explanation comfortably deals with all of these questions: people are just no damn good. It's our flawed, rotten nature. As long as you can indict abstract, untestable "human nature" as the problem of humanity, then there is no way to do anything about it. This gives you a moral holiday. You are freed from the responsibility of intervening in history to change things for the better. It comforts your own sense of powerlessness to think this way; it's a way of thinking rooted in powerlessness. A second familiar form of pre-scientific thought also prevents you from having to figure out rationally how reality works, so that you can avoid remaking society. This second mode is known as "lady luck." It's part of the strike-it-rich syndrome in mass culture, which you actualize by gambling. As long as luck determines your fortunes in life, you don't have to exercise your adult intelligence to tackle the genuine complexities which make social life happen. It is also sexist—women are considered as unpredictable as luck. Still another means of pre-scientific irrationalism in daily life is known as "brand-name loyalty." People become totemistically allied to a commercial product, like Dodge trucks or Borden's cheese. They avoid critically examining the quality of the item, and keep buying it with religious conviction in its goodness. It is easier to have faith than to be scientific, especially when organized religion, mass education, work and the media contain your practice of analytic reasoning, destroying your self-confidence.

An especially widespread and complex form of pre-scientism in everyday life is known as "common sense." This simultaneously helpful and harmful mode of thought has a sacred place in mass experience. People who don't exercise critical thought retreat to "common sense" as their way of seeing and knowing. For its religious and negative sides, John Berger describes it as a

> ...home-made ideology of those who have been deprived of fundamental learning, of those who have been kept ignorant...Common sense can only exist as a category insofar as it can be distinguished from the spirit of enquiry, from philosophy...It belongs to the ideology, of those who are socially passive, never understanding what or who has made their situation as it is...And when they justify something by saying, "It's only common-sense," this is frequently an apology for denying or betraying some of their deepest feelings or instincts.[19]

The deep feelings or instincts denied by common-sense exist as latent popular resources for transcendence. To the extent that common sense is a flight from reality, it is an irrationalizing force. However, there is its benign side as well. My students see "common sense" as an orientation to survival rules in daily life— when it's raining you take an umbrella, things screw in to the right and screw out to the left, you don't steal or goof off when the boss is looking. Those people without "common sense" are considered foolish, self-destructive, or disoriented. In either irrational or socially orienting forms, "common sense" functions as an adjustment ideology, displacing a mature grasp of *what can change* in the reality we find.

The pre-scientific flight from rationalism is a flight from the fears of your own inadequacy. This is easier to understand through the mass practice of hero-worship. Athletes, actors and actresses are hyped into media super-stars, glamorized in a way that prohibits objective measurement of their talents. Identifying with heroes fills the void of your own doubts about yourself. A lifetime of hearing how worthless you are also creates wounds which demand the infusion of star-worship. These wounds lead to other, more dangerous forms of behavior—racism and sexism. The rejection of rational thought, plus the need to resolve feelings of powerlessness, lead to power-mongering against women and non-whites by males who cannot react scientifically to their needs. Pre-scientific thinking supports the conviction that blacks are inferior and that women belong in the kitchen.

The intervention of critical learning is absolutely crucial here. A dehumanized, pre-scientific mind can accept the irrational dehumanization of other people. Contrarily, an adult, humanized person will be compelled to examine reality for truth and fiction, separating clarity from blind prejudice. The flight from understanding cause and effect is a defense against confronting the social process which has infantilized and disempowered you, thus avoiding the facts of weakness out of which strength can grow. By promoting a mass commitment to rational scrutiny, the liberatory class develops the popular resources needed to oppose the mystical thought underlying racism and sexism. Further, the conceptualization of liberatory learning as an *empowering* pedagogy is relevant here. People can find in themselves individually and together the feelings of power they used to seek in worshipping heroes, making purchases, expecting miracles and acting aggressively towards their class-peers.

Acceleration: Going Nowhere Fast

There is another dimension of popular consciousness which contributes to irrationality. It can be referred to as "acceleration." Where vocationalism levels the capacity for critical thought, and reification freezes and fragments mass reflection, acceleration speeds up mental processes beyond a pace suitable for critical analysis. The mind is conditioned to operate at a perceptual speed which repels careful scrutiny. Life in thought, and thought about life, are swept up into the rushed routines of existence.

Minds immersed in mass culture become habituated to a dizzying pace of life. There is a frenetic envelopment in noise, motion and color. The electronic mass media debase communication by pummeling the senses with loud, fast bursts of language. Radio, television, and illuminated, moving advertisements operate at a stunning audial and visual pace, using trite slogans and catchy images for persuason. They set an addicting standard of stimulation. This hyped use of words and pictures fits into the whole accelerated gestalt of daily life.

The acceleration effect of electronic communications is supported by the style of printed mass media. Advertising flyers, commodity packaging, flashy billboards, sensational tabloids, sports journals, family and gossip magazines, and the stationary lighted logos of chain stores, create a spectacular visual overload in everyday life. Quickly perceived and unnaturally amplified beyond human scale, these media monopolize attention. The slower conceptual skills needed to penetrate books and analytic discussions do not develop in the crowded milieu of mass culture. Acceleration creates only surface perception in people. You exercise only shallow habits of mind. Wherever you look, or whatever you read, you can't examine it in depth because it's happening too fast, or else you have no need to scrutinize it, because its message is so simple. Accelerated consciousness cannot perform rational inquiry of reality, but it is ideal for absorbing political and commercial slogans, for enjoying rock music, for processing headline news flashes and zinging burger advertisements.[20]

Companion accelerations in other phases of daily life create more perceptual interference to critical thought. The pace and congestion of urban and suburban traffic is one such speed-making phenomenon. The "fast get-away" on the weekend is another. The fast-food industry sells speedy food through service publicized by blasting media. Instant or processed foods you can buy at the supermarket allow fast-foods to penetrate domestic life with a style of rushing. Instant lotteries are now spreading, combining the gambling, strike-it-rich motif with the accelerated pace of life. Home remedies advertised in the media race each other for which can relieve headaches or upset stomachs faster. While airplanes roar overhead and dashing fire-engines siren their way through the streets, everyday life is routinely surrounded with machines accelerating our activity: elevators, escalators, revolving doors, telephones, electronic cash registers now using the universal product code, motorized toothbrushes, food processors, electric razors, etc. The rise of the totally enveloping disco culture ideally confirms the hysterical saturation of the senses, which dishabituates consciousness to reasoned reflection. At another level of abstraction, the speed of mass culture displays the "quickie" motif, as a form of macho sex, dehumanized eroticism, and as a generalized theme for social exchange. The pace of stimuli and demands keeps people off balance and exhausted, yet so addicted to the destructive speed of life that they keep looking for more.

Such addiction to high levels of surface stimulation reduces mass reception of serious printed texts and deliberate verbal exchanges. Minds accustomed to amplified effects feel uncomfortable with the slow pace of critical thought. Hence, liberatory learning is unfortunately dissonant with the aesthetics of mass culture. Critical dialogue and densely worded books offer a jarring change in perceptual speeds and intellectual demands. This discomfort is clearly visible in my classrooms. It is manifested by short attention spans, by the impatience of some students towards those who are committed to careful scrutiny, and by body-shaking, where people self-generate the stimulation they need. Developing tolerance for the slow pace of critical intellect is a serious task for the liberatory class. The use of comedy, mime, and sequentially decelerating techniques can help ease the transition from thought-denying acceleration. These pedagogical resources will be explored in the next chapter, as part of an overall approach to acceleration and other forms of false consciousness.

As an anti-critical force, acceleration realizes the cliché of "going nowhere fast." It is reified motion, action without progress. People are kept very busy rushing through a crowded social field, at the end of which they feel no more whole or free than at the beginning. They finish the day as powerless as when they started. Their self-doubt has not been resolved. Tired from running, they remain in debt, looking for a better job, caught in traffic, wondering how to make ends meet, searching for a good mechanic or doctor or larger living space, or needing a more fulfilling love life. Liberatory culture has to wedge itself into this contradictory crack. The everyday rush is compelling but it is fundamentally a distraction from the unsolved problems of daily life. A transcendent classroom has to penetrate the distraction to expose the still alienating realities of work, family life, sex relations, race hostility, unemployment and vocationalized schooling. A conceptual study of these issues can change both the pace and quality of mass perception.

Mystification: The Little Woman and the Welfare Cadillac

Besides being immersed in the rush of daily life, people are also submerged in a host of cultural mystifications, which offer false answers to social questions. Reification stands in the way of seeing systematic wholes; pre-scientism discourages a search for rational explanations to authentic problems; acceleration makes the mind work too fast to probe deeply into anything; then, what more needs to be done to interfere with critical thought? Why even more ideological baggage, in the form of mystifications, to further manipulate popular intelligence? One reason is that despite all the cultural instruments propelling false consciousness, people still live with critical resources, and with genuine problems they want solved. To distort remaining intellect and to answer the longing for explanations, mass culture distributes mystifications.

The irrational base on which a pyramid of mystifications rests has already been laid through vocationalism, reification, pre-scientism and acceleration. Mystifications offer uncritical minds false ways to put it all together, to see an illusory whole, to integrate the confusing pieces into fraudulent truth or unity. Cultural myths, ideas, values, clichés and assertions are generated from many sources—church, school, politicians, media, business. Some are old and durable—America is the Promised Land—while some are new and spread quickly—America needs nuclear power to free us from the greedy Arab oil countries. Many are sexist—the Little Woman belongs in the kitchen, and many are racist—blacks use welfare to buy Cadillacs. Some serve as political prophylaxis against radicalism—better dead than red, the Red Menace versus the Free World, you can't fight city hall. Some promote macho individualism—every man's home is his castle, be your own boss, look out for number one. They can include pre-scientific faith in "human nature," "lady luck" and "name brands," but they also offer a larger world-view. The full range of mystifications includes practical advice on surviving hostile social relations as well as simple explanations for why so much is going wrong in society. Many people wonder, Why aren't things working out? Why isn't life easier than it is? Why is there unemployment, crime, pollution? Why does everything cost so much and work so badly?

If the people who asked these questions could find critical instead of mystical answers, the system would face great opposition. As it is, despite all the interferences to thought, there is persistent strike and protest activity, as well as much unorganized resistance in the form of sabotage, theft and vandalism. To distract people from their problems and questions, to divide them against each other so that they will not unite against the social order, and to ease people into a fatalistic acceptance of the status quo as the best of all possible worlds, an enormous range of mystifications filters into every piece of daily life.

The system of mystifications is very complex. They can be single statements, like "the grass is always greener," a phrase which summarily dismisses human aspiration as mere jealousy of the other person's success. Popular sayings like, "give him an inch and he'll take a foot" or "if you're so smart why ain't you rich?" offer a simple and comforting wisdom which rejects the need for serious reflection. Infantilized mass consciousness fears the confusion and complexity of life, so it looks to clichés like "mind your own business" and "keep your nose clean" to offer meaning as well as instructions. In addition to assertions which define and direct behavior, there are stereotypic conceptions which fortify social divisions. Such divisive conceptions include the Little Woman, the Bitch, the Welfare Cadillac, the greenhorn and the greaseball, the Honcho, and Number One. These clichés set off groups and individuals from each other, based on differences in sex, race and power. Words such as nigger, spic, mick, kike, wop, cunt, dyke, fag, are condensed linguistic expressions for whole mystified fields of belief which alienate oppressed groups from each other. Further, there are assertions which demonstrate a mystified self-conception, like "the Little Man." Reich was particularly concerned about this mystification of "the Little Man," "who is enslaved and craves authority and is at the same time rebellious."[21] He saw such mystified consciousness as a base for fascism.

In some instances of mystification, a single conception can be an umbrella for a trans-institutional practice. The case of "blaming the victim" demonstrates this. In a book with the rubric as its title, William Ryan discussed "blaming the victim" as a refusal to see "social problems as social."[21] Instead, individuals are blamed for their failure in a society which allegedly offers everyone opportunity. The person is indicted instead of the system. The answer to deviance, poverty or injustice is to change yourself, not the social order. The process of "blaming the victim" supports a righteous and defensive mass arrogance against the more oppressed sectors of the population. Men who live in a disempowering culture can support their own damaged egos by concluding how weak women are; thus, women don't deserve equal pay to men or equal athletic programs in the schools. Whites can soothe their own doubts about their social worth by feeling how blacks deserve the poverty they live in; if only blacks were as enterprising as whites, they could make life work for them," is one way racial mystification blames the victim. There is a flip-side to "blaming the victim" which makes it such a strong disguise of the systemic sources of oppression: "blaming the victim" feeds off "blaming yourself." Sexism in men and racism in whites is supported by self-doubt and irrationalism in the oppressing group. A life spent in a depressant mass culture, where the institutions are dominating you and "cooling you out" (See Chapter One), leaves people in a powerless anxiety. They have learned to blame themselves for their failures in society. Dehumanized by class-enemies they can't see or fight, they choose to gain some cultural compensation by fighting class-peers whose differences they can see. Raising consciousness about the structured failure built into the system is a key task of the liberatory class, vis à vis mystification.

In some important instances, the production of mystifications should be viewed through the action of organized sub-sectors, like the schools which do the "cooling-out" of mass aspirations. Beyond the vocationalization of popular thought and feeling by mass education, there are two other examples of sub-systems developing mystified consciousness: conservative politics and the spectator sports business. The emergence of the political tendency known as the "New Right" offers a good example of mystified ideology forming itself around concrete issues.[23] The "New Right" offers false remedies, distracting from the real problems of American life, under an umbrella of slogans: censor books in school, stop ERA, repeal abortion, keep the Panama Canal, stop forced busing, deport alien workers, restore capital punishment, no gay rights, cut taxes and government waste, go back-to-basics in the schools, and end reverse discrimination (a la Bakke). While these mystifications will not solve the basic problems of mass life, they gain strength from their linguistic concreteness and from their promise of some immediate goal or relief. Further, they are supported by the deepest levels of irrational thought developed in false consciousness: a powerlessness which fears both scientific inquiry and natural sexuality, the base on which racial, sexual and national chauvinisms rest. As a further example of sub-sector activity promoting mystification, the sports culture is ideal. It massifies people away from class-consciousness. The sports fan experiences de-politicized identity—not a worker or citizen or trade union member, but a Yankee or Red Sox fan. Athletic spectacles are notorious for their evocation of patriotism, with flags, marine color guards, national anthem, and tri-color bunting. Politicians are drawn to the ceremonial glamor, where working-class Bostonians become more angry at working-class New Yorkers than either are at the bosses or the system. While "blaming the victim" is a trans-institutional process dividing people, the sports culture is an example of a single institution separating what should be a common humanity. Compounding these divisive forces is another strong mystification that begins in family life but has become generalized in a non-institutional way in American society: ethnic identity. The phenomenon of the "hyphenated American" creates even more division in a populace already segmented by race, region and religion.

All mystifying clichés and processes, whether operative in one or many institutions, or whether stitched into daily life non-institutionally, need to be abstracted from common usage so that they can be rationally examined. By pulling them out from the fabric of daily life, the liberatory class can promote a transcendent re-experience of them. Many mystifications have names which are household words. Their linguistic familiarity is a current strength and potential weakness. Their vulnerability lies in their very legitimacy. When examined in a liberatory learning process, these mystifications make the students feel at home. The critical discourse begins with common currency. As the consequences and facticity of any mystification are scrutinized, the class expels itself from routine allegiance to false belief, while expelling the cliché from its routine possession of consciousness. In the case of a mystifying process whose shape is invisible and name unknown—like "blaming the victim"—the liberatory class will be revelatory, standing virtually alone as a vehicle for demystification in mass life.

Oh Say Can You Speak: The Non-Practice of Democracy

Mass culture can no more permit critical thought than it can allow the practice of democracy. Both these activities threaten domination. They can develop in people an autonomy which would jar the class hierarchies underpinning American life. Social relations are over-organized, so that people grow up rarely exercising self-discipline, self-organization, collective work styles, or group deliberation. In the family, in court, on the policed streets, at work, in church, in school, in unions, in voluntary associations, and in all the public and private institutions from Yankee Stadium to hospitals to unemployment offices, bureaucracy and hierarchy reign. A culture-wide addiction to and resentment of authority results. People become dependent on the very authorities they despise.

Despite the non-practice of democracy in everyday life, there is an awesome number of democratic mystifications. Clichés abound: the Free World, the New World, the Promised Land, God's Country, the land of the free, sweet land of liberty, land of opportunity, bill of rights, human rights. A contradictory basis underlies these terms. They emerged from the heroic period of American history when white settlers fled repressive European regimes and faced the hardships of pioneer life. As religious and political refugees, they ran from the poverty and white terror of the Old World. For blacks brought forcibly to America as slaves, the story is obviously different. Africans could not enter America with the kinds of Utopian feelings held by many white colonialists.

The high standard of living in America continues to attract immigrants from poorer countries. Moreover, American democracy is still appealing to fugitives from police states. This suggests that the democratic mystifications in American life have to be approached gingerly. The first white settlers survived the rigors of the frontier. Later immigrants survived the exploitation of industrial life. Their descendants have respectful roots in all the toil and aspiration invested so far in the making of American life. Non-whites have a different investment in the state of American democracy, after three centuries of fighting first slavery and then racism. People are justifiably sentimental about the sacrifices each generation has made for freedom and nation-building. Because these sentiments, especially among whites, are not critical or class-conscious, they can be parlayed into patriotic mystifications. Extricating popular achievement, Utopianism, and resistance from allegiance to the state and to corporate life is an intricate task for the liberatory classroom. The critical dissociation of class-identity from corporate-identity can be aided by examining labor history and the subsequent massive development of public and private bureaucracies. The imposing and dehumanizing presence of state and corporation in daily life contradicts the national mystification of democracy. Raising awareness of this contradictory announcement and denial of freedom is of strategic importance.

Race oppression has left minorities clearer on the question of national liberty, but the denial of democracy in everyday life is a general experience. People pay a price for talking back to parents, bosses, teachers, supervisors, cops, judges, landlords, credit-managers, and bureaucrats. Their superiors on the job are all appointed from the top, impervious to democratic discipline from below. At the same time, people exercise virtually no power over the officials they elect. The only local power the system permits involves supporting racism—whites are allowed to prohibit blacks and Latins from entering neighborhood schools or housing. Themselves economically pressed and power-starved, some whites have taken an opportunity to vote limits on their property taxes, used to support social programs for the poor and non-white; they also have been organized to use their voting power against gay rights. At the same time, they know how to wildcat against companies and unions denouncing unauthorized strikes. Such a chaotic and polarized political situation—the few rulers over the divided and mystified people—encourages episodic as well as self-destructive rebellion. Periodically and unpredictably, bottled-up people explode. This can lead to wildcats as well as to race riots, to sitdowns as well as to looting sprees. The absence of democratic forms in daily life retards the development of organizational skills needed for sustained political resistance. The oppressed themselves are most endangered by uncritical swings from resignation to disorganized rebellion, yet this is precisely the eccentric behavior conditioned by authoritarian mass culture.

Small Talk, Big Talk

Another consequence of the non-practice of freedom in daily life is an impatience with "talk." Ordered around by superiors who don't allow you to talk back, people are socialized into controlled "action." In the important institutional settings of mass culture, there is little dialogue and many commands. Thus, the official side of life includes an enforced silence which dishabituates people from gaining the experience of group discussion of policy. In a critical classroom, where mutual dialogue is a key learning process, the mass inexperience with "talk" poses serious problems.

Working people talk a lot among themselves, but grow quiet in the presence of authorities. To talk a lot in an institution, at work, at school, or in front of superiors, is to be guilty of collaborating with the enemy. Or, if you become too talkative, you open yourself to suspicion by your boss. If your talk in a classroom is too enthusiastic, you'll be thought of as a brown-nose or ass-kisser. If your talk is too rebellious, the teacher will consider you a trouble-maker. If you are articulate enough to stand up to the boss or teacher and get away with it, you'll earn the respect of superiors and peers. Because a power struggle surrounds the use of words in every institution of life, there are tense rules and high prices to pay for talking. At the very least, supervisors discourage people talking to each other because it interferes with productivity; in school, teachers dissuade students from talking to each other, or out of turn, not only to maintain order but also to maintain the teacher as the sole regulator of the talking.

The problematic nature of "talk" in mass culture has a sexist dimension as well as an undemocratic one. In my classes, women have talked with more ease than men. In general, women students find it easier to take public risks by engaging in critical debate. The men are cloaked in a formidable silence, fearing to be proved wrong in their opinions or feelings. Their linguistic style is abrupt and terminal; they are more likely to voice strong conclusions instead of partaking in an evolving dialogue. This kind of reaction is not uniform or universal, but there is a strong male defensiveness against the humiliation of being wrong. Some men have rationalized their withdrawal by saying that *women* talk and argue all the time. To talk too much is to be silly like a woman. Going public with your thoughts and feelings is a threat to macho dignity. Talking a lot in class means commitment to the process; commitment suggests feeling that the discussion matters to you; admitting publicly that something matters to you is a surrender of male coolness, a giving up of the disguised toughness where you tell the world you can make it on your own. Talking openly and seriously in a group is a statement that you need the others, and the men are reluctant to let on that they need anything from anybody. Their aloofness develops over the years, from hearing how worthless they are, from feeling inadequate in meeting the demands of others.

The male denial of talk is a kind of performance anxiety. Further, silence is a form of defense as well as resistance—it prevents the enemy from knowing what you think or feel, and using it against you. It also sabotages a controlling process that needs your verbal collaboration. In a culture where superiors regularly humiliate subordinates, it becomes understandable for students (especially men) to stay self-protectively silent in class. The power struggle involved in the politics of talking impressed Freire so much that he keeps emphasizing the "culture of silence" which surrounds the oppressed.[24] Finding the students' authentic and critical voice is so central to the liberatory process that Freire uses the words "dialogue" and "dialogic" in expressing the shape of transcendent learning.

The politics of talking in mass culture confront a dialogic process with numerous obstacles. It often appears to working people that articulateness is a class luxury. The rich can afford to sit and talk for hours. The boss jaws on the phone, his feet up on the desk. Politicians talk and talk, stealing the people's money and getting nothing done. Discussion is a privilege, not a democratically distributed right. Worse yet, the language of the powerful is not equivalent to the language of everyday life. Non-elite English, both white and black, is not the same as the Standard Usage taught in the schools and used by the authorities. Working people know that they will betray their inferior class-background by simply speaking. Why should they open themselves to judgment in front of a college-educated, articulate teacher? They are verbally intimidated in the presence of the elite, but in private, in their own idiom, they invent marvellous stories and satires. They cannot talk freely while a superior is present, which is why such a dramatic silence begins when the teacher enters the classroom.

This alienation of their language from power holds back their political development. It makes people accessible to manipulation by sloganeers. The other side of imposed silence is manipulated talk. Politically and commercially, mass culture fills people with countless words. Daily life is flooded with acceptable phrases, ideas, clichés, conceptions, slogans, seductions, and opinions. The language of Free World politics, macho sex and sports, big money, fast cars, flashy purchases, lurid movies, screeching music, and sensational crime, fill everyday talk. The words appropriate to critical reflection are virtually non-existent. So much needs to be done with langauge and democracy in a liberatory class. Both teacher and students need awareness about their patterns of discourse. The politics of language in school and in mass culture needs exposure. Where do we talk and how do we talk? What do our words mean? When are we silent and when do we speak? Which words do we use and not use? Detached scrutiny on our speaking and non-speaking is one way to jar students and teachers from immersion in their uncritical use of words. A critical discussion about uncritical talk opens up the possibility of transcending the linguistic limits of daily life.

Merry-Go-Rounding: The Problems of Private Life

The analysis so far indicates that mass experience is crowded with interferences to critical thought. The penetration of consciousness is multi-dimensional. The regressive modes of thought suggested by vocationalism, reification, pre-scientism, acceleration, mystification and anti-democratism, draw strength from their mutually supporting features. They are further strengthened by their appearance and reappearance in routine environs—school, family life, work, play, consumerism, religion, sex and race relations, media, and politics. Added to these interferences is another force which is not a way of thinking as much as it is a condition of living. *The demands of private life* need to be considered as another obstacle to the mass development of critical thinking.

On the non-elite campuses, non residential worker-students are not just college students. While attending community college, they are also parents, spouses and wage earners. Their many non-academic responsibilities include holding down paying jobs, doing housework and raising children. If they have not yet become parents, they are children with responsibility for other siblings or for older members of their extended families. Besides shopping, cooking, cleaning, laundry, home repairs and shuttling relatives to doctors, they spend a lot of time commuting from home to school to work and back to school or home again.

Older and younger worker-students feel harassed by the rigors of family life. However, both age groups experience a generation gap which disturbs their ability to dialogue. Younger students in their punk, hitter, hippie or even straight modes, express life-styles that irritate their elders. Conversely, the moderate demeanor of older students reminds the younger ones of their parents, who are the authorities in family life, setting limits and making demands. Meanwhile, the older segment sees their own children's rebelliousness mirrored by the young people's style in class. This leads to defensiveness on the part of both groups. As a divisive situation in daily life, the generation gap is an ideal theme for class projects; chapters in the ped-agogical section of this book will report some teaching experi-ences based on it. At this juncture, it matters to note that both groups feel oppressed and need reconciliation with the other. In general, the older section is more prepared for serious academic work than the younger one. On the one hand, they need more from college. Their family responsibilities are larger so they have immediate hopes about the college degree advancing them economically. Further, they feel they blew their big chance for school when they were young and wild, and now want to make this second chance really work. They have been sobered by years of making ends meet (they call it The School of Hard Knocks). Unlike the younger ones who have grown up surrounded by TV and rock music culture, the older students are less penetrated by the acceleration effect of mass life. Thus, they are able to concentrate with more ease. The youthful cohort is not only more dominated by mass culture, but it's also more antsy for experience, after eighteen infantile years of being bottled-up by school and family life. They want to encounter the world as grown-ups, so they are at the wrong age to sit and examine life with a deliberate intelligence. They long for a spacious sexual and social life, not for a scholarly one.

Young and old are crowded together wherever they are—home, school, highways, buses, trains, supermarkets, post-offices, banks or hospitals. Life is congested with noise and demands. Because the young lack full-time work, they don't have the money to leave home and live in their own places. Cramped in family quarters, they live day-to-day as young adults in a space which denies their adult autonomy. They have no choice but to find open territory by hanging out on street-corners, or in vacant lots, abandoned buildings and basements. Their search for unorganized space and time takes them to old cars, where they find the privacy they need for sex. Jalopies also offer them a sense of power, motion, and freedom, missing in their parents' homes, their teacher's classrooms, and their bosses' shops. The car in this social matrix offers a dehumanizing route to power. Backseat sex is a comic cultural legend, but it's also a scene of macho conquest. The aggressive men's use of cars against women is generalized socially against everyone by their wreck-less driving habits. The barbaric potential of the car expresses again the mechanical distortion of life which Reich feared. Social relations themselves have conditioned this eventuality, because mass culture fails to provide creative work, well-paid labor, private housing, critical learning, and non-sexist and non-racist models for adult life, all the things which young people especially need.

The Madding Crowd

Consider student life in the green-house college town. When you leave the family and the lower grades which infantilized you, the chance for autonomous adulthood is greater. In an articifial community of peers (the residential campus), your intellectual, sexual, artistic, emotional and political growth does not have to compete with the immediate limits of work and family chores, or commuting, or distracting non-academic street life. The elite college setting is far more nurturing of human development than the commuter campus. The residential school not only offers plusher facilities, smaller classes, more financial aid, more libraries, and more liberal arts, but it simply concentrates its nurturance into a self-enclosed space, so there is more free time and easier access to what you need.

In contrast, the dispersed lives of worker-students make them hurry away from class. They need to rush to their next course in a tightly-packed schedule, or need to catch a bus or pick up the kids or get to a burger joint for a four-hour shift. On a larger scale, they need to graduate as fast as they can, and zoom into the job market, degree in hand, looking for work. This leaves little time to lounge before or after class. They are less free to hang out and talk about art, politics, film, love, war and the meaning of life. A hard core of the most motivated and the most backward students do manage to stay on campus, the first seeking out professors for conversation, and the second making connections in the lounge and cafeteria, where they hang out, smoke dope, gamble, play ping pong and blast radios. Between these polar fringes is the vast majority which has little time to party, talk, attend a club or political meeting, or go to a march, rally, teach-in, lecture or poetry reading. Harassed and fragmented lives prevent the many who would stay on campus from pursuing their own development.

The shortage of free time and open space, for the privacy you need for study and for sex, retards not only critical thought and emotional growth, but also class solidarity. The liberatory ideas of communal life or collective deliberation or cooperative action surface as *more* threats to freedom. As far as worker-students can tell, they need to be accountable to *fewer* people, not more. They look for a lower profile of demands and responsibilities. Overwhelmed by family life, by teachers, by authorities and institutions, their gut feeling of freedom involves separation from social life, not collective social reconstruction. Non-accountability is a fantasy which emerges from an over-organized life.

The American Dream itself speaks to this need for autonomy—
buy your own land, be your own boss, strike it rich and enjoy an
independent income, hit the road in a van. A liberatory class
committed to group process will encounter anti-social weariness.
Students arrive with conflicting needs to "get away from it all" as
well as to "get together." Their real dreams for human community compete with their fears of even more dominating responsibilities. The contradiction here is intense: They are too isolated
and too involved at the same time. Social life is present with
demands and absent with supports. Their degree of social
isolation leads to the desire for more isolation. Atomized persons
in tedious jobs and in isolated families have so much to do, that
they long for a leisured disconnection from life. In addressing
this problem, the liberatory class needs what Mills suggested as a
public context for "clarifying one's knowledge of one's self:"

> The knowledgeable man in the genuine public is able to
> turn his personal troubles into social issues, to see their
> relevance for his community and his community's
> relevance for them. He understands that what he thinks
> and feels as personal troubles are very often not only
> that but problems shared by others and indeed not
> subject to solution by any one individual but only by
> modifications of the structure of the group in which he
> lives and sometimes the structure of the entire society.[25]

Life in the Parking Lot: Campus Etiquette and Aesthetics

There are large numbers of students who reject the vocationalization of their characters. They do what they can to fight
their way out of reification, acceleration and pre-scientism. The
absence of democracy in daily life is as annoying to them as is the
presence of too many domestic demands. This fraction of the
student group is interested in critical consciousness, questioning
the mystifications which flood mass culture. Racism, sexism, the
corporate order, the shape of everyday routines are becoming
problematic. Worsening social problems and exposure to critical
ideas has helped promote the development of this fragment.
Once in motion, such emerging students face the uninviting
reality of their community college. In terms of aesthetics and
social relations, the community campuses themselves become

further obstacles to critical thought.

Rural two-year schools enjoy a more sylvan milieu than urban ones, but they are generally cheaply constructed around a giant parking lot, near a highway. Comfortable lounges are few. Teacher offices are rarely private. There are simply not many places to sit quietly and talk. The noisy cafeteria smells of stale tuna fish and has a sticky floor stained with spilled coke and coffee. The library is small, overcrowded and distracting from the constant sound of shuffling feet. The surfaces of floors, chairs, tables, walls and doors communicate unyeilding messages: concrete, steel, asphalt, formica, fiberglass, mason-blocks, brick, tile, aluminum. A cold flourescent light bathes these textures. The cheapness, the coldness, the drabness and the hardness of the surfaces combine with the bad food, functional design of exteriors, and roaring noise of the expressway, to tell you that you should leave this place, that you and this college are not very important in American higher education. This kind of depressant aesthetic lowers aspirations. It weakens the motivations needed for serious intellectual growth. Everyone knows how comfortably furnished the elite schools are, so the repulsive environ of the worker-college is just one more judgment on the worthlessness of the students who go there. They respond to being third-class citizens by rejecting the academic work put in front of them and by vandalizing the milieu which recks of inequality and dehumanization.

Compounding the aesthetic incentive to leave, reject or damage the campus, are the negative social relations. The interaction between the students and the college staffs is often discouraging. The secretaries and janitors respond unevenly to the worker-students, who are their class peers. They can be helpful or hostile or just plain uninterested. The students don't know what to expect when they enter an office of the college looking for help. The mood swings of the non-academic staff, from defensive mistrust to sympathy to disregard, signal to students that they are not important enough to command respect. The non-teaching staff, drawn from the working class, feels privileged to be working at a college, but they are defensive in front of class peers who are on campus as college-attenders, not as employees. Lack of education makes the employed staff feel inferior. Still, many admire the students and offer intricate help; others, overworked, are annoyed at students who ask a million questions, hand in forms late, and need special attention. The bureaucratic rigamarole is confusing to everyone, in a time when the community college is still being shaped. The rules change frequently during an institution's formative period, making it hard for students to adjust to the red tape. They fill out the wrong forms right or the right forms wrong, but either way, the deadline was yesterday. The bureaucracy creates byzantine requirements which further interfere with learning, so it's reasonable for students to become impatient with the endless layers of regulations, written in an English few of them ever use. Their frustration triggers the annoyance of the secretaries who must deal with them. Adding to this unfortunate conflict among worker-peers is the fact that the janitorial staff is a domestic squad which must pick up after the students. So, they view students in terms of the mess they make. These situations are plain enough to observe if you talk with people on campus, listen to them relating, and watch what's going on. Some secretaries have mistaken me for a student, and have abruptly ordered me out of an office where I wanted to use a telephone. In enforcing the college rules against students' use of equipment, their voices have been unmistakably severe.

It would be unfair to characterize all worker-staff responses this way, but the point needs to be made, in terms of social relations which repel students from taking academic life ser- iously. Worker-students cannot count on the solidarity of their own class-peers, whose loyalty is badly divided by their own self- doubts and by their need to enforce rules made by superiors who can fire them. This ambiguous situation is worsened by the response of the academic staff to the students. The academic encounter is even more repelling than that with secretaries and janitors. Students begin with militarized registration, get passed on to counselors who have too many students to contend with, hear few answers, strange lingo and baffling directions, and wind up getting flung into a course like Jonah being spit out of the whale, because that class fit the schedule or was the only one still open. In such a depersonalized milieu, you come before a commuting teacher who will dash away from class and campus as quickly as the students. As middle-class professionals, the teaching staff is even more alienated from the students than are the secretaries and grounds crew. The language and demeanor of professors and worker-students are comically incompatible. The funky roughness of students disturbs professorial repose, generating a genteel paranoia about student violence, which keeps teachers on their toes. The class hour begins, and with lecture notes in hand, the professor starts bellowing the day's lesson, racing the clock. Clearly, there are supportive and creative teachers throughout the two-year network, doing critical education under the worst of conditions. Yet, the preponderant student experience is that of the aloofness and disdain of their professors. This is hardly surprising, given the training of the teacher group. The professoriat has as much to overcome as the students, in terms of designing education as a liberatory exercise.

Repulsive aesthetics and oppressive social relations have dogged students throughout their years in the mass education system. The drab decor and alienating interaction of the community college only continues the negative character of the lower grades. Twelve years of lower education has left another legacy which students and teachers must contend with—cognitive underdevelopment. For all their processing through the many layers of public schooling, college freshmen and freshwomen arrive with weak literacy, low bases of information, and unevolved conceptual skills. The liberatory class will have to deal not only with many bad feelings about school, but it will also have to present critical problems at the same time that it develops the cognitive faculties needed to handle critical inquiry. Nothing can be taken for granted here. The liberatory enterprise is pulled in many directions at once, as it evolves in a social field full of obstacles. The critical teacher who begins the study and teaching of mass reality starts without knowing what the students know and don't know. The encouraging news is that despite all the interferences, critical thinking happens regularly, in classes where students display a startling richness of intelligence and humanity.

Jumping Hurdles: Resources for Reconstruction

The interferences to critical thought are instructive as well as pervasive. Their comprehensive operation in daily life teaches us a number of lessons. First is how threatened the social order is by the popular emergence of critical thinking. Why would any culture evolve so much false consciousness unless its survival depended on mystification? The many impediments laid in front of mass intellectualism demonstrate that the political stakes are high. The struggle for critical consciousness is nothing less than a battle for a new social design. The epic proportion of this task is inspiring, but in times of low mass insurgency and much reactionary politics, it is difficult to see how our work in single classrooms fits into the whole. The development of an empowering pedagogy is a long process of cultural revolution. This form of cultural politics can be aided by keeping in mind a number of resources: a conceptual negation of the social interferences to critical thought; the educational experiments of Freire and his notion of "class suicide"; and the many strengths, skills and knowledges students themselves bring to class.

A model for transcendent learning can be designed by conceiving the *opposite* to the social field preventing liberatory thought. At an abstract level, liberatory transcendence involves the externalization of false consciousness. Mass culture is inside each mind no less than each person is inside mass culture. Critical education is a long process of desocialization, as each feature of dominated thought is expelled from consciousness. Programmatically, where mass schooling stresses vocationalism, liberatory culture promotes critical liberal arts, the integration of mental with manual arts, and the serious exploration of science and sentience in learning. A rational examination of thought, feeling and action in everyday life will serve as an antidote to pre-scientific mysticism. A focus on systemic questions can help reverse the fragmented perception represented by reification. Liberatory learning looks towards social mediations and interactive processes. In response to acceleration, the critical class develops modes for deliberate scrutiny. Experiments are needed with techniques for slowing down perception, through meditation, careful observation, and successively deeper phases of inquiry into a single issue. These kind of processes will prepare consciousness to reject the many kinds of mystifications circulating in mass culture. As a final negation of the interferences, the liberatory model includes the practice of democracy. An authority-dependent people can gain skills of self-discipline and self-organization only by taking responsibility for their learning. An egalitarian mode of education distributes a humanizing experience of shared power, which is incompatible with the subordination and power-mongering conditioned by mass culture. Overall, liberatory education can be thought of as a social practice out-of-sync with mass experience, yet rooted critically in the reality of daily life. Its form and content is transcendence of the given.

Two aspects of the given order will change slower than consciousness: the demands of private life and the repulsive aesthetics and social relations of the community college. Critical learning is an act of study which can lead to a study of action. Ideas change faster than institutions, so at the term's end, some features of false consciousness will be challenged, while such distractions as commuting and the crowded school library will remain just as oppressive. In fact, they may be more oppressive than before, because the consciousness of oppression will have been raised. This new critical awareness can be a prelude to the social action needed to change the structures of daily life. However, while there is a real connection between transcendent thought and social action, it is not immediate or mechanical. The redevelopment of people and society is a prolonged dialectical process, with advances, reversals, leaps, small steps, twists, and ironic, unexpected turns. This led Marx to call the process of social change an old mole, burrowing intricate and invisible channels underground, until one day its head bursts through the surface, quite unexpectedly. The French philosopher Paul Nizan captured the dialectics of revolutionary change through a similar metaphor. For him, the reality we see and act on is an outer shell under which enormous forces are developing, until they break through and reorder social life.[26]

In the prolonged process of critical learning, the change in the character of the teacher has been referred to by Freire as "class suicide."[27] This involves a transformation of class allegiance, away from the elite style conditioned by university training. However, the intellectual does not become modeled by mass culture and its brands of false consciousness. Neither is the university character a model for student development, because it is so removed from the circumstance of working, living and feeling in daily life. To criticize the mode of intellectuals is not to glamorize the students, whose character is not a model for the teacher. The teacher's investigation of daily life, and attendant reevaluation of his or her pedagogical mode, are preparation for initiating a process which transforms everyone involved. Both teachers and students become something different than what they started out. The teacher surrenders the mystique of power and expertise, while using his or her conceptual understanding of reality to provoke critical consciousness in the students, through which they reject their own class character. Teacher and students assume the personalities of people jointly designing a liberatory culture for themselves. These transformations are the optimum results of the liberatory process; most experiments in critical education will achieve partial realization. The role of teacher as initiator remains indispensable, because students have not yet been able to start it by themselves.

Down from the Pedestal

There are rewards for being on an academic pedestal: a sense of power, the admiration of an audience, acceptance by other professors for playing within the rules. Yet, there are burdens as well: alienation from students, a need to appear formidable, a fear of failing to meet the expectations of colleagues and students, the constant pressure to put on a good show, the defensiveness that accompanies the exercise of power over others. One aid to teachers easing their transition from an authority-model of education is an appreciation of the resources in students for the making of liberatory culture.

First among the resources is the problematic nature of daily life. People are short on cash while being alienated from the wage-labor they must perform to pay their bills. Unemployment is a common reality staring them in the face. The job shortage is only one of the harassing scarcities in everyday experience. Familiar commodities like gas and sugar, meat and wool, cotton and paper, rise mysteriously in price. Added to these dramatic cost increases is the general inflation rate. There doesn't seem to be enough of anything you need—parking space, mass transit, home mortgages, playgrounds, good schools, or carts in the supermarket. There is a decline in the quality of social life which especially deteriorates family relations: street crime, drug and alcohol addiction, strewn garbage, poor health care and mental services, and run-down housing. In addition to these culture-wide problems, certain segments of the population suffer surplus oppression. Females do the notorious "double-shift"—wage-earning job on the outside and domestic duties at home. They are paid less than men for the same work, and cannot move freely about society on their own. They are subject to rape and sexual harassment on the job, and on the street. Another group experiencing extra-oppression is the non-white sector. People of color find racism in virtually every corner of daily life. They are routine victims of police violence as well as institutionalized prejudice. The high profile of sexual and racial issues makes them obvious themes for investigations. By locating itself there and in the other unresolved problems of mass experience, the liberatory class legitimizes critical learning. It takes its stand against oppression through an unambiguous interest in the concrete problems faced by students.

The transparent oppressions of daily life are one resource for liberatory learning, but so are the unrecognized problems. There are oppressive features of culture which are not so obvious as high rent or the rush hour. The kinds of experience which are routinely or invisibly oppressive include the disco culture, fashion fads, spectator sports, advertisements, fast foods, noisy cars and wreckless driving, sexist and racist uses of language. Provoking a critical sense of routine dehumanization is a difficult task for a critical classroom. It's far easier to launch debate around unemployment or crime than it is to discuss the commerical control of leisure time, or the macho encounters between men and women, or the reflex racism in everyday conversation. The resource here lies in critically uncovering how these activities lead to self and social injury.

Besides the acknowledged and unacknowledged problems of everyday life, there is a further resource in certain strengths, skills and sentiments which students bring to class. One of the most prominent resources is a strong popular dislike for arbitrary power. People are socialized to submit to authority, but they retain a rebellious distrust of teachers, bosses, cops, judges, bureaucrats, and big outfits like corporations. They sentimentally want the little guy to make it in a world of big powers. Every day, they feel burdened by order-giving superiors, who they think of as arrogant parasites. Wrapped up in this feeling is pride in the genuine work they are able to do, as well as a nostalgic commitment to frontier, egalitarian America. Their pioneer-immigrant legacy disposes them to favor fair play, social justice, equal rights and open opportunities. The confusion of holding these sentiments in a society which allows little practice of democracy, and which divides the people racially and sexually, is great; it leads masses of people to support the denial of equality to sub-groups, like non-whites, women workers and homosexuals. Underlying their formal commitment to freedom and their practical rejection of equality is a still strong suspicion of organized authority. One concrete expression of democracy is their healthy disregard for decorum. They relate to each other in an up-front, refreshingly unceremonial way, quite unlike the formalities of the upper classes. Further, they long for a life close to nature. Industrial pollution is disgusting to them, even though they can be mystified by the corporations into equating ecology with loss of jobs, and nuclear expansion with greater employment. In their ideal society, there will be no scheming politicians, no payoffs, no freeloaders (welfare people or millionaires), no special favors—all the familiar corruptions of their present world. While their powerlessness attracts them to the power of uniforms, parades and weapons, they can also relate to war as a terrible waste of wealth and people, especially when adventures like Vietnam make imperialism glaring while the communist threat is so intangible.

Caught in a hostile and disempowering culture, they remain remarkably strong and good-natured. When treated with respect and equality, in class, their hidden resources open up. Savvy about life's nitty-gritty demands, they maintain a lively sense of friendship and comedy. They love good stories, satires, exaggerations, tall and bawdy tales (a strange mixture of good-humored kidding with aggressive sexist, racist and self-hating narratives). Side by side with anger and aggression is their modesty. They don't act spoiled, as if the world owes them something. They demonstrate an admirable seriousness, in meaning what they say and saying what they mean, and honoring commitments once they make them. Intellectually, they have barely been allowed to test their minds. Yet, they have more brain-power than they show in class or on the job. In an authoritarian setting like the traditional classroom, they perform worse than they can.

They will be surprisingly literate once their defenses lower. When they want to learn, they learn *fast*. Finally, the diversity of practical work-skills they bring to school is awesome.

Without recognizing and using these resources, a critical teacher would be unable to begin a liberatory process. Faced by all the social interference to critical thought, and by the university model of learning, the teacher and students need to use popular strengths to undo the damage of mass culture. On the one hand, it's fair to say that conditions are difficult for promoting liberatory education. Many objective realities point to this being hard times to start a transcendent offensive in school or daily life. On the other hand, the unresolved problems of everyday living are growing worse; every major institution of American life is in worse shape now than ten years ago—school, family, work, health care, housing, mass transit, the two-party system, welfare. Besides energy and minority activism, the political stage is still alive with constituencies, from women to gays to the handicapped to seniors to rank-and-file caucuses in the unions. Whatever the political profile in society-at-large, liberatory education make its contribution. The forces of domination are only as large as the unsolved problems of culture. If the division and mystification of the people appear immense, they are tailored to be big enough to cover the giant contradictions of an irrational social order.

The building of a liberatory pedagogy begins from the facts of domination and social pressure. It is an enterprise supported by the refusal of teachers and students to surrender their humanity or their future. Beneath false consciousness, there are resources which survive the acidity of mass culture, waiting for a reconstructed life.

Notes

1. Stanley Aronowitz, "Mass Culture and the Eclipse of Reason: The Implications for Pedagogy," *College English*, April, 1977, pp. 768-774.

2. *Ibid.*, p. 768.

3. See Freire's *Education for Critical Consciousness* (Seabury, New York, 1973), especially the first section, "Education as the Practice of Freedom." Also, the theory of "concientization" or teaching for critical consciousness is discussed most directly in the first two chapters of Freire's *Pedagogy of the Oppressed* (Seabury, New York, 1970) and in the first essay on the adult literacy process in Freire's *Cultural Action for Freedom* (Penguin, Baltimore, 1975). An informative report on the Freirian technique can be found in Cynthia Brown's pamphlet *Literacy in 30 Hours*. Brown's essay is an expanded version of a paper first appearing in 1974 in *Social Policy* magazine. Her association with the Open Learning Center at Berkeley addresses the question of the American adaptation of Freire's methodology. Brown's pamphlet is available from Writers and Readers Publishing Cooperative, 9-19 Rupert St., London WIV 7FS, England.

4. The most detailed account of how Freire and his teams examine the concrete reality of their students is in *Pedagogy in Process* (Seabury, New York, 1978). The first half of this book is Freire's "letter-report" to the reader, about how he and the other teachers educated themselves into the situation of Guinea-Bissau, the newly liberated territory where they were asked to assist in literacy programs. Believing that experiments cannot be repeated but need to be reinvented, Freire made numerous visits to Guinea-Bissau, and exchanged detailed letters with the education ministry there, prior to co-developing a program for that country.

5. Freire, *Cultural Action for Freedom*, p. 29 and p. 30.

6. "The Other Face of Bread" by The Workers' University, *Cross Currents* (Pushcart Press, New York, 1977) translated by Emmanuel L. Papparella. This collectively written document first appeared in the Italian monthly *Humanitas*. It is the expression of a group of Italian migrant workers living in Brussels, representing their group reflection and action on their oppressive situation.

7. Freire, *Pedagogy in Process*, p. 78.

8. Studs Terkel, *Working* (Pantheon, New York, 1972), p. 29. For more perspective on how people feel about their life in work, see also Barbara Garson's *All the Livelong Day* (Penguin, New York, 1977).

9. Wilhelm Reich, *The Mass Psychology of Fascism* (Noonday, New York, 1971), p. 335. The consequences of performing alienated labor in a machine culture greatly preoccupied Reich. He saw the frustration and rigidity leading to the exclusion of rational thought, compassionate feeling and natural sexuality, a situation which supports fascist mentality.

10. Terkel, *Working*, p. xi, p. 29, and p. 160. In his introduction, Terkel is compelled to notice how great a fear of machines exists in his worker-subjects. In their remarks, the working people he interviewed frequently refer to the machines as a force of their dehumanization, better cared for by the bosses than the humans who work them. This theme of machine-oppression is one of the few unifying threads in Terkel's sprawling report.

11. C. Wright Mills, *The Power Elite* (Oxford, New York, 1956), p. 318.

12. *Ibid.*, p. 319.

13. Harry Braverman, *Labor and Monopoly Capital* (Monthly Review, New York, 1974). See especially part two, "Science and Mechanization." This work is a brilliant investigation of the dehumanizing effects of corporate automation. The focus is mainly on the "degradation of labor" through the imposition of class-based mechanization and the division of labor. The implications for other dimensions of culture, such as schooling and family life, are discussed suggestively, but need more elaboration than Braverman could include in this single book.

14. Freire, *Pedagogy of the Oppressed*, pp. 48-49.

15. Georg Lukács,, *History and Class Consciousness* (MIT Press, Cambridge, 1971). See the chapters "Class Consciousness" and "Reification and the Consciousness of the Proletariat." Lukács' suggestion, vis a vis false consciousness, that "the many individual wills active in history for the most part produce results quite other than those intended—often quite the opposite"(p. 47),and that reified action "fails subjectively to reach its self-appointed goals, while furthering and realizing the *objective* aims of society of which it is ignorant and which it did not choose"(p. 50), are good starting points for examining the ironies of dominated thought. An ancillary question is relevant here: While it makes sense for irrational thought to result in unintended or opposite results, the dialectics of social change suggest that rational, class-conscious thought and action will also have unpredictable, unforeseeable consequences. The distinctions between a dehumanized social process and a humane one seem to lie less in knowing exactly what the shape of the future will be than in the value-structure on which the future rests.

16. *Ibid.*, pp. 50-53.

17. *Ibid.*, pp. 89-90.

18. Freire, *Cultural Action for Freedom*, pp. 40-42.

19. John Berger, *A Fortunate Man* (Writers and Readers, London, 1976), p. 102.

20. For the ideological content of printed advertising, consult Chapter 7 of John Berger's *Way of Seeing* (Penguin, New York, 1973). In part, Berger's analysis locates ads as a future-denying force, which promises what commodities can't deliver—an ideal future if only you

buy this or that. This false appeal crowds out genuine Utopian thought.

21. Reich, *The Mass Psychology of Fascism*, p. xv. Reich saw the mentality of the "little man" as ripe for reactionary politics, as long as his real problems, authority-dependence mixed with rebelliousness, were played out in a culture of domination. Two considerations of the American "little man" present this problem in a U.S. context, even though they lack the radical depth Reich brought to bear on the issue: Patricia Cayo Sexton and Brendan Sexton, *Blue Collars and Hard Hats* (Vintage, New York, 1971), especially their chapters on "Grievances" and "Equality," and Richard Sennett and Jonathan Cobb, *The Hidden Injuries of Class* (Vintage, New York, 1973), a more sophisticated assessment than offered by the Sextons. For a sensitive account of alienation in the worker-family, see *Worlds of Pain* (Basic, New York, 1976), by Lillian Breslow Rubin.

22. William Ryan, *Blaming the Victim* (Vintage, New York, 1971), p. 16. The operation of this process in the school system is discussed in Ryan's second chapter especially. For other accounts, see Burton Clark's "The Cooling-Out Function in Higher Education," Annie Stein's "Strategies for Failure," and Sherry Gorelick's "Open Admissions: Design for Failure?" cited in introduction and first chapter of this book.

23. For a current assessment of New Right politics and the New Left, see "Sex, Family and the New Left: Anti-Feminism as a Political Force," by Linda Gordon and Allen Hunter, *Radical America*, winter, 1977-78.

24. See chapters 2 and 3 in Freire's *Pedagogy of the Oppressed*.

25. Mills, *The Power Elite*, p. 318.

26. Paul Nizan, *Antoine Bloyé* (Monthly Review, New York, 1973). Nizan's novel about a peasant who rises to become a mid-level railway official, offers an insightful account of the self-repression accompanying upward mobility. Dickens offered a similar view through the character of Bradley Headstone, in *Our Mutual Friend*. To achieve respectability and success, worker-children have to surrender their naturalness to the mechanical demands of the work-world. Repressed, morbid and alienated characters result. Nizan focuses on the vocational training in school which facilitates this manipulation of class character:

> Antoine receives a scholarship to secondary school, a scholarship for special instruction, of course...No one thinks of teaching Antoine Latin, much less Greek...He will not be a man of culture, he will not sprinkle his speech with bouquets ...Sons of farmers, artisans and minor functionaries receive special instruction. What use would they have for the humanities? The laurels of the liberal arts are not for their brows. Arts of free men? Free men who have incomes.(p. 43)

Bloyé moves up economically, through a narrow mastery of technical knowledge. He lives an arid life, contained sexually, emotionally, politically and intellectually.

27. While Freire speaks consistently of the need for reconciliation between teachers and students, his thoughts on this question are pursued most concretely in *Pedagogy in Process*. Earlier, in *Pedagogy of the Oppressed*, Freire had elaborated the dialogic theory which underlies his practice of democratic pedagogy. By the later work, *Pedagogy in Process*, he considers the issue of teacher transformation through the idea of "class suicide", enunciated by Amilcar Cabral in the struggle to free Guinea-Bissau from Portuguese rule. Freire agrees with Cabral that the university-trained intelligentsia and the urban middle-class elite can play a significant role in the revolutionary process if they can transform their own class background, and identify with the needs of the oppressed. Without their own "class suicide," however, the elite are unfit to teach or lead the oppressed. Freire sees the political role of the transformed elite as indispensable, but the threat to freedom by an unreconstructed intelligentsia is great enough for him to recommend training unpolitical peasants as teachers before choosing unpolitical youth from Guinea-Bissau's urban middle-class (p. 82, *Pedagogy in Process*).

PART TWO

RECONSTRUCTED LEARNING

...their English teachers would wince and cover their ears and give them flunking grades and so on whenever they failed to speak like English aristocrats...

Kurt Vonnegut, *Breakfast of Champions*

Teachers sometimes talk about things the students know nothing about and expect the students to comment on the discussion but if they do not know anything about it they cannot participate.

Student in one of my classes

Knowledge about things is static. There is no quarantee in any amount of information, even if skillfully conveyed, that an intelligent attitude of mind will be formed.

John Dewey, "Democracy and Education"

Being conscious...is not simply a formula or slogan. It is a radical form of being.

Paulo Freire, *Pedagogy-in-Process*

CHAPTER THREE

EXTRAORDINARILY
RE—EXPERIENCING THE ORDINARY:

Theory of Critical Teaching

Sunday Evening Angst

Sunday night is one of the cruellest times of the week. Blue Monday follows soon after, the cause of Sunday evening anxiety. The start of every new week sees a hundred million Americans going off to work, while another sixty million march to school. The realm of ordinary routines is simply enormous. The ordinary experiences of life—school, work, family—not only fill time, but they also shape language, behavior and imagination. In the face of unbroken routines, life's Utopian possibilities fade. Liberatory culture resists this eventuality. Like a riptide, it cuts a disruptive path across the domesticating flow of events.

As a part of liberatory culture, critical teaching challenges the limits on thought and feeling. A critical classroom pushes against the conditioned boundaries of consciousness. The enveloping realm of the routine is extracted from its habitual foundations. When the class examines familiar situations in an unfamiliar way, transcendent changes become possible. Such an animation of consciousness can be formulated as *extraordinarily re-experiencing the ordinary*. This key rubric locates an empowering theory of knowledge in the re-perception of reality.

The transcendent appreciation of the ordinary sets an

overall parameter for liberatory learning. Starting from this conception, we can synthesize other contours for an exercise in critical education:

- social life in dialogue
- self-regulation of process
- withering away of the teacher: variant functions, oscillating distances
- symbolic separation: expulsion and re-entry into mass experience
- contextual skill-development
- conceptual exercises
- self-created media and texts
- ego-restoration
- character-structure awareness
- integrative study formats: component group work, collective work styles
- organic evolution/evaluation versus behavioral syllabi and testing: self-measurement, feedback sessions, peer and mutual assessments
- comedy as a learning resource: merging work and pleasure, comic language as a popular means of resistance
- the convertible classroom: spatial functions and the profile of student needs.

This systematic outline will be elaborated in the coming pages. It is best appreciated as a flexible agenda of pedagogical resources. As a variety of liberatory modes, it can't be applied in a cookbook way, and it can't guarantee automatic success. Taken together, the conceptions are an assembly of frameworks in-progress, having emerged from my teaching experience, and from my familiarity with Freirian and progressive education practices. Such a liberatory system can be useful in provoking critical reflection by teachers and students. Yet, it can propel extraordinary learning only by its adaptation to the ordinary circumstances of each classroom.

Ordinary/Extraordinary: Dialogic and Dialectic Process

As a seminal conception of liberatory theory, *extraordinarily re-experiencing the ordinary* involves the externalization of false consciousness. Critical learning challenges alienation by connecting student awareness to the mesh between interior psyche and external control. Dissociating mass psychology from mass culture involves designing courses which jointly address self-in-society and social-relations-in-self. This is a way of knowing which can extroject false ideas from consciousness. Freire called this active transcendence of domination "conscientization," a learning process larger than literacy and a teaching style different than the delivery of compelling lectures.

In the Freirian system, social practice is the thing studied, while "dialogue" is the form of study. As conceived in a politicized pedagogy, dialogue is a democratic model of social relations, used to problematize the undemocratic quality of social life. The dialogue form for learning itself contradicts hierarchical society and its mass schooling. The form and content of the class dialectically support each other, as the practice of freedom through the study of oppression. From his roots in liberation theology, Freire posited dialogue as a critical and criticism-stimulating activity. Not only egalitarian, it is also mobilizing, the pedagogical means to advance political consciousness. He distinguished "horizontal" dialogue as a liberating pedagogy from "vertical" anti-dialogue as an oppressive pedagogy:

DIALOGUE
A with B =communication
            intercommunication
Relation of "empathy" between two "poles" who are engaged in a joint search.
MATRIX: Loving, humble, hopeful, trusting, critical.

ANTI—DIALOGUE
A
< | over
B=communique
Relation of "empathy" is broken.
MATRIX: Loveless, arrogant, hopeless, mistrustful, acritical.[1]

The key feature of this method is the transition it can effect from one state of consciousness to another. The transcendent possibilities of dialogic learning lie in its political and moral values, which are incompatible with social oppression. The structure of learning itself challenges structures of control.

As a transcendent mode of teaching, dialogics integrate a theory of discourse, subject matter and political power. This radically egalitarian method is not automatically grasped by left or dissident teachers. The act of study needs to be thought of as an act of cultural democratization; democratic relations in class legitimize the critique of oppression; students experience freedom while examining the forces which impede freedom. The practice of democracy in study is the study of democracy in practice. This dialectic action disrupts the routine submission to authority in and out of school. Ordinary roles become problematic—the teacher no longer issues commands and the students no longer can fall back on authority-dependence. The extraordinary disruption of familiar order empowers students.

An egalitarian class is by its nature a humanizing reconstruction of social life, where so little democracy is permitted. Transcendent teaching is innately Utopian, humanistic and interactive, in sharp contrast to the pragmatic, programmed and mechanistic modes predominant in mass education. In resisting the authoritarian style of mass culture in school, liberatory learning rejects the behaviorism of rote lessons and machine testing. Liberatory theory can be analyzed and systematized, but each liberatory class cannot be standardized. The structure of each class is shaped from the inside by an interaction of teacher and students. Each semester's work is most authentically described at its conclusion, after its organic growth from a base in liberatory ideas and methods.

Counter-Structures: Doing, Un-Doing, Re-Doing

The dialogic method asserts counter-structures against behavioral models. It dis-orders reality with modes for self-ordering. An example of this is the methodology of literacy teaching used by Freire.[2] He and his associates employed flexible agendas for each session and a variety of pedagogical materials. Before using phonetic cards to teach the alphabet, the Freirian teams showed slides to the class, to provoke a long discussion on the culture-making powers of humans. In addition to phonetic cards and pictorial representations, there is also systematic teacher-training. The design of transcendent counter-structure is an art which demands a high level of consciousness in the teacher who initiates the process. Freire found that

> A major problem in setting up the program is instructing the teams of coordinators. Teaching the purely technical aspect of the procedure is not difficult; the difficulty lies rather in the creation of a new attitude—that of dialogue, so absent in our own upbringing and education. The coordinators must be converted to dialogue in order to carry out education rather than domestication.[3]

Throughout his writing, Freire remarks on the need for teacher reconstruction, which will facilitate the reconciliation of teachers and students. This theme receives its greatest prominence in *Pedagogy in Process*, the report of his work with the revolutionary government in Guinea-Bissau.[4] His insistent use of the term "class suicide" is not a melodramatic approach to the problem of teacherly manner. Instead of self-flagellation or guilt-tripping, Freire rather realistically assesses how indispensable the teacher is to the liberatory learning process. It is a difficult task to use dialogue as the means to systematically and problematically *re-present* to students what they have unsystematically and uncritically taught the teacher. The teacher is the architect of this un-doing and re-doing. The extraordinary re-experience of the ordinary cannot begin or proceed without the teacher's counter-structures. This is an inspiring and awesome situation for teachers, who so often feel trapped in the slough of despond. So much can be gained or lost in the project of liberatory teaching.

Conversions: The Object-Subject Switch

The teacher who changes to liberatory modes accepts responsibility for a process which converts students from manipulated objects into active, critical subjects. This empowering conversion is the result of re-perceiving reality. The teacher can prepare for this eventuality by studying the students in advance of teaching, and by grasping the overall process as *self and social inquiry designed for consciousness-raising skill development*. This formulation asserts the integral development of the liberatory process in each student. For each class, the teacher qualitatively

assesses the initial levels of cognitive skills and political awareness, while listening to the thematic and linguistic profile of
student reality. Cognitive and affective growth, informational
resources and political awareness, emerge concurrently through
the critical study of life by critical lives in study. The structure of
values underlying these conceptions remains the same: social
practice is studied in the name of freedom, for critical consciousness; democracy and awareness develop through the form of
dialogue; dialogue externalizes false consciousness, changing
students from re-active objects into society-making subjects; the
object-subject switch is a social psychology for empowerment;
power through study creates the conditions for reconstructing
social practice.

The conversion of popular consciousness from mass to
liberatory culture mobilizes students into a struggle for "ownership of self."[5] The dramatic distinction between owning yourself
or being owned involves a democratic or a massified form for
society, a humanized or de-humanized model of social relations.
The humanization of reality starts with humanization of students into subjects, who insert themselves into history. Reflecting on subject-making dialogics, Joel Spring writes "To be
human is to be an actor who makes choices and seeks to guide
one's own destiny. To be free, to be an actor, means knowing
who one is and how one has been shaped by the surrounding
social world."[6] Liberatory teaching thus leads a symbolic exodus
from oppression.

The Withering Away of the Teacher:
Separation, Transformation, Re-Integration

One goal of liberatory learning is for the teacher to become
expendable. At the start and along the way, the teacher is
indispensable as a change agent. Yet, the need to create students
into self-regulating subjects requires that the teacher as organizer fade as the students emerge. It is useful to examine how the
teacher's profile changes, how the evolution of the liberatory
process demands and then rejects direction.

The critical learning initiated by the teacher effects a
symbolic expulsion of students from daily life so that they may
re-enter with critical consciousness. The separation, transfor-

mation and re-integration of students can be looked at from a number of perspectives. First, from an epistemological point of view, there is the method of abstraction which dissociates routine thought, behavior, language and situations. Single features of everyday life are isolated as themes for study. This is the method which uproots the ordinary pieces of experience for extra-ordinary reflection. A critical dialogue around an abstracted part of life permits students to gain detachment from the structure of social relations inside and outside their minds. Abstraction serves to evict mass culture from thought. A reflective detachment on daily life is a means to push yourself away from the ordinary by pushing the ordinary away from you. This is the starting point of separation, which allows a transformative process to begin. A second aspect of dissociating from routine consciousness is less metaphysical. It involves the classroom being a physical reality separate in time and space from the other dimensions of living. The temporary separation permitted to the classroom, as a formal study space apart from the routines of earning money, commuting, raising children or arranging leisure-time, allows it room to experiment with reflection on all aspects of social life. A third way of understanding the symbolic separation achieved by the liberatory class is to see the sessions as an experiential matrix distinct from the emotional, political, social and intellectual values familiar to the rest of life. The experience of separation can only occur if these dimensions are arranged to trip the onrushing flow of experience. The liberatory classroom is a break from routines which offers a study of routines so that the familiar shape of life is appreciated with criticism rather than acceptance. As a separate zone for consciousness change, the liberatory classroom can break with the flow of events, the students' routine immersion in mass culture. The object-subject switch relates to this process of separation. Students are separated from the culture which has made them into manipulable objects, and with critical consciousness replacing false thought, they leave the class as subjects, that is, as people mentally armed against domination. If the liberatory process takes hold, then expulsion/reconstruction/re-entry represents a model for humanization through learning. In a society devoted to humane social relations, philosophical and physical separation will not be crucial to liberatory growth. All institutions and situations would promote critical awareness. In mass culture, separation is fundamental to transcendent change.

The person responsible for provoking separation and critical re-entry is the teacher. By identifying, abstracting and problematizing the most important themes of student experience, the teacher detaches students from their reality and then re-presents the material for their systematic scrutiny. As the process evolves, one measurement of student development is how much direction the teacher needs to offer. If separation-reconstruction and the object-subject conversion are progressing, then the teacher will have to offer less direction and more support in other ways. This internal, organic test of development—assessing how much direction the teacher is responsible for—is a means for determining the progress of humanization. When the liberatory process is working well, the learners themselves assume more responsibility for the class. The students' emergence as subjects involves their growing self-regulation, which suggests that the teacher will simply regulate the class less. A successful class begins preparing students with the critical skills they need to pursue learning. They become their own systematizers, organizers and cultural analysts.

This ideal eventuality—the full subjective emergence of the students and the withering away of the teacher—means that the initiating/organizing function has become generalized in class, distributed to the group rather than an expertise possessed by one person. The class can then set for itself more advanced problems, which may require calling in specialists at the discretion of the group or doing special investigations of a body of knowledge. In my own teaching practice, several of these moments have occurred. It was refreshing and startling to feel the process lifted from me into the class as a whole. Most often, this kind of development was only partial. The progress towards subjective emergence and self-regulation is a very difficult one: it is not a direct march forward, but is rather full of advances and regressions, inconsistencies, surprises and reversals. The classes which did become self-organizing did not order me out of the room. In fact, the more autonomous the students, the more they wanted my presence. Perhaps they enjoyed the sense of power in disciplining me into my role in the process. Perhaps they wanted me around for reassurance, in case something went wrong. Perhaps they simply enjoyed my participation in the reconstructive process. In any event, as my teacher/initiator role receded in the most advanced classes, I found myself assuming a number of other functions. The first new role was that of *peer-discussant*, a member of the dialogue on equal terms with all the others in class. As long as the process moved ahead, I could be peer-discussant and other things too; but when it broke down in ways the class itself could not repair, I needed to separate myself out from the group to become problematizer/coordinator again. Instances of regression are the acid-tests of dialogic education; the temptation for the teacher to lecture is great. Re-focusing the class on its thematic problem tests the teacher's own evolving skill as a cultural organizer.

Given this conception of liberatory education, the teacher's function is in constant motion in class. The teacher accepts a variety of roles, at oscillating distances from the action. The teacher is the person whose intellectual skills make her or him responsible for provoking conceptual literacy in the critical study of a subject area. However, as the process takes, the teacher is not always the leading factor in class. After catalyzing discussion, at moments of the greatest success, the teacher experiences a dissolution, blending into the group deliberation. At moments of partial or full breakdown, the teacher experiences her or his role reconstituted, separated out for the restoration of the process.

Listening: Ready for Anything

A liberatory learning process is very demanding on the teacher. Changing roles and operating at varying distances from the activity requires that the teacher pay careful attention to what's going on. At every moment, the teacher must be a sensitive listener, to assess the forward, lateral or regressive motion of the session. There will be ideal moments for intervention, withdrawal and re-entry. A process which unsettles the routines of life is itself unsettling and non-routine.

The teacher needs to come to class with an agenda, but must be ready for anything, committed to letting go when the discussion is searching for an organic form. The teacher's initiating agenda and pedagogical materials start a process which keeps redesigning itself in-progress. By offering problem-statements, the teacher begins as provocateur of conceptual inquiry, but eventually the class can set its own agenda by reflecting on its previous session, thus making each phase of its own development grounded in a recognition of its growth so far. As the responsibility of self-reflection generalizes in class, the spectrum of roles performed by the teacher become much broader than those of initiator/coordinator and peer-discussant. At times, the teacher may simply be a *convenor* of the class hours. In other circumstances, the teacher may be called upon to be a *facilitator* of a special study or project needed by the class. Still other functions are *advocate* for a perspective missing in the discussion or *adversary* to a line of thought or to a kind of oppressive behavior appearing in the discussion. The class may call upon the teacher to be a *lecturer* on a body of information or a problem about literacy or about conceptual habits of mind, which will propel the class across an impasse. On occasion, the teacher may serve as *recorder* of the sessions, whose minutes enable the class to examine its own learning process. Sometimes the teacher will need to be a *mediator* for divisive tendencies in the class, and at other times the teacher will be a *clearinghouse* or *librarian* through which resource materials pass. A process which mobilizes the critical consciousness of the students places the teacher into a mobile complex of roles. Down from the pedestal and out from behind the lectern, the teacher leaves behind the simplicity of lectures and term papers for something much more rigorous and compelling.

Working in a matrix of roles and functions, the teacher finds that her or his responsibilities increase and decrease at the same time. There are moments when the teacher plays a high profile role, in the initiation of the dialogue and in restoring the process along the way. The teacher is the class member with the greatest command of critical literacy and academic discipline, so the passing on of these skills begins with the initiative of the instructor. Yet, as the class develops, it adjusts the teacher's profile. An unorthodox and self-shaping process brings with it many surprises and rewards. When initiative begins to pass to the class, a great weight is taken from the teacher, whose experience of reconciliation with the class is inspiring. Quite simply, as the students' sense of responsiblity emerges, the responsibilities of the teacher ease. One of the larger rewards in this development is the unconventional pace of growth. Students learn so quickly once they emerge as subjects of the learning process. In the object-subject switch, self-regulation decreases alienation, and alienation is the largest learning problem of students. The quick pace of learning in the non-alienated classroom raises a fundamental challenge to the behavioral/mechanical modes of education—one lesson plan for each class hour, four class lessons each week, fifteen class weeks each term, two terms a year, etc. These arbitrary and regimented time frames for learning become strikingly inappropriate, once the liberatory process takes hold. People then learn in remarkably brief and unpredictable spans and moments, reflecting their organic needs. This organic time span in liberatory learning concretely humanizes education. Education is not ruled or timed by an alienating institution but sets its own chronology. What this means in practice is that single sessions may be longer or shorter than the time allotted for them by the schedule grid; single courses may actually finish before semester's end, or may need one and a half, two or three terms to mature. Time itself is one of the controlling routines of life challenged by an extraordinary process. When a class acknowledges that its learning has ended before the term is officially over, or that its work is not complete by end-term, it has an experience of being in command of its own education. The authenticity of this moment is exciting, after so many years of being ruled by artificial, clocked regimens. The teacher has a place in this authentic community of learners, no longer responsible for furiously filling the air with words, in those painfully slow weeks dragging on to final exams.

This ideal development of teacher and students, where both mutually evolve the class, permits the students to grow into an intellectual character which is not mere mimicry of the professorial style. Through a prolonged process, the transfer of initiative opens up unfamiliar personality development. A venerable architecture of power, like the temple of the Phillistines, falls unexpectedly around us. People pass beyond the ordinary models of life.

Using Daily Life: Hamburgers and the Ordinariversity

The irony of liberatory learning is that profound changes can occur through a critical study of ordinary life. Transcendence lies in the reversal of everyday conditioning. University training has left teachers with little experience in mass culture or in problem-posing dialogics. The turn in pedagogy towards daily life can open vast resources of subject matter. For every class and discipline, themes lie around us.

Further, the adaptation of study to the situations of mass life will make intellectual work of tangible relevance to students. This will be a novelty to them. Prior years of mass schooling have been ridiculously remote from their needs, so school itself has helped invalidate mental work. As it now stands, the power of the mainstream runs separately from the power of structural thought. Bringing the two together is a simple idea. It will also be catalytic.

For this project, some conceptual shapes or objectives are useful to bear in mind. One of the first operational shapes for liberatory teaching could be called *contextual skill-development*. This suggests that cognitive skills—reading, writing, comprehension, laboratory techniques, etc.—will be developed through a problematic examination of a real context, drawn from student life. As a basic method, contextual skill-development points to teaching introductory techniques through materials or activities which express a critical view of daily life. Traditionally, an academic discipline tends to teach its special body of knowledge abstractly, conservatively or narcissistically. The examples drawn in texts or lectures relate to no one's experience, or promote the experience of an elite, or else are simply couched within the discipline's own terminology. This prevents the study of any discipline from being a critical encounter with social life. The results are so absurd that the orthodox disciplines become their own worst enemies, repelling the masses of students from taking their methods seriously. Students leave such history, psychology and chemistry classes little wiser about the concrete problems they live with. The liquidation of their interests from academics serves to liquidate academic life from their interests. The idea of contextual cognition asserts the need to integrate concrete reality into formal study, so that the shape of official knowledge is transformed.

If skills are not learned in a problematic context drawn from experience, then the teaching will serve to domesticate the students to the methods of the discipline. The course will involve the submission and adjustment of the learners to the transmitted expertise of the teacher. This kind of passive structure for education will preclude the students separating from and then reentering their experience. The memorizing form of study has been called by Freire the "banking system" of education, in which professors make deposits of knowledge in the empty accounts of their students' minds:

> The role of the educator is not to "fill" the educatee with "knowledge," technical or otherwise. It is rather to attempt to move towards a new way of thinking in both educator and educatee, through the dialogical relationships between both. The flow is in both directions. The best student in physics or mathematics, at school or university, is not one who memorizes formulae but one who is aware of the reason for them...In the process of problematization, any step made by a subject to penetrate the problem-situation continually opens up new roads...This is why educators continue to learn.[7]

The teacher's conviction that she or he can learn important things from the students is a keystone of this process. Without that belief, the educator will be rejecting student reality as a rich resource for thematic problems. Also, the teacher who does not seek to learn from the class will not listen carefully to what students offer, and hence will condition students into nonspeaking. With a feeling for student resources, the liberatory teacher can embark on the experimental design of problem-models for each discipline. These models can animate an authentic encounter between student consciousness, reality and intellectual methods. Skills developed through consideration of an experiential problem will make education an ongoing process of life—a state of being rather than a course in an institution. Critical learning enters life because learning has absorbed life as its source for problematic themes. Without this dialectic between an academic discipline and reality, the transcendent conversion of students from objects into subjects is not possible.

The concrete contents for problem-posing education need to

be relevant to each class situation. Some examples of literacy, conceptual and aesthetic courses will be presented in the coming chapters, drawn from my own teaching. I can refer to several of them briefly, to give some practical reality to the theory. In a number of my classes, we studied hamburgers or made video plays from our experience or investigated family life through the writing of marriage contracts. Each class began with a very familiar feature of experience—what Freire would call the "codification," or representation of an ordinary piece of reality, abstracted from its habitual place in society, as a theme for class study. We studied each object or situation structurally, using writing, reading, speaking and analysis to unveil the meaning of this event in our lives and in the totality of social life. In the case of the hamburger we recreated the largely invisible commodity relations which deliver a fried piece of dead beef to our palates. I brought hamburgers to class so that the familiar object would be as close at hand as possible, for the launching of unfamiliar analysis. The separation and re-entry from this exercise was rewarding, as the dialogue moved to consider "junk food" versus "health food," and the need to cooperatize the school cafeteria. In another class, one which studied dramatic writing, both literacy skills and awareness grew through the students' self-design of scripts based on their lives. The study of literary form was also a study of their lives. In our sessions, we discussed the meaning of their reality as well as the means for their aesthetic re-presentation of real life. The final teaching example involves a class which examined sexist dimensions of family life through the writing of marriage contracts. The contracts were literate documents which exercised numerous skills— writing, reading, organizing, editing, group and individual composing, etc. This project facilitated critical awareness because the emerging goal became the writing of a contract for an egalitarian marriage. There were long and interesting debates on how to shape equality in male-female bonding.

In each of these exercises, the classes had a chance to develop literacy skills through a real context. They also were called upon to use conceptual habits of mind. *Conceptual exercise* is as important as the development of literacy. The structural perception of social life depends on the command of analytic methods. To this end, techniques for rigorous scrutiny need to be integrated into the problem-contexts posed to the class. My teaching has left me optimistic that conceptual habits can emerge in the course of a few months. Some conceptual paradigms for teaching structural thought will be offered in the next section. There are analytic capabilities in each student, which are rarely exercised. Through rational analysis, the class not only reverses mysticism in its mind, but it simultaneously exposes the shape of social life and the unused powers of thought in every brain. By using their conceptual skills, students reverse their own disempowering consciousness. They gain an immediate sense of power which accompanies their emerging awareness of reality. Together, the sense of power and the clarity about self and society serve to restore the self-confidence eroded through years of depressant schooling. The restorative implications of analytic thought need recognition, especially when its context involves revealing the structure of social relations which have disempowered the students.

Creation and Re-Creation: Shaping the Re-Shaping

Contextual and conceptual studies are pedagogical foundations for expelling false consciousness. Along with democratic dialogue, they are the basic vehicles for conscientization. Each vehicle has a distinctly egalitarian character. A class of equals critically examining everyday life is the kind of setting to mobilize people as subjects of their own learning process. This interest in democracy and daily life is by itself a means to delegitimize the absence of democracy in our day to day experience. At the same time that social life is demystified, the students inside the process are validated, for powers they possess but have not been taught to use. Such development is provoked by a teacher whose success can be measured by the gradual dissolution and replacement of her or his teaching function.

The teacher is an exorcist confronting a panoply of dybbuks. Having expelled anti-dialogue from her or his own teaching style, the person who provokes liberatory learning must then investigate the students' world, gain some working measure of the level of literacy and politics extant, and then design the thematic problems which will develop skills and awareness. Building on the foundations of dialogue, contextual and conceptual study, there are more advanced modes for facilitating transcendent education. One of these pedagogical techniques could be called *self-creation of media and texts*.

The liberatory class can gain a lot from writing its own texts and designing its own forms of communications. These activities could complement the critical study of printed works and mass media which habitually fill school and daily life. The preparation of its own expressions is an active way for the class to criticize the debased communications and art which surround it. As part of the process, students can create printed, plastic and visual media to give presence to their own idiom. These expressions would magnify their own voices against the sensory saturation of mass culture. Each self-creation could serve as an object of reflection as well as a process of development. By examining the product, the class can gain some detached evaluation on its own progress.

The act of separation from routine reality can be aided through creating your own media and art. This activity pushes away the enveloping world. It changes people from being passive consumers of expression to being creators of meaning. In these efforts, it is reasonable to expect amateurism as well as mimicry of the forms found in everyday life. The class projects need to be evaluated from the bottom up and from inside the process, rather than in comparison to commercial culture or high art. Each class expression registers a certain moment of development. The value can be assessed in terms of where the class began and where it has come to. My own classes have done slide-shows, newspapers, and small texts, as well as video plays. The pride each class has taken in its self-designed media has propelled their emerging presence as critics of culture. There have been lessons even in the projects which went awry.

Diving into the Wreck

Besides action-projects like self-created media or the writing of marriage contracts, there are reconstructive techniques which relate to the *work-style* of the class. One purpose of a liberatory form for class interaction is the restoration of community. Mass culture interferes with the self-organizing capacities people can use for designing common purpose. The liberatory class can address this problem through collective work styles, self and mutual instruction, and peer/group evaluation. These activities are *integrative study formats* which speak to the alienation and atomization of students through mass culture. Isolated from each other, and alienated from their own powers, students need collective vehicles for two key developmental processes: *ego-restoration* and *character-structure awareness*. For the object-subject switch to succeed, the liberatory class must challenge the ego-damaged characters of the students. Years of processing through the institutions of mass society have left students divided, frustrated, and defensive about their own skills. Integrative study formats offer peer-group validation. That is, the students need to appreciate each other as competent, effective and worthy human beings. They don't enter class feeling this way. Their conditioned self-images interfere with their taking command of the learning process. Each student through group interaction has to shed her or his disempowered character. This can be achieved through modes of study which depend on critical peer transactions. The object-subject switch revolves around a turn away from authority-dependence, towards self-regulation. The kind of self-validation here is not simply a person-centered turn-to-yourself. Because disempowerment is social, empowerment has to be social. In the liberatory matrix, reconstruction involves people-in-a-process and a process-in-people. This dialectic permits an encounter between self and the cultural conditions which interfere with critical growth.

Collective work is a bonding experience for people who live with a low level of solidarity. A developmental rule-of-thumb is that people generally rise or sink to the amount of responsibility placed in them. A cooperative style of work in the liberatory class locates decision-making among students who have reacted to orders all their lives. Thus, an exercise in collective work and group deliberation is therapeutically restoring. A class project which cannot get done without student cooperation structures a high level of mutual responsibility into the pedagogy. The idea, once again, involves the withering away of the teacher, which is another way of formulating the withering away of authority-dependence, through the delegation of responsibility into a community of learners. One technique which eases the gener-alizing of power from the teacher to a group of equals is the *component method*. This simple idea calls for breaking down a large theme—like "work"—into smaller units or sub-themes. The activity of breaking a theme into component parts is itself a conceptual analysis helpful in developing structural perception. Each sub-theme is a problem which a grouping of students can develop for class presentation. After each group has discussed its single dimension, the class as a whole reconvenes for a dialogue which reconstitutes a focus on the larger theme.

The component method not only offers the students an exercise in the conceptual deconstruction of a theme, but it also deconstructs the teacher-centered learning process. Through component analysis, in their sub-groups, the students will have to look to each other more and to the teacher less. The single teacher in the room cannot be continually present in each group. Less supervised in their own work-teams, the students will need to supervise themselves, or else the study will not get done. Such a process structures the retreat of the teacher from direction and opens space for the advance of self-regulation. Within each sub-group, peer-instruction will replace teacher instruction, given that the teacher is only intermittently available. When the class as a whole re-convenes to receive each team's deliberation, students will again be addressing each other. The gradual emergence of a dialogue among peers, mediated by a commonly acknowledged problem, is another in-process test of development. The more students talk to each other about their deliberations on the problem-theme, the more they are emerging as subjects. This is not the same thing as scheduling a mechanical debate between students on an issue, or having students raise hands to ask the teacher's permission to speak. Peer-dialogue through component analysis involves students addressing each other without mediation by the teacher, but only mediated by a commitment to the inquiry. This simple idea amounts to an extraordinary change in the classroom gestalt. Teachers and students have become so conditioned to having all talk pass through the teacher's authority, that no one in class will have experience in self-regulating dialogue. As a skill, democratic discussion becomes easier the more you practice it. Some ways to ease into it include having a rotating chairperson for the sessions, and exchanging hand-raising with self-discipline, that is, people who want to talk can defer to each other, the first rights to the floor going to whoever has not yet spoken.

The democratization of social relations in the classroom will not be automatic. Regression to authority will be continual. In the sub-groups, students may set up a replica of their old schooling. The most advanced student in the team can dominate the others, become the new teacher-authority, and sabotage the collective process through anti-dialogue. To deal with the students' re-assertion of hierarchy, it helps to ask each member of the team to take part in issuing a verbal report, when the class as a whole reconvenes to hear the group deliberations. The most aggressive students and the most passive will each play out their own forms of alienated behavior, so the teacher has to study the reconciliation of the students with each other as well as the teacher's reconciliation with the class. Another problem can emerge when each team reports. The groups may start talking to the whole class, but as they go on, their words become directed more and more towards the teacher. When I notice this happening I try to do a few things. First, I refuse to make eye-contact with the people who have begun addressing their remarks only for my appreciation. This dissolves my presence as a focal point and encourages the talking student to generalize her or his discourse to the whole class. If I sense that I am the only one to whom a question or issue is addressed, I next rephrase the committee report as a question for class discussion, and resist responding myself. This helps wither my presence and decondition the students' authority-focus. Still another way to subjectivize student focus is to take the issue addressed to me and not simply raise it as a question for discussion, but either throw it to another of the teams for comment, or to ask each person in class to draw on their own experience or opinions for an answer. For example, in dialogue around the theme of work, at moments where the discussion-reports are giving me too high a profile as primary respondent, I can ask each person in class to list and talk about the worst jobs he or she has ever had and the best jobs she or he can imagine having. This not only generalizes the dialogue away from the teacher but it also offers a way to practice the structural perception of ordinary experience. The discussion then stays centered on the students' critical discovery.

Collective work process and peer education can address the problems of social fragmentation and self-doubting egos. They build confidence and community. In addition, the activity of testing for development should be supportive and organic. So far, internal and egalitarian measurements of the process have shaped up around the withering away of the teacher and the advance of student self-regulation. Concretely, these developments can be evaluated by determining how much direction the teacher needs to offer and how much peer-dialogue is emerging in the class. These are appropriate vehicles for assessing an interactive and democratic process. A standardized testing instrument brought in from the outside, or designed by the teacher separate from the class, would only contradict the emergence of students as subjects. Similarly, the liberatory class resists levels of learning; it is not easy to standardize it as a stepping-stone to higher level courses. An authentic learning process rejects mechanical agendas or limits on its growth. This does not mean that cognitive as well as affective and political growth cannot be determined. By comparing the class' early, middle and late expressions, projects, dialogues, writings, interactions and component team-work, it is apparent what progress is being made in literacy and conceptual thought. This kind of in-progress and in-process evaluation is an extraordinary challenge to the ordinary shape of power. Institutional testing through the agency of an empowered teacher is a way of keeping students paralyzed as objects. The liberatory class rejects alienation through its own means of organic self-measurement.

The ideal is for evaluation to be a learning activity consistent with the process. A class session can begin with group reflection on the work done so far, and it can end with mutual feedback on the day's interaction. Students can offer verbal and written evaluations of themselves, each other and their sub-groups. Each person can reflect on how much or how little distance has been traveled since the sessions began. The teacher can offer group and individual assessments, and should receive both collective and personal evaluations of his or her role from the students. The two most concrete problems with implementing this approach is that students need to be socialized into self-evaluation and that the institutions we work for will insist on behavioral testing and grading. Both the students below the liberatory teacher and the authorities above will attempt to impose mechanical models on teachers who attempt liberatory experiments. From the students' point of view, democratic discipline will be unfamiliar, disturbing, demanding, and appealing. It's common for a period of classroom anarchy to accompany the transition from orthodox to liberatory structure. The teacher can only create the conditions for the practice of freedom, and cannot command anyone to be free, so the consciousness in each class will determine the limits of egalitarian reconstruction. From the institutional point of view, some experiments may be tolerated, some encouraged for window-dressing or as contained ghettoes for trouble-making teachers and students, and many will be discouraged by administrative fiat. In each school or college, teachers need to assess what level of liberatory learning they can assert, given student consciousness and institutional politics. Mass alienation and bureaucratic repression set limits on all phases of a critical pedagogy. Caught in the middle, the teacher needs to remember that liberatory learning is not a professorial conspiracy, but is rather a mutual effort of teacher and students. This suggests that it can only work if the students cooperate, and that the students are a mass of potential allies. They are, in fact, the ones who have the most to gain by the success of democratic learning. This is a support teachers can turn to. Liberatory teachers are not doing things *for* the students or *to* the students, but rather are launching a process *with* them. The difficulties in this enterprise should be apparent, but the energies released in students justify high expectations.

Counter-disciplines:
Changes and the Changed

As conceived so far, liberatory learning proceeds along a broad pedagogical front: the form of democratic dialogue, the use of themes from daily life, the empowering object-subject switch, the mutual transformation of teacher and student, contextual and conceptual skill-development, variant roles and oscillating distances for the teacher, self-created media and texts, integrative study formats and internal evaluation. To these modes for animating critical consciousness must be added the need for interdisciplinary approaches to study, for unearthing hidden social histories, and for problem-contexts appropriate for the extrojection of racism and sexism.

Cross-disciplinary study asserts an integral intellectualism

against the academy's fragmentation of thought. Holistic intellect is transdisciplinary as well as critical. If transcendent
learning rejects rote lessons, syllabi, and mechanical testing, it
also resists limits set by a single discipline's methods. The critical
study of themes from everyday life needs to be carried out in the
broadest terms possible, for the problem-statements of a class to
have wide implications. The problematic study of social practice
stretches out not only in time and space but also across the
boundaries separating academic departments. Concretely, my
class' study of hamburgers not only involved English and
philosophy in our use of writing, reading, and conceptual
analysis, but it also included economics in the study of the
commodity relations which bring hamburgers to market, history and sociology in an assessment of what the everyday diet
was like prior to the rise of the hamburger, and health science in
terms of the nutritional value of the ruling burger. The ensuing
attempt by one class to cooperatize the school cafeteria subsequently provided an active lesson in the politics of social change.
The transcendent value of this cross-disciplinary, problematic,
and experiential approach is that it simultaneously considers the
specific and the general. Hamburgers are an immediate part of
life which can be studied for their systematic expression of social
relations. This need for thematic problems to be studied in an
interdisciplinary way and for uniting specific with general
implications, underlies the codifications of experience used by
Freire and his literacy teams. Starting with an ordinary theme
from the daily life of Guinea-Bissau—the production of rice—
Freire goes on to elaborate a series of expanding contexts which
connect a specific item to its whole cultural milieu.[8] From the
agronomy of rice in the area of the literacy class he proceeds to
ask questions about the geography of the whole country vis á vis
rice production, and then world geography. Following the
international problem of rice production, the expanding circle of
interest moves to the politics of rice, in terms of government
planning and national defense of the newly liberated country.
Then, Freire points to the history of rice cultivation in the
particular nation and in the world. Lastly, as a final disciplinary
context, he considers rice and health, health and work, work and
education, education and national reconstruction.[9]

The interdisciplinary approach, in a liberatory framework, is the most potent means to free consciousness from the limits of the particular. It takes an immediate feature of culture and develops systematic and holistic awareness of the reproduction of social life. This education into the deepest and broadest implications of daily life expands consciousness; it animates an understanding of what any small part of life means. From this base, another kind of learning can emerge—the unveiling of hidden social history. People living in a dominated culture are kept from knowing the long history of popular resistance to domination. The problematization of a familiar piece of existence can remedy this by expanding outward and backward in time and space to those social struggles once or still alive. To raise awareness about ongoing and past resistance is to unfreeze historical consciousness. As long as the mass media and the schools can keep the history of resistance hidden, people will lose touch with their history-making powers.

Ending the censorship of history is an important operation for the liberatory class. There is no single means to do this, but the context of each discipline and each thematic study of experience has to set the conditions under which awareness of popular resistance is raised. The importance of this historical restoration for subjective emergence cannot be overestimated. The object-subject switch rests on a reconstruction of identity. The new identity for students will be shaped around their autonomy, their detachment from the control of mass culture. It is strengthening to know the many circumstances where people have refused to adjust to control, and have fought back instead. Without these kinds of models, the only tangible shapes of freedom will be those false ones now invading consciousness, in the form of "striking it rich" or buying a bigger car or "being your own boss" or taking out your frustration on a class-peer (racism and sexism). For a dominated people to enter history as makers of society, they need to know that they don't have to in-vent the wheel. It is discouraging to feel alone or to feel that you must begin from scratch. Emerging people need a consciousness of who their allies are, in past generations and in the present time. This is an especially high profile issue in the American sit-uation, where the political experience of each new generation is so discontinuous from the previous one, and where racism is a long historical feature of public and private life. The design of pedagogical problems which unify class-peers now divided by race and sex, and which provoke consciousness of the episodes of popular resistance to authority, will be critical remedies for the effects of mass culture and censored schooling. Practically, in my own classes, these issues entered the dialogue in the context of other questions. In studying conceptual thought in a Utopia course, I would offer the class articles on a wide variety of autonomous social actions now underway. When the discussions evolved close to issues of trade unionism, or women's rights, or race oppression, or the systemic differences between capitalism and socialism, I would experiment with ways to make historical study integral to our dialogue. In this pedagogical area, it would be most helpful for liberatory teachers in the social sciences to take the lead in developing models. The approach to historical awareness needs to be more than anecdotal and schematic, because consciousness of social history is a paradigm for character structure. By changing the historical imagination, the liberatory class alters perception about the roots and shape of culture; by changing perception, critical education restructures self-in-society and society-in-self. Revealing the dimensions of class, race and sex in history amounts to revealing who you are, who you have been, and who you can be.

A Little Laughter:
The Resources of Comedy

Alienation in mass culture, as the largest learning problem, separates students from their own history and history-making power. It also divides them from each other and from the teacher. This situation forces the liberatory class to effect multiple reconciliations. A complex process of self and social reconstruction is accompanied by unavoidable tensions. The lowering of defensive rigidity and conditioned responses opens up inspiring energy as well as threatening uneasiness. One valuable resource in easing this progress is comedy. A comic atmosphere relaxes the fears attending desocialization. Further, comedy helps demystify the professional aura of the teacher. Through sharing humor with the class, the instructor comes down from the pedestal, in the process of withering away.

The merging of study and comedy has other counter-alienating effects as well. An amusing milieu brings together intellectual and emotional experience. Comedy serves to reduce the sharp social alienation of work from pleasure, when it becomes an integral feature of class interaction. In mass culture, schooling is a form of alienated activity, a prolonged preparation for the alienated domain of work. Both school and work are sharply divided from private life and leisure. The result is anti-intellectualism in both domains. Work and study are so empty of creative fulfillment that leisure time takes on an exaggerated lust for pleasure. A culture which so divides work from pleasure creates a dehumanizing dualism in social life: work is regimented labor for money, study is regimented intellectualism for grades, so free time is the over-burdened sphere of good times. The dreary realities of school and work create a magnified need for compensatory pleasure, which the leisure-time industry aggressively exploits. The noisy distractions of commercial culture are only as large as the denial of pleasure in daily life.

Critical education needs to challenge the ordinary monopoly on fun held by the free-time industry. If transcendent learning does not draw on the refreshments of playing, it will be experienced as another grim excercise, just like the school and work everyone has already had enough of. If study can assimilate the energy of play, it will attack a basic reification of daily life— the bargain struck between working now so you can have fun later. This deal keeps people frozen in a life pattern of powerlessness because leisure is as dominated as school and work.[10] Mass adjustment to the polarization of labor and pleasure fixes neurotic patterns into everyday experience. Something is always missing. Frustration piles up. You go out to have a good time and when it's over you're still in the same place. The liberatory class can disrupt this routine of life by experimenting with comic styles of pedagogy, by not accepting the liquidation of fun from study, by constructing an integration of thought and feeling.

There is yet another reason to examine comedy as a resource for liberatory culture. Laughter, like singing, is not only a potentially bonding experience for people, but there are verbal forms of popular resistance rooted in comic uses of language. People can experience solidarity through song and comic moments; they also share a style of comic discourse which is their grass-roots possession. In school, at work, in the streets, at home, at parties or while commuting, a popular response to domination is to make fun of your superiors. People satirize their oppressors through sarcasm, parody, ad hominem and reductio. These verbal and gestural modes are a rich means through which to separate yourself from the authority figures over you. They amount to a linguistic underground, where a culture of resistance is kept alive. By buffooning the teacher, the boss, the cop, the judge, the parent, or the bureaucrat, you keep alive your knowledge of being separate from the order oppressing you. When these comic acts surface, the superior is usually incensed, and you can expect punishment. The fact that satire is not permitted to subordinates as a means of discourse only insures that it will continue as a valued means of self-assertion. As long as authorities can be injured enough to respond with punishment, then comic uses of language will survive as a weapon of the underdog.

The widespread use of satire as a means of separation from authority and self-assertion is a promising area of mass autonomy. Further, satire is not the only form of popular autonomy through comic language; and popular speech is not the only dimension of mass life which needs study for the shape of autonomous expression. The range of dominated and un-dominated behavior is something teachers must discover and translate into concrete pedagogy. For example, students tell each other all kinds of jokes and stories, some satiric, some self-parodic, some outrightly racist and sexist, some just plain clever and hilarious. It makes sense for a liberatory class to locate the healthy and the unhealthy uses of comedy. There are more resisting roots in mass experience than university intellectuals are able to identify; graduate training is better suited for comprehending the field of mass culture as one of dominated consciousness. There is a dual resource available through comedy: appreciating popular satire as indigenous resistance and appreciating comedy as an influence on pedagogical style. Both the form and content of the class can be healthily transformed by the dialectic assimilation of comedy.

A comedy-appreciating teacher will better evaluate the speaking and the silence of the students. A humorous class flowing through the comic folkways of the students will become a serious place to enjoy change, and an enjoyable place to change seriously. Through experimentation in making pleasure co-exist supportively with rigor, the studies will emerge as something different than the clownish, controlled milieu where a professor indulges as the entertainer. Comedy can be an unexpected landmark in a liberatory frontier.

The Convertible Classroom:
A Space for All Reasons

The comprehensive agenda for a liberatory classroom can be thought of as resistance to the dystopic possibilities of mass culture. The popular emergence of critical thought is a bulwark against barbarism. Comedy joins the other egalitarian, humanizing and epistemological resources useful for propelling consciousness growth. The re-perception of the ordinary and the subjective emergence of students are exhilarating moments in the process. The dialogic study of daily life can animate transcendent development, but liberatory change can also degenerate. There are no guarantees that consciousness will keep moving ahead—it can regress. Many forces condition its shape, requiring a pedagogical theory and practice as panoramic as the field in which consciousness forms. As a companion to the mobile complex of roles and functions for the teacher, the liberatory classroom also assumes a variety of convertible modes. The classroom changes its form so as to adapt to the profile of student needs. Each mode fulfills a concrete developmental service: workshop, studio, skill and counseling center, consciousness-raising group, kiosk news service, and library.

The workshop form provides a round-table milieu suitable for dialogue. It is a visual dis-assembly of the familiar classroom gestalt. A class arranged in rows facing the teacher is very alienating to students who have been regimented in this manner for so many years. The circle-seating idea has been experimented for a long time now in alternate education settings. My own experience with it has been positive. In some cases, where we cannot move chairs, I have simply sat in the rows to avoid having all eyes focused on a talking teacher at the front. The important thing is to interrupt ordinary expectations of what class structure will be. The workshop model is one way to deconstruct the familiar and open up the chance for unusual growth. The teacher will find it easier to wither in a workshop once the idea of the "front of the room" is problematized. In this kind of space, the students' dialogue and their self-creations are the focus. As a corollary to the seminar function of the workshop is its operation as a studio space. The classroom will need to offer a quiet space for deliberation as a whole and in groups. For those times when the session divides for a component method study, the separate work-teams will need to use the space for sub-group activities. This will include the study as well as the creation of a wide variety of materials—printed, audial, visual. The studio function is especially critical in the mass colleges, where a shortage of meeting rooms interferes with student development. The changeover from workshop-seminar to studio-group work will be a refreshing flow in and out of forms, stimulating attention.

A third spatial mode for the liberatory class is that of skills and counseling center. In these functions, the learning process attempts to address basic needs. The class dialogue can be a place where living as well as academic resources are exchanged. Students will have a complex melange of needs—informational, conceptual, personal, academic, financial. The thematic studies themselves need to shape interaction around this existential architecture. In addition, the students and the teacher can share special information, as a verbal bulletin board, which can assist the people in class with concrete problems around finding a job, an apartment, good classes to enroll in, or other colleges worth transferring to. Further, some students may need extra assistance in an academic skill or in navigating through the school bureaucracy. If these needs are ignored, they will only interfere with the development of critical thought. If these needs are farmed out to alienating sub-units of the school, they will again interfere with the students' emerging critical consciousness. There is a terrain of needs which cannot be easily assimilated into the problem-themes for class study, and which will not be addressed humanely by special agencies within the school machine. In the domain of immediate and excess need, the liberatory classroom converts to a skills and counseling center.

This function amounts to designing the session as a transcendent miniature of the entire school. When the skills and counseling functions are assimilated back into the classroom from their stations as separate units in the education plant, they need to avoid replicating the external bureaucracy. For the students' needs to be met, they must have a partisan environment in which to dialogue. This is a very hard thing for them to find. The institutions through which they pass are almost uniform in rejecting their interests. For a classroom to reverse the effects of mass alienation, it needs to present itself as unequivocally identified with the students. From another angle, the approach to excess and immediate need is not simply an issue of student partisanism, but is also supportive of interdisciplinary study. The practice of farming out skills and counseling needs to specialized units encourages teachers to withdraw behind the walls of their compartment learning. Over-specialization is an academic disease which exalts abstract knowledge while rejecting concrete student reality. By addressing the fundamental skills and counseling needs of students, liberatory teachers demystify their own position. The class then shapes itself from the bottom up.

As a partisan and convertible space, where ordinary behavior and social life are examined in transcendent ways, the classroom will often emerge as a consciousness-raising group. This form suggests that the encounter is more than cognitive and the relations are not business-like. The repetitive routines of life are enveloping enough to preclude consciousness-raising situations. Therefore, the awareness function of the classroom may provide most students with their only access to breaking with mass culture. In the consciousness-raising format, the liberatory class attempts personality change. The brief span of the class will permit only the beginnings of profound change, but this is part of the liberatory agenda notably absent from mass education and notably monopolized by "human development" encounters available only to the elite. Generalizing this experience will make the benefits of personal growth into a popular process of social change. In its consciousness-raising mode, the liberatory classroom can fruitfully explore power dualities and oppressive role models—teacher-student, boss-worker, white-black, male-female, parent-child, straight-gay. A discussion which abstracts us from these routine interactions can be very developmental, psychologically in our understanding of self and other, and philosophically in terms of the conceptual analysis necessary to grasp the systematic nature of these power transactions.

Another form through which the classroom achieves consciousness-raising is different than the psychological and philosophical realms just discussed. The liberatory class can be a place where culturally censored information is exchanged. This is its kiosk and news-service role. Announcements of political events not covered by the mass media can be made here; all kinds of newspapers, periodicals, books, pamphlets, posters and magazines can be shared. The students' local candy stores offer a uniform assortment of reading materials. The broadcast media and mass circulation dailies similarly manage news into censored shape. This makes the liberatory class a lone and essential source of critical information, which can disrupt the neat encirclement of thought in daily life.

The liberatory classroom assumes its variety of functions in an irregular manner. There is no standard operating procedure for when to convert from one spatial mode to another. The teacher once again plays an indispensable role in socializing the students into these possiblities. After all, the students will arrive in class alienated from school, which means that they will not take the initiative in redesigning the process of study or the shape of the classroom. In fact, they will have largely given up expecting school to shape itself around their needs. It will be surprising news to them that the teacher, the process, the time and the space can be reconstructed in their interests.

Getting There from Here

There is a reassuring simplicity in the old ways of teaching. They may not work very well, but they are a solid tradition to fall back on—the hour-long lesson, the documented lecture, the socratic discussion, the course outline and sturdy reading list, the separate canon for each academic discipline, the term paper and final exam. It is well organized and very busy. The irony of this order is not simply the static knowledge it produces, but also the alienation it provokes. The situation calls for transcendent reconstruction.

The liberatory system outlined in this chapter is one useful starting point for educational redesign. As a schema, it synthesizes Freirian and progressive learning ideas into a working theory extracted from my own teaching experiments. The crux of liberatory theory rests in the empowering animation of critical consciousness, through the students' object-subject switch, in an egalitarian, experience-based dialogue, initiated by a teacher functioning in a mobile complex of roles. This theory should be adapted, amended, re-invented, used or discarded, depending on the requirements of the specific teaching situation. Philosophy needs to shape itself around reality because theory best serves liberatory culture when it is "grounded theory," that is, reflection emerging from concrete practice. When we think critically about our action, then we can act critically on our thinking. Teaching is the most important social practice of intellectuals, so reflection on pedagogy can do a lot in extraordinarily redesigning the ordinary work of a teacher.

My own teaching experiences, reported concretely in the next section, proved to be a comprehensive re-education for me. In developing with my students a structural appreciation of social life, I found myself investigating whole fields of knowledge I had not entered before. There were breakthroughs and dead-ends, advances and regressions. The scope of the problems was matched by the shape of the rewards. In starting the long break with the past, I saw possibilities which suggested more possibilities. As each course emerged, I felt myself looking at terrain I never saw before, through windows I never knew existed.

Notes

1. Paulo Freire, *Education for Critical Consciousness* (Seabury, New York, 1973), pp. 45-46.

2. *Ibid.*, pp. 63-84. Freire reproduces some of the slides-representations he used in Brazil to animate critical thinking prior to the start of literacy teaching.

3. *Ibid.*, p. 52.

4. Paulo Freire, *Pedagogy in Process* (Seabury, New York, 1978).

5. Joel Spring, *A Primer of Libertarian Education* (Free Life, New York, 1975), see chapter two on "Ownership of Self."

6. *Ibid.*, p. 63.

7. Freire, *Education for Critical Consciousness*, p. 125, p. 153.

8. Freire, *Pedagogy in Process*, pp. 117-118.

9. *Ibid.*, p. 118.

10. Stanley Aronowitz, *False Promises* (McGraw-Hill, New York, 1973), see chapter two, "Colonized Leisure, Trivalized Work."

CHAPTER FOUR

MONDAY MORNING:

Critical Literacy and the Theme of "Work"

Introduction: Reports of Teaching Practice

From coast to coast, Monday morning fever grips the start of each school week. The old forms of discipline collapse under the weight of new alienation. Teachers and students face each other as confused combatants. What can be done? Where do we begin when the time clocks sound for Monday's early class?

Ironically, we have no choice but to begin from the best possible place—where we are. Education for critical thought begins with the concrete situation of each class. It can work only by being grounded in the limits and possibilities of each course, each academic department, each school, and each locale. The theoretical outline in the previous chapter can be creatively adapted for each locus of learning. New theory and new practice will both emerge from sharing reflections on teaching experiments, in an educational project which is definable only as people act and reflect on it in-process.

Because Freire is a rich resource of pedagogical frameworks, it can be helpful to look more concretely at the teaching practice of his literacy teams.[1] Prior to scheduling classes, Freirian educators study the life and language of their prospective students. These sociological inquiries permit them to discover a small number of key words from daily life—called "generative words"—which will be used for both problematizing experience and for literacy teaching. The generative words, like "brick," "rice," "slum" or "wealth," suggest social themes around which consciousness can be raised. They are also selected for their trisyllabic structure (tijolo, ti-jo-lo, "brick" in Portuguese), so that each word can be broken up into phonetic pieces and then recombined to make new words. Each generative word is "codified," that is, presented in a visual form, prior to being written out. Visual codification in the form of a slide permits a class dialogue to begin around the thematic content of the word, without pre-literacy interfering with the learners' ability to reflect critically. Following a discussion of the cultural situation suggested by the picture, the word itself is presented in written form. In this way, literacy flows from social critique, through images, conversation and writing rooted in the concrete lives of the students.

Before any codification or generative word is introduced, the Freirian teams train themselves in the technique of dialogue, in addition to their study of local conditions. Further, the pictures and words through which writing and reading will be taught are not offered in the first class sessions. The initial meetings are wholly devoted to a group of pictures concerning the distinction between nature and culture. The intent is to raise consciousness about the human power to make culture, as demonstrated in the everyday lives of those people in class. Critical consciousness begins with an encounter between students and their human capacity to transform the world. This dialogue on humans as hunters, farmers, builders, tool-makers, etc., proceeds through a series of ten pictures, the last of which represents the literacy class itself, as the latest act of the students in transforming themselves and their reality, through the activity of learning to read and write. Such an exploration begins the re-perception of self and society, in an empowering format. The discovery of self as a culture-maker and of culture as the making of human activity propels the class forward into sessions devoted to literacy. Freirian teams have found that using the dialogic method, they need only seventeen generative words and some thirty hours of classes, to provoke basic literacy. The first trisyllabic generative words progressively give way to more complicated ones, in sound and structure, as the students gain facility with the written code of their speech.

This pedagogical style, emerging for pre-literate peasants in the Third World, has lessons for educators who work in the metropoles of the West, teaching for an urbanized, post-literate, and industrial constituency. Domination by mass culture, in an advanced society like the U.S., has left the population either functionally illiterate or uncritically literate, and politically undeveloped. The need for conscientization exists, to counter the interferences to critical thought in daily life. The questions of dialogic pedagogy, cultural democracy, critical awareness and structural perception are urgently relevant in this technically advanced culture. The extension of social control through state institutions like the schools, and the dissemination of commercial culture through electronic media, make the situation ripe for a humanizing pedagogy. The specifics of this pedagogy cannot be mechanically lifted from Brazil or Guinea-Bissau to North America, but need to be evolved right here. In the last decade, there have been numerous educational experiments, growing out of the radical politics of the 60s.[2] The following chapters record one more, from the Open Admissions years of the City University of New York, 1971-1977. The egalitarian character of Open Admissions de-stabilized New York's public academy long enough for experiments in liberatory teaching. The results were only partial, but still rewarding. Like other experiments under-way at the time, they showed how much can be learned even under difficult conditions, once the old ways were left be-hind. Critical education can be a compelling force for de-sociali-zation. Both mass culture and false consciousness are strangely vulnerable to critical classrooms, here in the center of the First World.

Problematizing Daily Life: Literacy and the Theme of Work

Work! You can't live with it and you can't live without it. My students have a hard time finding jobs, and a hard time keeping the bad jobs they find. They resent their low wages and menial tasks, but how can you live without an income? So, they fade into and out of a wide variety of jobs below their capabilities, as clerks, helpers, "gofers," messengers, typists, loaders, burger pushers, cashiers, pump-jockeys and salespersons. Their experience of work is not happy, but work itself can be a dynamic theme for class study.

In a number of classes, I experimented with the theme of

work as the subject matter for language teaching. The project related to a variety of operational goals elaborated in the previous chapter: self and peer education, collective work styles, the withering away of the teacher, the turn to daily life for material, and the emergence of students as subjects of a structural learning exercise. By examining work as a means to develop literacy and consciousness, I wanted to do more than merge popular experience with awareness. As a literacy project, the study of work was built on the language skills students brought to class. The resources I drew upon were not only experiential. Work autobiography served as the program content of the study, while the students' existing speaking, listening, reading and writing capacities were the linguistic base for deepening literacy.

The approach which emerged was textured, integral and successively more demanding. It combined the activities of composing, editing, verbalizing, conceptualizing and reading. From the verbal and biographical backgrounds of the students, we moved eventually to considerations of work-oriented changes in society as a whole. In the end, I understood this methodology as an alternative to the "back-to-basics" phenomenon, which exalts the value of traditional study in grammar. The liberatory approach—experiential, sequential and integral—does not impose grammar on culture, but rather shapes literacy from resources in student reality.

Preparing for the Study: Easing Alienation, Exercising Resources

It's a tricky business to organize an untraditional class in a traditional school. Freire and his associates took more time to prepare for the start of their class sessions, by studying the student population. The classes they offered to pre-literate peasants were carried out in a non-institutional setting. Once inside a school, many alienating factors come into play, distancing the students from the act of learning. To ease this situation of student hostility, I practice lowering my presence in class as soon as possible. On the first day, I say my name and the title of the course, and little else. Instead of delivering a lecture on the course material, I ask each student to come to the board, write his or her name, and spend a few minutes telling all of us who they are, why they are in the class, what jobs they have now or have had, where they live, etc. This introductory sign-in withers my presence while magnifying the voice of the students. They do far more talking than me, from the beginning. In addition, as they introduce themselves to each other, they begin making bonds— some live in the same neighborhood, or are enrolled in the same programs, or have worked in the same places, or need rides to school, or announce their need for a job, which someone else may help out with. I introduce myself last and talk to the kinds of material the students have raised in their own self-presentations. On occasion, I've asked the class to write for me the kind of opening speech they *expect* me to deliver or that they would *like* me to deliver. We read these short compositions aloud, and compare people's expectations from the course.

I do share with the class the style of pedagogy I will offer and explain my commitment to it. One of the first exercises I ask people to do helps concretize the self-educative, non-punitive approach to literacy: free writing.[3] This technique has become more familiar as a non-traditional writing exercise. The goal is to develop composing skills, by having students write for a timed period, without stopping to correct. This spontaneous writing is an athletic exercise to develop compositional fluidity. In daily life, there are few occasions to write. Depressant English classes have convinced many students that they can't write, read, speak or think correctly. The simple act of composing non-stop is a way to reverse the retarding effects of prior experience. As an impromptu exercise, the free writing is not read, corrected or graded, by the teacher. It is not written to answer a question set by the instructor. The non-punitive milieu surrounding it permits students to exercise their human talent to compose, without feeling threatened by authority. Week by week, the amount of writing students complete in the timed period invariably increases. Their growing facility with words is ego-restorative. It is validating to notice your increasing command of a language activity.

With the sign-ins and free writing setting a non-authoritarian tone to the sessions, and with the student voices and composing skills being the predominant action so far, a base has been established for introducing more demanding literacy exercises.

Biography and Pre-Writing: Resources in Memory

Most students possess more language skills than they will display in school. The turn towards student reality and student voices can release their hidden talents. Autobiography, memory and the power to make mental images are concrete, initial resources for deepening literacy. Two provocative themes on which students write willingly are "the worst teacher I ever had" and "the most dangerous moment in my life." I ask students to write a good sized paragraph on each of these subjects.

For this phase of the writing, I present a "pre-writing" method, a tool students can use to help them generate well-written material. Pre-writing involves organizing the material prior to putting it into paragraph and theme form. A simple means for this includes three steps: Think—Itemize—Write. First, close your eyes and get a good mental picture of what you're going to write about. Then, begin listing all the things you're seeing. Last, from your written list, write your composition, checking back later to see that you've put into your sentences all the items you listed from your thoughts.

Pre-writing offers students a way to systematize their thoughts for writing. The successive activities of mental imaging, itemizing, and then composing, generate written matter in sequentially more demanding phases. The simplest level of making mental pictures moves on to harder levels of transferring images into words and phrases listed on a page. Then, those pieces need to be transformed into coherent sentences and paragraphs. This method makes students aware of resources they already possess. Their visual imaginations can serve as propellants into more difficult acts of composing. The sequential approach avoids the confrontation with the blank page, in front of which students can sit in paralyzed anguish, until they just decide to write chaotically off the top of their heads. Between paralysis and disorder lies the student's own power to systematize what he or she knows. Pre-writing helps begin this, while the themes of "worst teacher" and "dangerous moment" offer students appealing topics from their own lives. They have been waiting for a chance to share public blasts at their teachers, and are curious to hear each others' perils.

There is another fundamental means to use student language resources as a support for the best writing students can do. This second method can be called the "dictation sequence." The key feature here is connecting spoken language to written language. Dictation involves not only mental imagery, but also speaking, listening and composing, in a phased technique. The dictation sequence begins by asking students to break into groups of two. One member of the team will be dictating his or her verbal thoughts on the theme for composition, while the second member of the unit will record, on paper, verbatim, what the person speaks. Then, the two change places, the recorder becoming the speaker and the speaker becoming the composer. The students are asked to gain a sharp mental picture of the things they want to speak before they begin talking to their partners, and each recorder is urged to ask the other to speak as slowly as necessary to get every word down. This is a style of writing which encourages peer relations. The students have to cooperate to get the work done; the teacher does not monitor them. They need to listen carefully to each other, something they are conditioned against through the teacher-centered schooling in their pasts. The same progressive difficulty of the pre-writing method is also present in this dictation mode. From simple mental imaging we progress to speaking out loud what we see in our minds to recording on paper the words we hear spoken. In their native idiom, students have strong speaking skills, so it is a great resource to have composition evolve from their verbal talent. Further, it is important to make clear that the written language of our culture is nothing more than encoded speech. Students should make a connection between their speaking language and the act of writing language on paper. That literate activity is now dissociated from them, because they have been required in authoritarian classrooms to encode a language which they do not speak—Standard English. By transcribing the language of a peer, they validate their own native speech, which once it is put on paper with respectful care, turns out to be a far richer resource than they had imagined.

The pre-writing and dictation methods are writing techniques which develop self-confidence and awareness. They are also literacy modes which students can "take away" with them from class. They can use these simple exercises on their own, without need of teachers or grammar books. The more they practice it, the better they become, without teacher supervision. Even the style of it in class, as an activity, where you are thrown onto your own memory, images, or ability to listen to a peer, encourages the withering away of the teacher and the subjective emergence of the students. Neither a teacher nor a textbook are the centers of this self and peer education. These modes naturally support the workshop format for class discussion, in which people write and then read their own work for each other as an audience of peers. This serves to decentralize the responsibility for reaction, criticism, discipline, and correctness from the teacher to the peer group.

These simple exercises in literacy, here developed around the specific experiential themes of bad teachers and dangerous moments, have led to a good deal of discussion in class. The writings on teachers have been especially fertile for deeper scrutiny. It helps for students to get their anti-school feelings out in the open, instead of only acting them out in alienated behavior. An open confrontation with teacher-repulsion in students is a way to work through an interference to critical thought. The students have taken the opportunity to pour out a litany of oppressive memories, vis á vis their schooling. It has been a relief for me as the teacher and for them as students to be in a school space where this reality need not be hidden. From the sharing of experiences and impressions, we have occasionally moved on to a conceptual exercise based in the same thematic material. I asked several classes to write a short piece which draws on all we've heard so far, and answers the general question: What is a bad teacher? This involves the simple philosophical operation of abstracting a general case from specific details; it's a foundation for structural perception, and a logical base for categorical understanding. The model of the bad teacher which they develop serves me as a caution in designing my demeanor. During this exercise, I act as recorder, standing at the board, listing the qualities which they abstract from their experiences as the paradigm for bad teacher: too much or too little discipline, doesn't allow students to ask questions, doesn't answer questions, talks so fast people can't follow, talks so slow people fall asleep, gives too much homework, always yelling at students, makes fun of students. At this point, some classes have gone on to practice "negation," that is, designing the opposite of the bad teacher, to arrive at a model of a good teacher. Other classes have returned to their personal histories to record the best teachers they have had, and then develop the general category from experience. In either case, they gain a more conceptual command of a rather ordinary feature of their lives. Still, they do not think in a transcendent fashion, even as they practice critical scrutiny; they do not yet articulate the model good teacher as one who practices liberatory values. This kind of thinking is far down the road. With some critical analysis underway through writing and dialogue on experience, the time has been ripe for introducing a second problem-theme, "work," and another self-educating technique, "voicing."

"Once I Built a Railroad": The Self-Correcting Voice

The class writings so far have unearthed and systematized rather interesting material. In preparing autobiographical compositions, the students have not only exercised literacy and conceptual skills, but they have also been working together, and have begun a study process which is validating their lives. Their personal experiences are acknowledged as things worthy of serious attention in class. This is a beginning in restoring self-esteem after the years of depressant schooling they have had. Our next step in this project was my request that students write a composition answering this question: What is the worst job you ever had? For those few who had not yet been employed, I asked for an account of what they considered the worst job around, one they would hate to wind up doing.

I asked that people use the three step, think-itemize-write pre-writing method I had introduced earlier. When their brief chronicles are ready, I take the opportunity to discuss an exercise in self-correction which we employ for the balance of the sessions: voicing. Voicing is a self-editing tool which calls on students to use the natural grammar in their speaking voices. The method is simple: after composing, you read out loud what you've written. The grammar in your speech will automatically correct errors made by your writing hand. All you have to do is carefully listen to your own voice as you read; wherever you stumble or hesitate, your strong speaking skills are being interfered with by your less developed writing skills. This developmental distinction between speech and encoding offers students a self-educating method which uses one of their strengths to remediate one of their weaknesses, without the learning activity passing through a teacher or grammar book. This is possible, epistemologically, because speaking is mastered earlier in life and through a different means than the mastery of reading and writing. The ability to speak a language is a skill normally and automatically acquired as long as a child hears language in the early years of its life. As an older and more exercised language facility, speaking is deeply rooted in children before they begin the formal study of reading and writing in school. In addition, there is a political interference complicating the transition from speaking a language to encoding and decoding it on paper. The child who naturally learns to speak through her or his family environment is taught to read by an institution of the state or church, in a regimented setting, and in a form of language which is dissonant to the conversational rigor of everyday life. These alienating factors widen the gap between the formal study of language and the informal learning of speech. The result is a dissociation of students from their own speech, as a rich comunicative resource and as a self-educative tool vis á vis strengthening their powers of composition. The practice of self-editing through voicing helps correct this problem.

My students do not know that they already have grammar in their voices. Good grammar has become mystified as something only English teachers and textbooks have. Students feel condemned merely by opening their mouths. It is ego-restoring to value something as crucial as your own speech.

Vocalized self-correction is a simple way to begin literacy study from student resources. It is a form of self-study on several levels: you use it to study your own experience while studying your own speech and writing. Such textured language activity integrates skill-development with consciousness-raising. One problem in this method is that student speech has been limited in its styles, dialects and lexicons by mass culture. It is not their autonomous creation, but is rather a socially conditioned product. Still, their speech, as well as their reading and writing, is more developed than they show in traditional school settings. Speaking is also an athletic skill they take for granted. To focus conscious attention on their mastery of talking, I have asked them to analyze speech into components. Speaking involves drawing on images and vocabulary in the mind, moves to the taking in of air and the modulated release of a stream of air through nasal, mouth and throat cavities, across a supple and mobile tongue, to moving lips, which together are expertly trained to form the sounds desired. This sequential action includes knowledge of cadence and rhythm, which is the grammatical way the voice achieves emphasis, phrasing of words and punctuation. By systematically recognizing the virtuosity of their speech, students continue a literacy-provoking self-study. The knowledge gained in this way is empowering. They contain within themselves the resources to gain the literacy which has eluded them.

With an understanding of their own mastery of speech, it becomes easier for students to accept how their voices can be a self-help device. The legitimation of voicing is achieved by the practice of it, rather than through the teacher's delivery of a lecture. One problem which the teacher can point out is that the rigorous voice will *insist* on reading correctly. As students search for their own errors, their demanding tongues will so swiftly read the correct thing that the eye will not be allowed to see the actual errors on the page. The speaking voice is a stronger language instrument than the reading eye, so for voicing to become the best help it can be, the eye has to be strengthened.

At first, students will not even know that they are automatically correcting errors as they speak. While voicing our writings aloud in class, in chorus, each person attending to her or his own work, the individual will unknowingly speak correctly what has been written incorrectly. To remedy this, we do voicing in pairs. One student reads her or his composition out loud while the other follows silently along, reading with the eyes. Whenever the speaker passes over something that the reader notices, the silent partner points it out to the other. Eventually, as this exercise is practiced, each person's eyes become more alert to the instant corrections of the voice, so that paired voicing is less necessary. Through this kind of language class, students pay more attention to their own writings and to each other's writings than ever before. It's unfamiliar for them to be looking so closely together at what each of them has done. Usually, only the teacher does that, and shares bad news with you, one by one. Like the dictation sequence, voicing withers the teacher and enhances peer relations. With these basic literacy methods, we can move into a discussion of the subject matter, "work," which unifies the class at the level of their common experiences.

The Worst Jobs: Composite Theme Development

After asking people in class to compose a piece on the worst jobs they ever had or on the worst job they can imagine, we devote a number of sessions to pre-writing, voicing and self-correcting. With the theme developed through these techniques, I ask two students to volunteer to read their compositions to the rest of us. As they read, the saga of bad work experiences stirs a lot of interest. Students spontaneously dialogue on jobs they have held in common. Just about everyone has something to offer to the conversation. To gain a deeper scrutiny of the theme, I ask the class to write two lists: What did the two worst jobs we just heard have in common, and what was different about them? We hear the two reports again before doing this simple structural exercise. At the board, I serve as recorder, making two lists, one titled "in common" and the other "not in common." As a basic conceptual habit of mind, the task of abstracting features of an experience around an organizing principle initiates the class into critical reflection on an ordinary subject. No one in class has trouble distinguishing some similarities from some differences, As each student reads her or his lists, I compile a composite of the responses at the board, as a public record of our deliberation so far.

The two lists need examination. Are they valid? Are there any items in the lists which contradict other items? Any claims made to add or remove an item has to appeal back to the original reports read to us. We sometimes ask the two student volunteers to read their work again, so that we can decide the validity of the lists. The principles underlying the lists are what provoke the development of critical thinking. I ask for careful attention to the items. If one of the personal stories of worst jobs referred to routine kitchen work for low pay in a burger house while a second related digging ditches in summer for minimum wages, then the experiential material allows us to draw general conclusions around salary and the kind of work, but has not offered us enough information to contrast work-hours and routine-ness or interaction with co-workers on the job. If we find details missing that we must know, we are able to ask one of the volunteers to give us more reportage. Critical education in this mode has its sources of data close at hand. An exercise like this one helps clarify what it means to make a reasoned judgement on a body of material. We structure a mass of details into categories of meaning. The mind practices re-perceiving reality into meaning-ful shapes.

Most of my students have never looked this closely at their jobs, their writings, each other, or the teacher. The careful attention to detail is what their English teachers have lectured to them under the rubrics of "paragraph development" and "theme organization." Studied as a rhetorical lesson instead of as a lesson in critically re-perceiving reality, "paragraph develop-ment" has of course not developed inside my students. By preparing composite lists, we construct a systematic breakdown of a discrete corner of life. By asking the original volunteers for further details, we gain a wealth of information which leads into a still more advanced phase of conceptual analysis: structural decomposition of "work." I ask the following question after we have continued unearthing more and more information: What are all the aspects of a job? This takes us again to the activity of abstracting a general case from specific examples. The class writes new lists of the components of "work": wages, hours, benefits, location, duration of employment, boss, co-workers, kind of work, special training, etc. The higher level of abstrac-tion sets a model for a structural analysis of any subject.

Conceptual Composition: Going Deeper and Deeper

With this much practice in developing an idea, we have sometimes gone on to write more precise analyses of the two job reports, and sometimes, for a little refreshing change, we have had two new volunteers read their accounts to us, and then have compared their reports. These early exercises in critical scrutiny begin to produce more thorough writing on the topic, but the development towards conceptual habits of mind requires more exercise. To go on with our problem-theme and literacy work, I next ask four students to read their worst job reports, and call upon the rest of us to attempt a more conceptual composition: What do the worst jobs have in common as Worst Jobs? This task involves abstracting a category of knowledge. Students write on the whole dimension of marginal labor, not on any one or two bad jobs. This phase of the inquiry has often given me the feel of take-off, as I stand at the board, listening to each student read out her or his piece on worst jobs. I make a composite list again of the qualities they identify as characterizing dead-end labor. Their thinking here is the most thorough so far, as they extract from their reality the general features of alienated work: low pay, no power to make decisions, little responsibility, routine and repetitious tasks, no creativity or independence, etc. With a well-developed conceptual model for the worst conditions of work, it's simple enough to practice developing the negation. The students easily produce a characterization of the best jobs around. These jobs have high pay, creative work, power and prestige, responsibility, and require special training or education. When I ask them to list which jobs in society fulfill this model of the best work, they come up with doctor, lawyer, architect, author, singer, athlete, executive, model, artist and pilot. With this material in such developed form, the next exercise is composing an answer to the following question: What's the difference between the best and worst jobs in society?

Up to this point, we have been gaining conceptual and writing skills through the systematic analysis of work in social life. These exercises offer a clear means to perceive what had previously been for students a rather chaotic rush of impressions. The development of critical scrutiny is valuable, but it can remain a largely empirical skill, that is, it can be an act of static knowledge, a training in describing the shape of something. Empirical observation is an important intellectual skill, but it is a foundation for transcendent thought, not the goal. Students who practice these conceptual exercises have been transforming themselves into people who can observe carefully and who can generalize but they do not yet have a commitment to transform what they have abstracted.

Some progress towards transcendent perception can be gained by diversifying the dualisms set up so far. We have been writing about bad and good teachers, worst and best jobs. I next ask the class to consider that terrain of labor known as "union jobs." A convenient place to begin this is to question the economic benefits offered through unionized employment. The list of material advantages in union jobs sets them up as one distinct notch higher than the world of worst jobs. The students compile a benefits list which includes fixed hourly rates plus periodic increments, sick pay, overtime, paid vacations and pension plans, etc. This systematic analysis of the union job is revelatory to all those who have not yet worked in an organized office, shop or plant. The knowledge of trade unionism is uneven and unclear among students, in a society where only a quarter of all jobs are unionized, and where the commercial media spread negative images of strikes and contract negotiations, announcing how wage settlements only increase the cost of living. The simple economic gains offered by unionizing stand out starkly when compared to the situations of the worst jobs we have analyzed. The moment when another section of social life—like trade unionism—takes systematic shape in the imagination is a pedagogical time rich in possibilities. The largely invisible history of labor struggles can be integrated here rather organically; the landmark dates of great strikes (1877, 1886, 1894, 1912, 1934, 1937, etc.) are of course unknown to almost every student. In addition, some imaginative writing can help clarify what class interests are involved in the flow of history. For example, students can be asked to compose a short speech from the point of view of corporate management and from the perspective of the workers, with each explaining in their own idioms why unions are good or bad. By creating persona speaking for each position, the students can clarify what each has to gain or to lose by the progress or regress of unionization. To expand the interdisciplinary character of this literacy exercise, it would be ideal to ask: Do wage increases really cause inflation? The students have a lively interest in this question, which permits the integration of formal economics into the discussion.

Through a consideration of a third shape of work—union jobs—and through interdisciplinary materials from labor history and economics, some transcendent thinking can be initiated into the critical scrutiny underway now for several weeks in class. Three central questions about labor suggest themselves as the obvious areas for a reconstructive dialogue around work— power, production, and distribution. How is work organized? What does work produce? How are the products and profits of labor distributed? These problems are systemic and grandiose. They need a concrete shape which can be phased in to the experiential and conceptual studies underway in the class. One simple means to focus attention on power is to ask: If you show up late for work and make mistakes, can the boss fire you? Of course, everyone says. Fine. If the boss shows up late for work and makes mistakes, can you fire him? Of course not, everyone says. Fine. This trivial fact of life provokes serious attention on an habitual injustice rooted in mass experience. How come people who do the same kind of thing at work do not have to pay the same price? This problematic discussion often leads to a dialogue on hierarchy. I have drawn pyramidal structures at the board and under it have put a variety of titles— hospital, school, bank, etc.—denoting some locations where students have worked. For each workplace pyramid, we have named the levels of bureaucratic power. Needless to say, students have systematically discovered themselves to be at the bottom of whatever pyramid we draw. I locate my own position in the college hierarchy, but the question of the bottom remains far more interesting. The bottom is not homogenous; the workforce is stratified in a variety of ways which interfere with its solidarity. What I ask next is: In how many ways is the rank and file at the bottom divided? Besides job titles and salary ranks and length of employment and location of work, etc., we also uncover features of sex, race and age as separating the bottom. Not only do power, pay and privilege decrease as we go down the pyramid, but the number of factors segmenting the workforce increase. The shape of this dialogue has varied from class to class, sometimes reaching dead-ends and sometimes going deeper. To focus continuing attention on the question of power and work organization, I take the opportunity at this point to introduce reading materials that propose transcendent ideas on labor. I also introduce a literacy technique which develops the students' ability to penetrate printed matter—pre-reading.

Work Re-Design: Pre-Reading and Re-Building

By this point, the class dialogue has matured enough to support the introduction of readings coordinated with the problem-theme. Because the literate act of decoding a text is as troubling for my students as writing a composition, I cannot hand out printed materials without offering techniques for close comprehension. Skill in reading has to be developed as we deal with serious texts relevant to an experiential theme. While I carefully choose reading matter on work-changes in society, I present to the class a systematic sequence which exercises their decoding skill. This sequence can be called "pre-reading."[4]

The simple first step in pre-reading is to stimulate interest in the text. The sensuous rush of mass media and rock music has so over-stimulated my students that they are dishabituated from the careful examination of a "slow" medium like the printed word. Pre-reading decelerates perception. Before any of them have to look at words, I mention the general topic covered by the reading selection and ask them to invent hypothetical questions which they think this text will answer. At first, this unfamiliar exercise receives a slow response. Having heard only the general topic of the reading, can you really imagine questions it will answer? I mention the topic again and sometimes offer a sample question. Eventually, someone comes up with one or two questions, then a third, fourth, fifth, and in a surprisingly short time, most of my classes have verbalized fifty to a hundred possible questions related to the general topic of the text, prior to having looked at the material. This type of preparation accomplishes a number of things besides using mental imaging and speaking as vehicles to prepare for reading. The speed of imagination and of speaking act as a deceleration bridge between the rush of mass culture and the deliberateness of close reading. Further, the authority of printed material is demystified. Ordinarily, through the authoritarian demeanor of mass schooling, an aura of expertise surrounds the dull texts handed out to students. In the case of pre-reading, the students' own thoughts and words on the reading topic are the starting points for the coordinated material. The text will be absorbed into the field of their language rather than they being ruled by it. This reversal is a concrete means to stimulate the students' subjective emergence in the learning process. Needless to say, after inventing dozens of potential questions to be answered by the text, the students become extremely curious to read it and find out how many are actually addressed. This stimulation of curiosity is a developmental test for the process as a whole. If students reject the reading material, then the critical process is not overcoming their alienation. If the pre-reading method of questioning provokes interest in the material, then the process has begun to restore a neglected intellectualism in the students.

The first technique for pre-reading—pre-questioning—is a method students can take away with them. After generating numerous preparatory questions on the reading material, the class can go right ahead and read the selection, taking note of how many questions are actually answered, or more extensive pre-reading can be used. An expanded form I experimented with in my classes involves a take-off on the dictation method of pre-writing. Before I hand out the printed matter, and after we have recorded all the preliminary questions we can invent about the topic, I ask students to copy down verbatim a few opening passages I read from the material. I read several paragraphs slowly and the students transcribe by dictation. Then, we voice their writings individually and in pairs, for immediate self-correction. Lastly, I hand out the text and ask students to compare their written versions to the original, noting where their encoding deviates from the print. This extended preparation develops close reading habits using the skills of careful listening and transcribing. Then, the eye is exercised in comparing two encoded forms. This is a rich way to extend the conscious connection between spoken and written language. At this point, I ask students to read the whole piece and write a summary of it. We hear each other's summaries aloud, and use this not only to develop comprehension skills, but as the means to begin a critique of the content of the reading.

In deciding what kinds of materials to introduce, I look for a few things. The selections should be in a reasonably colloquial idiom. If the language is jargonish, technical, abstract or formal, then it will alienate the attention of my students. Richly critical ideas and debate can be started from accessible language, so I scour the mass media, books, etc., for articles on the problem-theme of work. I like engagingly written things, but they must also suggest a problem, a critique or an idea of transition, for the class discussion to gain transcendent qualities. The readings have been selections from longer pieces or small articles xeroxed for class use. The range of material has been reasonably broad:

- about a failing steel plant taken over by the union, which managed to increase production 32%, saving the mill from bankruptcy.

- about a young auto worker from Detroit, whose chronic absenteeism and alienation perplex both the union and the corporation.

- about a college president who spends his sabbaticals doing menial work, discovering there the injustice of hierarchy.

- about a college teacher who spent time working in a piston plant and resented the absence of democracy on the job and the way he was laid- off without warning.

- about the occupational hazards of job stress and alienation, both contributing to heart disease.

- about a ghetto student working his way up from poverty and the worst jobs, living out the American Dream.

- about the glamorous and controversial pro basketballer Bill Walton, who mixed politics with his profession.

- about job redesign at Saab plants, where the work-team approach has been experimented with as an alternative to assembly line production.

- about the IGP insurance company in Washington, which has had worker control for a number of years.

- about a Michigan plant which eliminated most middle-level management, allowing the rank and file to organize its own work schedule, distributing supervisory wages to the workers as fringe benefits.

Each class does not get to read all the articles. There has never been enough time in the semester for that, and the shape of the class discussion has often made further reading not necessary or organic. The pieces that we do read provoke many questions for debate. We have gone on to do short compositions around such issues as: Can people manage their own work without supervisors? What would a fair policy be for wage levels? What alternative is there to hierarchy? While the study of the problem-theme of work has been deepening and diversifying, the compositional skill being exercised has so far remained mostly in the realm of short papers. To develop longer writing, we have gone on to write extended profiles of each other.

Profiling: Mining Personal Experience

Two of the articles we have read are in the form of profiles—the one on the ghetto student rising upward and the one on Bill Walton. The first is written personally as autobiography, while the second is a magazine feature by a professional writer. One way to continue the problem-dialogue while extending the awareness beyond the classroom is to ask students to write profiles of two working people, one around the age of twenty-five and the other over fifty. The goal would be for students to interview outside people so that they could compose comparative profiles of two generations of workers. To prepare for this ambitious exercise, the two profiles we read serve as preliminary models; yet, they do not go deep enough into the kinds of issues raised so far. For a more probing inquiry into job history, life style, and attitudes towards work and social life, we prepare our interview questions in advance. I ask each person to write down twenty questions they would want to ask their interviewees. We hear each other's lists out loud, and people are encouraged to borrow questions from the large pool they hear. Developing a model of questions is a starting point which helps develop critical scrutiny. Each student needs to draw upon our learning so far to understand the most important things to ask. The list of questions amounts to an in-process "test" of the course. It is a means to evaluate the amount of critical progress up to this point in the study. The design of questions for interviewing is a jointly conceptual and experiential task which grows naturally out of the material developed so far. Just how much structural perception exists now in each student will be dramatized by the listings. One useful means to advance the outside interviewing can be inside interviewing. Students can practice writing profiles of each other from their extended list of questions, as a pilot exercise prior to their doing it on non-members of the class.

The exercise in writing profiles generates a lot of material which will need to be sorted before a long composition can take shape. This sorting process demands conceptual scrutiny of the information each subject will offer the interviewer. An interesting variation of profiling, which can provoke attention on the categorical organization of an information mass, is to have the whole class interview one student. Each recording student will be hearing the same responses, but they will not produce the same profiles. By comparing the variant compositions, the class can have a useful discussion on the effective organization of the material. What were the best introductions and conclusions offered on this person's experience? Who emphasized which details and why? Who left out which crucial information? Which concrete details justified general interpretations made by the writer?

Overall, this problematic study of "work" offers one means to engage students in an extraordinary re-perception of something very ordinary. It not only develops literacy skills and consciousness relevant to the problem-theme, but it also validates students psychologically, because the exercise is based in their experience and in their language resources. By being sequential as well as experiential, it is a successively more demanding way to gain critical literacy. By using biography, speech and mental imaging, the class can develop conceptual habits of mind with surprising rapidity. Their mastery of reading and writing, the formal decoding and encoding of spoken language, appears to take longer than the development of structural thinking. Because the functions of reading and writing are harder to command than the verbal exercise of critical analysis, the written products of the class at the end of a single term will represent in most cases less conceptual reflection than the students can actually do. The excess skill in analysis will almost always be demonstrated best in the strongest language skill students possess—their speech. Thus, it is common for our class dialogue to remain more critical than our class compositions through most of the process. Both advance from where we started, but at different speeds. The best test of critical thought remains through dialogue, while the activities of reading and writing noticeably progress month by month. In the end, the work-world has achieved an unfamiliar shapely presence in thought and language. Work is not made less alienating, but critical thinking is less remote.

Notes

1. For the most concrete account of Freire's work in the classroom, see Cynthia Brown's monograph *Literacy in 30 Hours: Paulo Freire's Process in Northeast Brazil* (Writers and Readers Publishing Cooperative, London, 1975). In Freire's translated work, the most detailed description of his methods can be found in *Education for Critical Consciousness* (Seabury, New York, 1973).

2. The variety of educational experiments in the last ten years has been recorded in numerous books and magazines. Among the periodicals, *The Radical Teacher, College English* and *Ed-Centric* regularly published new modes for critical teaching. The works of Kozol (*Free Schools*) and Herb Kohl (*36 Children*) are among the most prominent in the field of pedagogical criticism. In the professions, radical caucuses like Science for the People and the Union for Radical Political Economy have had teaching committees publishing materials for the classroom. Several anthologies have gathered together some of the best work in radical education: *The Politics of Literature* by Louis Kampf and Paul Lauter, *Studies in Socialist Pedagogy* by Bertell Ollman and Theodore Norton, and *Teaching Human Dignity* by Miriam Wolf-Wasserman and Linda Hutchinson. Small teaching groups operate in different parts of the country, like the Teachers and Writers Collaborative in New York City, and like the Bay Area Radical Teachers Association, which until the mid-seventies published a journal called *No More Teacher's Dirty Looks*.

3. For discussion of free-writing and other student-centered, non-traditional approaches, see Ken Macrorie's *Uptaught* (Hayden, 1970) and Peter Elbow's *Writing Without Teachers* (Oxford, 1975).

4. I am indebted to Bill Bernhardt of Staten Island College for my introduction to pre-reading and free-writing. His book *Just Writing* (Teachers and Writers, New York, 1977) is a valuable resource.

APPENDIX

The Ten Commandments: Extended Exercise in Pre-Writing

Students find that writing long papers is a bewildering mystery. There must be some secret way to do it, and the teacher isn't letting on. From the student's point of view, the teacher's demand for a term paper is an alienating, threatening and arbitrary assault. From the teacher's point of view, after years of university education, the instructor can either write well or can lecture well on the mechanics of writing. In any case, whether the teacher can write well or not, she or he is the one in charge, making the judgements instead of being judged. It is habitually difficult for teachers, therefore, to understand the anxiety of their students. From a position of expertise and power, it takes an extraordinary effort to identify with the feelings of the powerless and inexpert. A simple remedy for this would be for teachers to study something they do poorly, each semester, so they will always be close to the feelings of a novice. This can help teachers know what the world and the class feel like from the eyes of their students. Another way to de-escalate student alienation is to demystify expertise constantly. An extended pre-writing method for long papers, derived from the shorter techniques discussed in this chapter, offers students one more self-educative vehicle they can take away from class. In both short and long form, sequential pre-writing demystifies composition.

The longer pre-writing method I have developed for some classes begins with a "brainstorm" and proceeds through ten steps to a finished paper. It starts from mental and verbal impressions easily accessible to students and moves through categories, sentences, paragraphing and theme-organization. Each developmental step leads naturally to the next. Students who complete any phase can be asked to tutor informally other students still at work. The process could be described like this:

1. *Brainstorm.* Start thinking about the problem-theme and list on a sheet of paper everything you know in your mind. The class will read its brainstorms to each other, and people can add anything they hear to their lists.

2. *Connecting.* With your composite list, draw lines on the page connecting all the items which belong together.

3. *Categorize.* Lift out from your composite list all the connected items, and rewrite them on a separate page, in groups.

4. *Equalize.* Notice which groups seem smaller than others and see if you can enlarge the short ones or divide the big ones.

5. *Titling.* Examine each group and decide an appropriate title for the items collected together. This title-word is the conceptual idea for turning the grouped items into a paragraph. The title suggests the general thesis of the sub-grouping.

6. *Ordering.* The titled groups will become paragraphs in the body of the paper. Look over the groups and ask which should be written out first, which second, etc. Reflect on the subject of each group, and judge where it should be placed in the whole paper.

7. *Paragraphing*. Translate each group into a paragraph, with each listed item serving as the idea for a sentence in the paragraph. After finishing a paragraph, check back to the list to see if all the items have been included.

8. *Framing*. The main body of the paper is written. Now write an introduction and a conclusion appropriate to the theme.

9. *Voicing*. Read the whole text out loud, individually and with a silent partner reading along with you.

10. *Self-Correct*. Rewrite for errors caught by the grammar in your voice.

This simple method is a tangible and self-explanatory means to aid the composing process. Like other literacy techniques, it takes time to master. One of its advantages is that it fills a gap left by voicing—namely, paragraphing. The voice can help with sentence structure and careless errors, but a range of spelling and paragraphing questions cannot be detected by the grammar in the voice. A reading voice does not contain such precise punctuation pauses to indicate the rhetorical transition between paragraphs, and it is a basically phonetic instrument, so it cannot account for the arbitrary spelling variations given to a single sound in the written code. The ten-step pre-writing method raises consciousness around the conceptual activity of paragraphing. Spelling naturally evolves as student alienation declines. The more students commit themselves to dialogue, reperception, reading and writing, the more carefully they discover the logic and illogic of their language's written code. If the teacher is impatient, perfectionist, or mechanical in using these methods, the potential for regress is great. Learning how to assimilate cognitive development into a problem-theme and into an experiential dialogue is the teacher's education. As an example of how the method can produce more systematic writing, I include here the first composition of a remedial student. He practiced the ten-step exercise during several class hours, and produced a rather accurate statement of the consciousness my students bring to our sessions. Following his paper, I've included preparatory steps for a second essay, on the college. It lacks the connecting lines between items, but note that I acted as recorder to assemble at the board all the items mentioned in class, and then for our next session prepared a ditto sheet reiterating the board list as the base for the next step in the process. Student writing served as a resource of issues for class dialogue. The first paper was the starting point for the problem-theme of work, while the second outline used the extended pre-writing method for the subject of our school:

"Tom"
(unedited student manuscripts)
Component Analysis List
"Work"

Paper route
Hassel with some people
Young woman answers door with no clothes
Christmas money
Riped off by middle man
Hostpital kitchen work
Lots of friends
Lots of sex with nurses
Many dates
Many unpleasent scenes
cruelty to patients
mentally disturbed individuals
thought
computer systems
New experience
Training
Riped off by bulshit line
Many different places
Planes
Helicopters
Many new people most phonies
beautiful girls
propositions
Sense of being older
lot of respect
many lonely nights away from home
alway wanting to be home
end it for school

"Jobs"

1. "Jobs"
Paper route
Hospital "computer"
Systems
Salvaging Metal
Training   Money
2. "People"
Hassels with some people
Many unpleasent scenes
Creulty to patients
Mentaly disturb people
3. "Women"
Young woman answers door naked
lots of sex
many dates
beautiful girls
propositions
4. "Robbed"
Riped off by middle man
Riped off by bulshit lines
5. "friends"
Lots of friends
Many new people most phonies
6. "Thought"
thought
end it for school
7. "Travel"
Planes
helicopters
8. "Age"
Sense of being older
respected
9. "Home"
Many lonely nights wanting to be home.

"Work" by "Tom"

I have had many jobs since I was twelve years of age. The first job was a paper route. Then a couple of years later I worked in a hospital. I worked there for about three years. After learning the hospital I went to work at "computer" systems. Now while in school I've been salvaging metals.

During my working career thus far I have met many different people. Some people gave me hassels, others were allright. I remember seeing horrible things done by people. The nurses used to have ways of punishing certain patients. Then there were the guys that just did sick things to the patients' food.

I remmember many experiences with women during my work career thus far. Once when I was collecting money on a saturday morning and a young women about twenty two answered the door in her birthday suit and asked me in. Well at twelve years old I was very shy and refused, then left. Now sometimes I regret leaving. At age sixteen everyone is into sex, so was I. It wasn't long after I started working at the hospital that the nurses started working on me. It was like you see in movies, people making love in linen closets, in unwalked stairways and in cars. I have traveled throughout the country in my work the last year in my work with computers and meet many women. The repairmen at this company traveled in pairs. So we did have a lot of night life. In bars we went to there were always women who wanted men. My friend would always help them out but I wouldn't. I don't know why but I didn't. I guess it was my loyalty to my mate.

One thing that has always been the same though is being ripped off. During my paper route days I was supposed to win prizes by gaining new customers. I gained customers for them alright but I never got the prizes. When I tried to collect the prizes I was always told they had not come in yet. In the hospital when it was time for a raise there was always some reason the couldn't come accross. I never tried to do anything about it but then one day I took a stand. I was working for "computer" systems on a salary basis. I listened to there bulshit about big raises for hard workers and worked my ass off and also work late nights for free like an ass. Then increase time came and they fucked me with a lousy five dollar raise. I was so pissed off I could have killed someone. That was the day I took my stand. The following week I was to go with my partner to Oaklahoma. Up to this time we had been doing the job quick and spending a minimum amount of money. The squeeze was on we arrived on Monday. On the plane we talked about increases and I found out he had also been screwed. So we pulled out our logic diagrams and he told me which I.C.'s were the hardest to get that we didn't have or did they have in stock. He knew which ones because he had recently worked in the procurement department. We found the real problem with the unit and phoned in the one we made up. They told us to wait there until they got us a I.C. which does division & multiplication. That was it we went out every day and night spending their money on presents for the family and our selves making up phony exspense reports. When we got back there were no questions asked. Things like this went on for about four months until I decided to go back to school. At the time I was leaving there were only two technicians my friend and I. The reason was that we worked for the cheapest pay and the others were laided off.

Since I've been attending school I have had two more jobs. I was ripped off in one and laid off in the other. The way I was ripped off was I worked with a guy who salvaged metals on the week end. I would bust my ass working as hard as he was but when the money came it didn't work out the way I figured. (For instance one week we found a load of copper, out of two thousand dollars I received seventy five dollars which I had to chase him for a week to get. This guy was a real prick. He finally got himself fucked because of the way he was. I think he considered himself Bill bad ass, you know one of the avengers. He said so. A guy a long ago ripped off a set of his torches. So to even the score he ripped off the guys tools and torches. He made one mistake, he got caught. Then after the way he screwed me he wanted me to help him by lying for him. Well I thought about it for a split second then told him to go fuck himself. I guess I should have done something to help him but I'm glad I didn't lie for him.

The job I now have at the gas station is going pretty good. I work about eight hours on Saturday. I used to work there three hours a night but was laid off when the gas shortage came about. The owner is a very generous man and the people I work with were great also. I think I will try to remain there as long as possible.

As for the future I am thinking seriously of becoming a cop. I wish to do so because I will be able to make fairly decent money and attend college while doing so. I believe I will always get ripped of no matter what. I know thats not a very optimistic attitude but thats the way it will be.

"Bill"
(unedited student manuscript)
"Our College"

Step No. 1   Listed on board

GOOD	BAD
Education Opportunity	Parking
Teacher/student involvement	Closing of school
Library availability	Dead weight taking valuable
Lab availability	space
Special help for students	Hard times to change a course
Gym and sports field	One person sends you to another
Meeting people	Recreation
Cafeteria	Cafeteria food is sad experience
Student lounge	Price of transportation
After class activities	Financial situation
Cafeteria	Relationship between teachers

Lounge
Lobrary
Parking Lot
Large classrooms
Bookstore
Good teachers
Help for students
Large campus
Easy to get in
Studnets and teachers
Library
School pace
Variety of subjects
Small for community College
Computer Lab
People are more friendly
The environment
Location
Skills center service
Transportation(near my house)
Best community college
More unity between the people
No requirements
Small amount of money
Teachers care
Students care
Nice study hall
Teachers willing to spend time
A place to sit down, relax and eat
Good phys ed dept.
Lots of pretty women
Lots of student discounts
Lots of social clubs
Make your own schedule
Free time to study or lounge
Student lounge has music and
    games
Student press
Clubs, tutors, bookstore,
    cafeteria
Choice of courses
Campus big
Clubs for free time
Own bookstore

Food in cafeteria
Registration process
size of class
Lack of chalk in classroom
Change in time schedule
Poor parking
Poor cafeteria
Poor counseling
Books are expensive
Overcrowding
Not easily accessible without car
Not enough teachers
Overcrowded classrooms
Price too high in cafeteria
Short on school supplies
Need more parking spaces
Too much open space and its cold
Overcrowded parking
Registration fee too high
Books very expensive
Penalty for dropping
Classes
Travel expense
Waiting for buses after class
Student lounge always dirty
Waiting on snack lines
Priveleged parking unfair
Jobs hard to come by
Too crowded
Must leave early to get a spot
Crowded and dirty
Cut downs from budget cuts
classes all full
Prices are high
Parking situation
Lack of communication
Too many rumors
Confusion in courses
Misplacement
Apathetic teachers
Class schedule hard on
    working people
Waste in book store
Some classes don't have books

Step No. 2 List Organized

GOOD	BAD
Education opportunity	Parking
variety of subjects	Priveleged/Overcrowded
skills center services	Price of Transportation
help for students	Not easily accessible campus
teachers care/involved	without car
VAC/vets services	Wait for buses after class
	Must leave early to get spot
Library and labs available	
bookstore	Cafeteria is sad experience
nice study hall	food is bad
good phys ed dept/gym, sports	prices too high
large classrooms & campus	poor service
computer lab	crowded and dirty
	waiting on snack lines
music, games in lounge	
relaxing in cafeteria	books very expensive
clubs for free time	some classes don't have books
after-class activities	apathetic teachers
meeting people/social clubs	lack of communicaation
people are more friendly	too many rumors
more unity between people	confusion in courses
no requirements	Closing of School
large course choice	size of classes
easy to get in	lack of chalk
school pace is slow	cut downs from budget cuts
small college	changes in time schedule
small amount of money	financial situation
discounts with student cards	not enough teachers
make own schedule	overcrowded classrooms
car travel	shortage of school supplies
parking lot for cars	hard to change courses
environment	one person sends you to another
location/setting	registration lines
transportation	poor counseling
public phones	penalty for dropping
posted information	class schedule hard on
	working students
	classes full
	student lounge dirty
	too crowded
	recreation

CHAPTER FIVE

LEARNING HOW TO LEARN:

Conceptual Thought in a Utopia Course

Political Imagination

Every teacher knows how little students have to show for all their years of schooling. The students know this too, and are angry. In a situation like this, it's easy enough to blame the victim. Teachers in frustration can turn against students for their lack of literacy and conceptual skills. Of course, the school system is the primary villain in this social melodrama, because the absence of critical literacy fits the kind of domesticated consciousness demanded by mass culture. A system based on hierarchical control is incompatible with an autonomous, thoughtful population, so it makes sense for the great mass of students to wind up with weak resources in English and analysis. Faced by this reality, critical educators in every discipline will have a hard time making their courses "sink in." The most visible pedagogical problem in any class is the underdevelopment of reading, writing and critical thought. These are the foundations for learning and transcendence.

To develop linguistic and philosophical resources in my students, I evolved a series of conceptual exercises offered in a Utopia course, and have used them in composition classes as well. At first, I was interested in Utopia as a theme before I had invented any conceptual teaching methods. The very idea of Utopia invited me into consciousness-raising teaching. Utopia stimulates the imagination; it speaks to the human power to reconstruct ourselves and our social relations. It is a place where politics and creativity coincide as well as collide. As I studied my students year by year, I was struck by the absence of transcendent thinking; there were very few spaces in their lives to invent options for themselves. Their sense of freedom, or happiness, or liberation was largely contained in the strike-it-rich, I'll-get-mine American Dream. The 60s had stimulated my political imagination, and now I thought that an inquiry into Utopia might do the same for my students. What emerged was an exercise in social analysis and conceptual thinking that went far beyond my own expectations for the course. The class was always well enrolled, attendance was high, and people sent their friends, mates, and relatives to take it the following term. I do think that the mere title "Utopia" acts as a magnet for the most advanced consciousness in the student constituency, just like the remedial courses I teach collect the least aspiring students. Yet, even if the Utopia class drew the most animated students, it will be plain from documents in the appendix to this chapter that their level of literacy and critical thought is still problematic, in need of much development. The process of that development has been the most inspiring teaching for me.

Structural Paradigms: Problems in Life and in Thought

Utopia taught as an inquiry into social life and as an exercise in social reconstruction has much to offer a liberatory class. It is an ideal subject through which to problematize any area of daily experience. Further, it can be taught through virtually any official department in a school, as each academic discipline can assimilate its methods and terminology into the theme of Utopia. Not only can a Utopia class be offered in many disciplines, but it is by itself a thematic study which encourages interdisciplinary approaches, as well as transcendent thinking. In the Utopia course I designed, language and logic skills emerged with critical thinking, under the formal sponsorship of an English department.

I begin the class like the others, with sign-ins at the board. After students have presented themselves to each other, and I have introduced myself, I next ask students to write down what Utopia means to them. These initial documents not only begin the course with my role in low profile and the student thought and language in motion, but it also serves me and them as a starting point vis á vis the level of literacy, critical thought and information about the subject. I listen carefully to my students' initial thoughts on Utopia, to gain immediate knowledge of the shape of consciousness and cognition extant in this group of students.

As each student reads her or his brief composition on Utopia, I act as recorder, sitting silently at my seat, taking notes on what each person offers. After everyone has read out loud, I then read back to the class what they as a whole have written to characterize Utopia. Usually, a number of people are stimulated by the composite reiteration of their writing, and have some questions to ask. Wherever possible, I try to locate the person whose original statement provoked the follow-up question, and encourage her or him to answer the question. This discussion format flows for an indeterminate time in an unpredictable direction, building up more and more curiosity about the subject. Eventually, there develops in class a desire for me to raise my profile, focus the debate on some questions, and share with them my starting points for appreciating Utopia. At this point, I act as a resource person, and offer a brief scheme for the literary and social action traditions which have been the peculiarly dual character of Utopia in Western society. I propose to the class that we can study Utopia as a literary tradition, as a history of various counter-communities, and as a form of critical consciousness. The suggestion that we can best understand Utopia by practicing Utopian thought stands as an appealing invitation to the class, and naturally leads us into a variety of exercises in conceptual analysis.

I present these methods through visual forms, which serve as paradigms for a conceptual habit of mind. The first form looks like this:

A Problem Solving Method

Life Description	Diagnosis	Reconstruction
Step one Observation	Step two Investigation	Step three Resolution

This three-step activity amounts to a problem-solving method. It moves from careful observation of something in the first part, to a contextual examination of it in the next section, to a reconstruction or resolution of its problematic nature, in the last step. The initial step calls upon students to exercise close scrutiny of an item and then to connect that empirical activity to their native language resources, in the writing of a detailed rendition. The simple act of reporting something in detail achieves a number of things. First of all, it is in contrast to the rushed mode of perception predominant in mass culture. Our first action decelerates the pace of mental life, so that a wider range of intellect and sensibility can be exercised. From another perspective, the development of empirical skills also develops literacy because observation is connected to writing, reading and speaking. The use of objects from daily life permits everyday experience as well as student language to be resources for deeper modes of critical thought, as in the sequential study of work reported in the previous chapter. The careful scrutiny of a familiar thing—like a classroom chair—allows students to create for themselves a studious milieu quite unlike the speeded environment surrounding the rest of their lives.

The second step of this exercise goes beyond description into analysis. It is social-historical, interpretative and value-based. I offer the term Diagnosis to denote step two as researching the problematic nature of the thing under observation. We ask: What is its human context? Who benefits how from it? What are its social roots and consequences? From this base in descriptive and diagnostic thought, we progress to the last part, Reconstruction. I ask students to write redesigns of the thing studied, so that the problems we uncovered are resolved. This final part exercises their creative imagination. As an overall method, this tripartite structure is offered as one paradigm for Utopian thinking. Those Utopians who write novels or build new communities do so with a lively sense of what they are seeing, rejecting and rebuilding in their social lives. Further, this methodology for developing critical consciousness is akin to Freire's techniques of social inquiry. He calls the first two steps coding/decoding, or codification/decodification, or surface and deep structure of the problem under study. Freire and his colleagues use visual codifications to provoke a dialogue which diagnoses (decodifies) the deep meaning of the social situation imaged before the students. This dialogue leads on to transcendent thought about ways to transform the situation (reconstruction). These are phases in the development of structural perception.

Because the development of structural perception is simultaneously a re-perception of the *ordinary*, the concrete subject under critical observation must be familiar. I usually ask the class to practice the three-part method on such things as chairs and hamburgers. This keeps the development of conceptual habits rooted in the transcendent turn to daily life. In the case of applying this method to the ordinary classroom chair, we first spend some time scrutinizing the fiberglass form-fit seats in the room, and then write out detailed descriptions of it. We read these compositions to each other, prizing microscopic attention to all apparent features. The chair, which is visually perceived very quickly, actually allows the eye to focus on a number of dimensions: the color, the materials, the molding into a single piece for the torso, the tubular chrome-plate legs in a crossing arch-like support for the seat, the small formica writing surface on the right side of each chair. It is rewarding to see how much vocabulary students can use when they carefully render something. A sense of confidence grows as I compile a composite description of the chair. To see something so thoroughly perceived is a refreshing experience for the class in a culture where so much rushes by or so much is remote from you (like the exercise of power through institutions).

With the chair carefully described, I then ask the class to attempt a social diagnosis. This part of the method has been very revealing. The familiar object under us turns out to be full of problems. At the very least, it's uncomfortable. Who designed it like that? Surely, the students wouldn't design or choose an uncomfortable chair for themselves. Whoever designed and selected it had certain things in mind when constructing and ordering a chair like this. We examine the social context of the chair in order to go beneath its appearance. As conceptual detectives, in dialogue, we discover that the chair functions to force a student's attention and conversation towards the teacher. (Some classes have spontaneously remedied this by suggesting we sit in a circle.) When these chairs are aligned in rows, they make it hard to rotate and speak to or look at your

peers. The chair is a hard, unyielding object, so it's difficult to relax in. Why are you prevented from relaxing in class? Because
you'll fall asleep, students answer. Why will you fall asleep if the
chair is comfortable? You don't fall asleep at the movies or at
home, when you sit in a comfortable chair, so why will you do it
here? Because the teacher is boring, they answer. So, if the
teacher is boring and puts you to sleep, the answer is to punish
you with a chair that keeps you awake, instead of punishing the
teacher for being a bore. Why not change the teacher so that education is exciting and inspiring? Do people fall asleep when they
are being offered something they really want? As we dialogue,
we focus on the hard, small writing surface bolted on to each
chair. In the old days, wooden desks allowed you to distract yourself by carving names and graffiti, but these new chairs eliminate
that. The chair's discomfort and impermeable surface are joined
by the bland colors, as hindrances to distraction. The tight construction also prevents slouching, reclining, leaning over and
foot-crossing. By now, the chair is no ordinary part of the classroom furnishings. It is emerging as a symbol of oppression. It is
being perceived as a discipline-device in which students must sit
upright, stiff and attentive, in front of a teacher whose activity
does not deserve the attention demanded from students. The
college chose this chair for its students, but for sure the
President and his deans do not sit on chairs like this. A quite
simple lesson in authoritarian rule grows from the recognition
that the people who must use the chair did not choose it, while
the people who choose it are not required to use it. A method
which began with the simple observation of an ordinary object
has begun to raise consciousness and uncover the deep ideology
of daily life.

Our pejorative analysis does acknowledge that a mass-
produced chair is cheaper to purchase and is more durable in a
heavily used public facility. Yet, do students at Harvard have to
sit on chairs like this? Some schools allow their students to be
comfortable. It's no accident that elite environs, no matter how
heavily used, are designed for aesthetic stimulation and for
comfort. Mass education is simply drab and regimented. Out of
such Diagnosis comes a flood of reportage about the students'
prior schooling. They share memories of boredom and abuse.
They marvel at their inability to remember what was taught. In

our talk, we distinguish between discipline and education, by analyzing all the other discipline devices employed by schools: grades, tests, demerits, standing in the corner, being physically hit, extra homework, no participation in sports and clubs, entries on the permanent record following a student through the grades, calling in parents, verbal humiliation, dress codes, hand-raising, etc. Each student has no trouble remembering these incidents, even though the cognitive content of their school years remains mysterious to them. We spend some time prac-ticing the "correct" and "incorrect" ways of sitting in the chair. This physical use of our bodies to realize a conceptual analysis really hits home. It is a strong moment of externalization and abstraction. People are now consciously practicing the shape of their oppression so as to be free from it. They are acting with reflection. The Utopia class has become a counter-class; they can use this school space to exorcise the damage of the previous school space. In this kind of conceptual exercise, students overcome an interference to critical thought by examining the interference itself.

From this point in an extended Diagnosis, they take easily to step three, the Reconstruction. I ask the students to redesign the chair so that it negates the worst features discovered in the Diagnosis. Each person writes out her or his vision of the chair she or he wants. They come up with ideas for large, wooden chairs, for upholstered seats with arms, for floor pillows, for big, old used couches, for clay-like soft chairs, and more. In their thoughts and in their writing, they gain a clear image of what they would do to transform the classroom. The simple question of furniture has been turned into a politicizing issue.

I ask students to practice this three-step method at home on any two things they want. Later on, I propose that they isolate the worst problem in their neighborhood and use the method for investigating it. Acting as secretary-recorder for these composi-tions, I read a selection to the class, and use them as starting points for discussing both the conceptual method and the items analysed. On some occasions, we have transferred the discussion of discipline and authority in school to the domain of the work-world. We take the reality of work through the three steps, especially focusing on the question of power. The figure of a domineering boss looms large in the writings and dialogue. I ask the class to use the Reconstruction phase to develop some models for non-authoritarian work. The ideas of "group democracy" and "peer discipline" have tended to emerge organically from these efforts. The debate on whether a democratic form of discipline can succeed is heated. Once again, daily life is the context for conceptual development while philosophy is validated because it is relevant to a concrete issue. Conceptual and experiential levels interact supportively here, in preparation for Utopia, the most radical critique of everyday life.

The World's Biggest Hamburger: An Extended Conceptual Paradigm

The trusty, modern American hamburger has served us for some of the most interesting conceptual exercises. After experimenting with the classroom chair as a provocateur of deep social analysis, I began searching for some other familiar item. The "car" in daily life is a good choice, but cars are too big to bring to class. One day, I walked into the college cafeteria, and was surrounded by the hot grease smell of frying burgers. My search ended.

I bought a hamburger and took it to class. What better way to extraordinarily re-experience the ordinary? The burger is the nexus of so many daily realities. It's not only the king of fast foods, the lunch/snack/dinner quickie meal, but it's also the source of wages for many students who work in the burger chains. In addition, the spread of fast food franchises is tied into the suburban dispersal of the American city. This dispersal is further connected to the automobilization of American life. The car, the suburbs, and the burger thus connect central themes of everyday life. So, I was able to hold in my hand a weighty interstice of mass experience. My students have eaten, cooked and sold countless numbers of hamburgers, but they have never reflected on all this activity. I brought a burger to class and interfered with a major uncritical flow of mass culture. It was a lucky break, played out on a hunch.

As with the chair, I asked students to examine the burger carefully, and write out a detailed description. We passed the burger from person to person, so that people could touch it, smell it, carefully look at its texture and color. The empirical reports were interesting. Close up, on reflection, many of the students found the hamburger repulsive. It was greasy; it was a mess of ugly colors; it was rubbery; it ran with ketchup; the lettuce was limp; the roll was stale, and so on. We were all surprised at this response. When I read back to the class a composite of their descriptions, the burger took a strongly negative shape. I next asked people to attempt a Diagnosis of this object. The obvious problem suggested by our work so far was: If the burger is unattractive, why do we eat so many of them? Why are there so many fast food restaurants? Why are so many things put on top of hamburgers? Are they nutritious? What did we do for restaurants before the fast-food empires began pushing the burger?

With the hamburger as the problem-theme of our inquiry, we developed in a number of directions. For the Reconstruction, one class wanted to act on our distinction between "junk food" and "health food." A class organizing committee emerged to cooperatize the college cafeteria, and have it offer a nutritious, fixed-price lunch. In other classes, we began evolving an extended conceptual paradigm to represent the total analysis of the burger. I had asked one class to recreate the entire production and distribution process which delivered a burger to a consumer. This recreation unveiled the largely invisible relations of commodity culture. It is empowering to systematize a grandiose model for the production of a simple piece of daily life. This kind of analysis enables students to connect the immediate with the general, as interactive dimensions of their experience. With conceptual thinking connecting the particular to the general, students gain a structural perception of the making of everyday life. Not only does such thought restore deliberate analysis to accelerated minds, but it also reverses the reification of intellect into fragmented pieces.

One long paradigm was especially rooted in appreciating comprehensive social change. The three-step Description-Diagnosis-Reconstruction method can be elaborated into a five step structure:

1.

X in the square is the theme or object under problematic study. In this first step it is described in great detail.

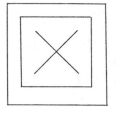

2.

The larger square represents X in its immediate social setting. How does X relate to other aspects of social life? What are the human consequences of X? This second step begins the deep contextual analysis of the codified theme. Example: the car. How do cars get made, sold, and delivered? Why do people buy the cars they do? Why do the cars look like they do? What other means of transport are available in society, and how do they compare to the car? What are all the things people use cars for?

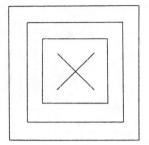

3.

The next large square represents the global relations of X. Does it exist in France, China or Afghanistan? Does our use of cars affect life elsewhere on the planet? Are building materials from other countries used? Are they built elsewhere? What do other countries do with or without cars? Why do they build them there and sell them here? Why would other countries send out raw materials to build cars someplace else? Who organizes this kind of system?

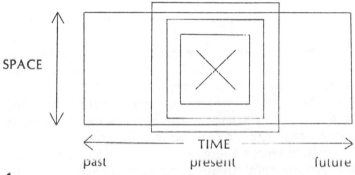

4.

The previous two steps have elaborated X in its immediate and global space. They unveil the social relations of X in the present time. The new rectangle moves backwards and forwards in time. This new dimension seeks to know how each student's life has been involved recently with X. Further, it probes the immediate future vis á vis X. Example: the car. When was the specific vehicle you use built? How does it change over time, as you use it? What determines how long you can use it? In terms of cars, what social changes will be effecting their use in the next few years?

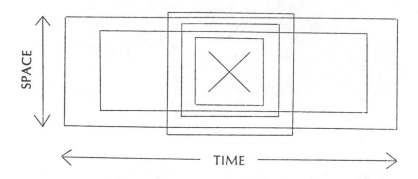

5.

The larger rectangle is the long-range time-span of X. When did it first enter human history? What did it replace? Why did it appear when it did? Has it changed since then? Who brought it into being and why? What will it look like ten or twenty years from now? *How could X look if it was reconstructed along different ideas? What changes are needed in it?*

The last step is the Utopian phase of the investigation. It calls upon students to re-invent the thing being studied, so that the future will not reproduce the present. As a conceptual method, this five-step paradigm locates a social relation in its complete time and space. It is a means to create historical consciousness. The kind of imagination which gets stimulated can serve as a base for discussing alternatives to the present society. For now, the burger and the car may be two ruling forces in daily life, but they weren't always with us and may not stay forever. At a certain point in time, society changed so as to produce hamburgers and cars, and in turn, these phenomena worked to change society. Students who gain the power to understand the transformation of society also gain the critical consciousness needed to invent their own transformations. Through our investigation, their perceptions of transport and food change. Talk emerges about non-polluting mass transit, about cooperative food service replacing the cafeteria's junk meals. The size of the system they live under still remains larger than the size of their critical thought, but their minds are expanding through a confrontation with reality.

Ringing Dinner-Bells: More Structural Paradigms

An important phase of development is gaining conceptual language with which to name the present and the reconstructed future. The absence of abstract thought is accompanied by the absence of abstract language in students. Words which denote general categories for a group of specific items are missing. The name of the system we live under is not clearly understood while the names of alternatives are vague as well. I don't remedy this situation by delivering a lecture on capitalism versus socialism, or hierarchy versus egalitarianism, or bureaucracy versus worker-control. If students ask to hear me talk on these issues, I respond in ways organic to the concrete questions under class discussion. What is most important is not for students to memorize a word like "capitalism," or to take notes on the meaning of "socialism." These kinds of knowledge can be useful only as part of a transformative education. The foundation for discriminating between social forms is critical consciousness, for without the ability to reason conceptually, the students cannot become their own agents of social change. They will always remain as objects of a manipulated historical process.

To create the conditions for their own subjective emergence in history, the liberatory study of Utopia develops their critical faculties. One method of special value focuses specifically on the process of abstraction. In class, I call it the "concept method." It is also tri-partite in structure:

The Concept Method

NAME	GENERAL DEFINITION	LIFE EXAMPLES
1.	2.	3.

This paradigm teaches people to invent generic concepts appropriate for related specifics drawn from experience. It encourages a dynamic appreciation of how a general idea is realized by concrete instances. In box 1, we put the name of something, like "junk food." In the second square, we write a brief general definition of the thing being studied. In the last box, we make a list of the many examples of the concept found in daily life. The third section answers the question: What would the concept look like if we saw it being lived out? This method allows students to examine a situation with many impressions, gather the impressions into groups, write out a few sentences which establish the general character of the grouped items, and then invent a short linguistic phrase which names the whole category of experience. In the case of "junk food," the exercise has come out looking like this:

NAME	GENERAL DEFINITION	LIFE EXAMPLES
Junk Food	Mass produced food that is cooked quickly in fast-food places, or bought, packaged and processed in supermarkets. Usually, it's low in nutrition.	Burgers fries canned fruits and vegetable packaged cereals cookies, cake donuts candy

This simple method can be applied to all kinds of situations. We can put "private car" or "mass transit" or "peer discipline" in the name column and work outward from there. Because the method is relational we can take a collection of items and work towards a general definition and a conceptual name. The paradigm allows us to move in any direction. We can

start even from the middle, with a general definition of something, like "a work situation structured so that each person has
equal control," and then move one way towards a name for that
social organization and then the other way towards concrete
examples of it. As an exercise in abstraction, it can provoke
critical consciousness when the routine situations of everyday
life are its subject content. For exercising the method, I list about
twenty concepts on the board and ask groups of students to
develop them through the paradigm, and present serially to the
whole class. The concepts I write down include "common sense,"
"lost cause," "broken home," "racism," "sexism," "inequality,"
"democracy," "student." As a way of focusing critical scrutiny on
habitual behavior, this method can also assimilate clichés of daily
life, like "strike it rich," "the grass is always greener," and "you
can't fight city hall." Such conceptual exercise linguistically demystifies experience.

After each group has worked on its concept and reported to
the class, I ask the groups to go back into committee and develop
the negation of their subject. This is an interesting phase of
study. The original committee reports had produced good
material for class discussion, while the new effort in designing all
three steps of the negation is a sequentially more demanding
task. The committees reconvene, take as much time as they need,
and then each goes to the board to lay out its three squares. Each
of the sections is demanding in itself, as they are three different
forms of perception—an abstract name, a general definition, and
an assembly of concrete illustrations of the general case. The
ability to perform negations in all three of these dimensions is
critical to their emerging consciousness. Negation is a fundamental feature of transcendent thought. For the study of our
course material, this methodology is useful in several ways.
Utopia can be understood as a negation of existing social
relations. Further, to understand the ideology of the present
society and of the Utopian communities we will study, we need
minds which can examine social life and abstract general values
from a welter of daily situations. The "concept method" facilitates these needs. As they use it, the students become startlingly
conceptual. In the course of a few months, their ability to do
abstraction can become razor sharp.

Bringing It All Back Home: Merging the Structural Methods

Through exercise in conceptual methods, the class dialogue becomes more richly analytic. The mind gets training in the skills of decoding reality. Out there in life, experience is always coming at you in too many little pieces or too many big pieces. Either way, you can't put it all together or absorb what it all means. The methods introduced in this class make it easier to structure what you see. Students begin to feel they they know where to put experiential details. With their abstraction abilities raised, I next ask them to look carefully at the two tri-partite paradigms, and see if there is a way to link them into a single structure. I draw them separately on the board, and let the class look them over. People begin suggesting some ways to do the linkage, and eventually they hit on a merged paradigm which some classes have called the "horseshoe," the "Utopia Graph," or the "open doughnut." This new structure is built by turning the first method on its side and connecting it to two concept paradigms, like this:

	NAME	GENERAL DEFINITION	LIFE EXAMPLES	
OLD IDEA in SOCIETY	example: authoritarianism		1.	**DESCRIPTION**
	↑ NEGATIONS ↓		2.	**DIAGNOSIS**
NEW IDEA in UTOPIA	"peer discipline" or "group democracy" NAME	GENERAL DEFINITION	LIFE EXAMPLES 3.	**RECONSTRUCTION**

This new form is possible because the third step of Reconstruction is a concrete description of a new, Utopian reality, while the first step of Description is the same process of empirical accounting which generates the Life Examples step of the "concept method." The two methods become linked at the level of experiential reality, with the problematic Diagnosis being the key bridge between them. The Diagnosis thus assumes a melodramatic role in bringing it all together, and it is fitting that it should. What is Diagnosis if not the moment of critical thought? The Diagnosis is the deep analysis of reality, the problematizing moment of inquiry, the animation of consciousness. The lesson in this linkage should not be lost. Through critical scrutiny, the kind of consciousness needed to design Utopia (transcendence) is achieved. Without diagnostic thinking, the bridge between the problem-present and the reconstructed future cannot be made. The future as a Utopian negation of the present rests on the development of diagnostic/reconstructive thought.

This enlarged structure is a more complete paradigm for a transcendent habit of mind. As a class exercise, it is more challenging than the tri-partite methods. It can be mastered in a number of ways. One of the simplest is to ask the class to offer material suitable for one of the seven squares, and then have committees generate the other six. In doing this, students are not merely studying Utopia as an academic notion. They have begun to model their own imaginations in a Utopian fashion. We are realizing our goal of entering Utopia through the consciousness of people who recreate social relations. This indirect road of study transforms the people who are studying the transformation of society. There are more landmarks along the way.

Circling In and Out: Tradition and Transcendence

The next developmental phase passes through a final paradigm, that of concentric circles:

I offer this figure as a representation of the dialectical flow between tradition and Utopia. The center of the circles is the society all of us are born into. Each rim outward represents phases of development, in a prolonged process of social and personal change which leads to radical reconstruction at the periphery. The last circle in the figure represents Utopia, the way of life most dissociated from the mainstream at the center. As you gain critical consciousness, you push yourself away from unreflective immersion at the center. You abstract the mainstream of your native culture so that you can study it. This is the process of expelling mass culture from yourself and expelling yourself from it. Pedagogically, Utopia studied in this way allows the externalization of false consciousness, because the center of the circles is synonymous with false thought. By gaining detachment on your habitual daily life, you begin transcending its limits. You no longer routinely go about your business, reproducing the situations which keep you trapped in the center. For my students, our Utopia class becomes their first critical rim away from immersion in the mainstream. Our own learning process is conceptualized in this paradigm as a break with the past.

Between mass culture at the center and Utopian negation at the edge, a great deal of time, space, thought and action exists. Alienation from the established order leads Utopians into critique, separation, and reconstruction. The outermost rim is where the most radical detachment can be found, but reconstructive change happens at each point along the way. It matters for students to see social change not only as their subjective responsibility, but also as something developmental. It's most familiar for my largely non-politicized students to have an all-or-nothing attitude towards social questions. For them, the seriousness of our social problems is obvious, yet they tend to think that if we can't have Utopia, then it's hopeless. Their imaginations do not include an idea of long historical struggle for social change. This makes sense given the history of insurgent politics in America, which is a discontinuous, episodic and special-interest story. The lack of historical continuity and of class-wide politics in everyday life prevents mass thought from focusing on protracted action for social change. Instead, thinking becomes manic-depressive; either we are hopelessly lost in the mainstream center, or else we flip out and rush to the Utopian rim. Several features of mass culture support this eccentric dualism: the "strike-it-rich" syndrome is a personal rags-to-riches fantasy; the "go west" and "be your own boss" ideas are dream-like elevations to individual freedom. The paradigm of concentric circles challenges this false consciousness by presenting to students a broader, integral and developmental conception of social change.

From the perspective of thought and action, humans are moving across the circles, out from the center, as they act to change their lives. As you put some distance between yourself and the mainstream, you pass through phases which have an indeterminate conclusion. You can keep moving out to the Utopian periphery, you can stop somewhere in the outer rims, or regress all the way to the center or to a circle closer to the starting point. There are radical Utopians living as cut-off as they can from the society they grew up in. There are people who live their whole lives in the mainstream. There are disillusioned Utopians who come back from the periphery. Further, the center, the developmental rims and the periphery exert a conditioning effect on each other. Each phase is influenced by the previous one and subsequently influences the next step in the process. People who gain critical consciousness begin shedding their old thought, but they take with them residual effects of their prior existence. Conversely, people who make a break from the mainstream culture develop new habits which begin to affect circles closer to the center. Some concrete evidence of this is easy enough to find in our readings of Utopian communities. There are religious settlements which reconstruct their economy along socialist lines not found at the center, but which observe Christian customs rooted in the ideology of the old culture. From another perspective, there are strong naturalist feelings in some Utopian communes which have been assimilated at the center, in terms of health foods, exercise, more open sexuality and an interest in crafts and plant-growing. To denote this last naturalist phenomenon in the mainstream culture we use the concept method to evolve the term "urban pastoralism."

The paradigm of concentric circles lends itself to a broad range of conceptual activity. I use it to develop a clear grasp of the mainstream, of intermediate phases out from the center, and of radical reconstruction at the edge. Our first exercise involves defining just what the center is. From there we go on to study a variety of rims detached from mass culture. With the center and some politicized options examined, we then focus attention on the Utopian periphery, by reading about actual settlements and a Utopian novel. With a richer texture of alternatives, student consciousness can bridge the gap between the rat race here and perfection there.

Mini-Texts: Writing Our Own Reality

To reach a working consensus on what the center of the circles is, we use the component method of group analysis. How would we characterize the average life in the mainstream? The document we produce from this question emerges as our self-designed report on American life. I ask the class to break down the large theme of life in mass culture into sub-themes. They come up with the following areas as the most important subjects for the inquiry: marriage, work, recreation, sex roles, education, childhood/adolescence, transportation, housing, retirement, diet/health, childraising, political beliefs, aspirations, and dress. A committee drafts a statement characterizing the few ways in which the vast majority of Americans live out each item. Each committee focuses on a single subject, and makes a verbal and written report to the whole class, which then debates the content of the analysis. I reproduce each committee's written report and assemble them all into a single document, called the mini-text, which serves us as a record of our own analysis of the starting point for detachment from the center. This document provokes a great deal of reading, writing, thinking, group exchange, peer dialogue and critical concern for accuracy. It emerges as a very uneven statement, in both thought and language. The students' commitment to the process is not uniform in the class, and neither are literacy and analytic resources evenly distributed. So, the individual committee reports express the levels of alienation and cognitive development for each sub-group of students. By being a characterization of student growth as well as of American life, the mini-text serves as an in-process test of the learning program.

The concentric paradigm and component method have proven valuable for characterizing the mainstream. The peer dialogue itself has served to bring retrograde committees into the critical process. Where a sub-group report is facile, poorly done or promoting an illusory image of its social subject, the discussion has been more rigorous than the original committee. A heated debate emerges on what amounts to the essentially pathological nature of ordinary life. A clearer sense grows that the routine pieces of experience are not working. This sensibility—developed through a dialogue, a document, and a conceptual paradigm—serves as the base for studying some intermediate options to the mainstream, and for judging just how far each departs from the center.

Drawing articles from newspapers and magazines, I offer to the class a variety of reports expressing critical reconstructions of traditional life. The alternatives include a feminist marriage contract, a college president who washes dishes in the school cafeteria, an anti-nuclear group joined by three high-paid engineers from General Electric, an ecology group campaigning against anti-environmental politicians, a neighborhood green-beauty group in the city, a tenants' union, a self-managed housing project, a food co-op in a black community and another in a white area, an auto repair garage run as a school and as a cooperative, and cooperative urban-restoration in two cities. I ask a committee to form for each article, to study it and lead class discussion on the following questions: How does the situation reported in your material depart from the average life in the mainstream? What general concepts can you invent to name these changes? Are the changes an improvement?

The dialogue on intermediate options has proven as interesting as the characterization of the mainstream in the mini-text. The debate on the value of each reconstruction has been vigorous. Spin-offs from the class sessions have included attempts to cooperatize the cafeteria into a student-run, nutritious service, and efforts to set up a cooperative used-book exchange on campus. Even though these projects eventually ended, their mere appearance was eventful for a de-politicized student body. Less dramatic transformations became visible through the students in class comparing their own lives to the options being discussed. The fact that these options were modest departures from tradition only strengthened the students' entry into them. They are like the conceptual exercises—phases in critical development. The breadth of options gives a rich texture to imaginations just beginning to think about social change.

Welcome to Utopia: The Pearly Gates at Last

Having considered the mainstream and some departures from it, we then focus on Utopia itself. Our study involves several current settlements and Skinner's *Walden II*. We read reports from a secular and a religious commune, and then read about an attempt in Virginia to set up a Skinnerian community (*A Walden Two Experiment* by Kathleen Kinkade). From these ongoing Utopian groups, we study Skinner's novel for its ideology and its concretely described social reconstruction. In each case, we compare the new situation to the mainstream and to the intermediate options. Using the concept method, we extract from the Utopia reports an ideological scheme which summarizes our general sense of reconstructive values:

1. *Self-Organization*—set up own work rules, schedules, governance, with ability to change rules.

2. *Egalitarianism*—open discussion of rules and issues; government open to everyone; one vote for each person; less bureaucracy and hierarchy; easy to remove leaders and change government; manual work shared by all.

3. *Collectivism*—sharing everything like jobs, knowledge, tools, expertise, money, goods, necessities, living space; no emphasis on careers, little emphasis on possessions.

4. *Experimentalism*—openness to new things, new ways of doing things, continuous testing of relationships, in work, in division of labor, in salary and in sexuality, etc.

5. *Holism*—attempt to merge work and play, home and the job, public and private lives; a rejection of living the alienated life, a piece of you here, a piece there.

6. *Aestheticism*—merging art and work, art and life; desire to liberate the creativity in each person, on the job and in spare time; greater emphasis on handicrafts and manual arts.

7. *Cooperatism*—desire to spread communal feeling; a criticism of individualism; emphasis on self-expression without encouraging selfishness; a moral concern with other people's needs and well-being.

8. *Pastoralism*—urge to live simpler life; less technology and machines; no waste or conspicuous consumption; organic food, loose clothes, natural hair; closeness to nature; emphasis on sincerity and simplicity.

9. *Activism*—participation in life; no spectatorism; urge to do and not just to watch; people encouraged to do as much as they can; people learning to do things for themselves; people do a variety of jobs, not tied to one job all the time.

10. *Tribalism*—home close to work; home as a place of work; all people thought of as family; each generation close to the others; no hostility between age groups; each generation teaches the next; responsibility for all people lived with; no family breakups; mutual dependence.

This schema begins evolving in the phase of the intermediate options we study, and continues to completion in the readings on Utopia. Along the way, we use this ideology in a number of derivative exercises. One project involved the writing of a "Free Labor Manifesto." This document outlined the conditions for non-alienated work. It called for an end to hierarchy, competition, dead-end labor and stratified salary scales. In other classes, we have focused on the existing hierarchy of a school or hospital, and redesigned the work on egalitarian principles. One of the most telling exercises drew upon the "open doughnut." We went back to the seven-step paradigm and placed the Utopian ideology points in the bottom section, under the "name" heading. Then we worked backwards to the negation of Utopia, up through the six other squares. The idea here was to start from Utopia and then develop an imaginary model for the opposite life, the one that the Utopians we study had abandoned. In recreating the prior lives of communalists, the students wind up presenting their own experience. Their lives become the anti-Utopian models which underlie the critical reconstruction of society. This has been an important connection which the conceptual study of Utopia allows students to discover for themselves. This phase of the process offers another in-progress test. The degree to which students use the paradigm for a critical assessment of their own lives in relation to Utopia demonstrates the level of cognitive and transcendent development.

The relational study of Utopia can be growth-provoking in other ways. When we approach *Walden II*, I ask students: What is the difference between happiness and freedom in your life and in the lives of the Walden people? The question of freedom has always been most important to the students, so I try to find a method to cut through the mystifications we all grew up with. One means to do this is to become concrete about the practice of freedom. For example, I ask three questions about practicing freedom: If you lived in Walden, what kinds of things would you be free to do? What kinds of things would you be free from? What kinds of things would you not be free to do? Each person makes a list of items for each question, and then I've put the composite lists on the board:

Free to:
    develop artistic and craft skills
    work at any job as long as space is open
    rotate jobs
    criticize management without fear of losing jobs
    eat at different hours
    have family life without having kids
    choose from a range of leisure-time activities
    eat in seven different dining rooms
    get expert training in skills and professions, no charge
    have privacy in own room
    take regular vacations

Free from:
    anti-social behavior; vandalism rape, mugging, etc.
    competitive behavior: competition for jobs, for parking,
        etc.
    aggressive sex in personal life
    hierarchy in salary levels, status differences
    epidemics spreading because of bad food, housing,
        sanitation, pollution

arguments with landlords and bosses
routine of 9 to 5 job
conspicuous consumption
manipulation through advertising
useless jobs

Not free to:
do anything you want to anybody at any time
start a job that is over-full
have more wealth or goods than anyone else
take something away from somebody else
show up late for work
keep leaving and returning to the community
talk about the community to outsiders
change the constitution of the community
remove managers or planners
vote on managers' decisions
serve more than one term as manager or planner
get special favors for friends or relatives
live well without working for what you get

A systematic breakdown like the above communicates the idea that complex scrutiny is needed to understand "freedom." This is a means to slow down and deepen perception. There is no simple egalitarianism in Skinner's Utopia, so the shallow and accelerated styles of intellect in mass culture are transformed through close conceptual analysis.

Taken as a whole, our study of Utopia is a study of self in society. The learning process offers a problem-theme for the development of critical consciousness. Utopia is assimilated as a critique of daily life. As a thing in itself, on the outer rim, it pulls people towards considering personal and social change. Such a conceptual study of society demands more patience and attention than my students have ever committed to intellectual work. They come to class looking for the Good Life or to be Complete Human Beings. These conceptions, from their own idiom, are important to them, but the Utopia class does not offer quick answers. The gradual nature of the class may be their first experience with a process of prolonged transformation. They slowly gain critical skills which help them use their own voices and their own intellects to design alternatives. Our growth together creates the conditions for more advanced studies in social life. With a critical appreciation of their reality, and with some exercise in ideology and conceptual methods, they gain the cognitive and political foundation needed for investigating the highly mystified questions of capitalism, socialism, imperialism, racism and sexism. The conceptual and dialogic approach, realized here through the theme of Utopia, develops the critical thought and subjective emergence missing in mass experience. Conceptual literacy, then, is not only a bridge to consciousness but is also an antidote to mass culture and a democratic prefiguration of future life and learning. This is a Utopian moment for people still ruled by the old order.

APPENDIX
Documents from the Utopia Classes
(from unedited student manuscripts)

The Hamburger Study

Major explanations of why the hamburger took over the U.S. food business:

Cheap meal   Quick meal
Convenient meal   Advertising blitz sold it to us
Fit in with the auto culture, the youth culture, and with suburbanization (drive-ins, shopping malls)
Standardized portions, limited menu, many items frozen—make it easy to run as centralized monopolized industry.
Uses cheap labor—little skill needed to cook and serve the food (High profits).
Plenty of ways to disguise it—ketchup, pickles, relish, etc.
Easy to vary—can add things to it to get quick variety.
Kids can eat there without trouble—hard furniture, colorful packaging.
Cheap family meal.

Cafeteria Reconstruction: Major Class Proposals:

1. Eliminate middleman to reduce prices—buy direct from farms and slaughterhouses, hire butchers, buy freezers to keep extra meat.
2. Unionize kitchen workers—Hire economist as manager, good cooks.
3. No private concession—school take it over and run it; students staff careteria as career training in food industry; student help will keep place clean.
4. More comfortable chairs and tables.
5. Full menu—fresh vegetables, choices.
6. Short menu—save money with fewer offerings
7. Cooperative—use the college itself as a school to train the people we need to make a food service coop work: student internships and student control in the cafeteria; cook our own goods; transport our own food; our own farms; work/study pay and academic credit for running the food service.
8. Build second level to relieve overcrowding; use downstairs cafeteria also.
9. Picnic tables outside for people to eat on; tables should be built by school shops.
10. Run a daily special.
11. Some kind of consciousness raising course to change students' attitudes to cafeteria?
12. No profit in running the cafeteria—nothing to gain by cutting quality of the food; people will be less piggy if students control it.

Plus these other ideas which were offered:
1. Have McDonald's take over the food service.
2. Design a food service where the plates and utensils are made of highly nutritious material; after eating the meal, you then eat the dishes, knives, forks and spoons.

Mini-Text One

CHILDHOOD AND CHILD-RAISING

Child-Raising

1. The typical American parent usually wants for his child things he never had the opportunity to achieve himself
2. A. Protection—Overprotection
   B. Roles of parents
     1)Mother—friend, easy to get around
     2)Father—strick discipline
   C. Parents try to form there childrens moral ideals according to there own.

We decided that how these forms of childraising are carried out affect childhood itself.

Childhood

1. This can exert great pressure on a childs growing up.
2. A. Resentment and dependence
   B. Children learn by imitation how they are expected to act in the outside world
     1)A child learns what tools he can use to get his way
   C. Children sometimes form 2 separat rolls
     1)For their parents (to keep peace)
     2)On the outside (their true feelings)

SEX ROLES

Sex roles are essentially based on stereotyped behavioral expectations, which have been integrated into our lives through a very dynamic socialization process. It is these roles that define women as subordinate and submissive, and men as agressive and independent. Yet, these imposed social roles are undergoing a major transition due to an awakening of women's consciousness.

Agressive & Independent Sex	*Subordinate & Submissive Sex*
1) Family Supporters and controllers	1) housekeepers
2) Political Activists within the family	2) childrearers
3) Initiators in sexual relationships	3) Victims of job discrimination, lower wages and rape
	4)Sexually exploited and placed on a pedestal

FAMILY LIFE

To establish themselves in their own social field

A) Father- provider the establisher of the social status of the family e.g. house, car (money)

B) Mother—coordinater of the household e.g. PTA—church groups

—coordinates household budget e.g. car insurance, food budget

—child-bearer

C) children—extensions of their parents e.g. boy scouts, school activities, church activities

—the children don't play that large of a role but without the children family unit would not be considered a family unit

—therefore the family has to establish themselves as a family e.g. do thing together with other families-picnics, parties

—family alone—vacations, Sunday drive visiting relatives

—have to have family pet or pets

—the problems of the family that the parents would have to contend with e.g. children—drugs, sexual problems, bad marks in schools, financial responsibilities of the parents for themselves and the children

—the average family does not get along with each other but they ,in most cases, get along well enough to survive.

Family life is becoming harder because society is becoming more complex.

TYPICAL WORK LIVES—(middle class)

The typical work life is a routine 9 to 5 job. The purpose is to make money. The job usually has a confining system for high advancement. Because of monatony the typical work life is physically and mentally exhausting. It is separate from family and home life. It means having a superior who usually doesn't remember what it was like to be at the bottom.

Most people suppress their feelings about the work they do. If they do think about it they rationalize their feelings by thinking that it can't be changed. They spend their lives looking forward to weekends and dreading Mondays. Months are spent saving money for the typical two week vacation to go to the same place they went last year. Television is the main form of entertainment and going to the local movie theater is a night on the town. All in all, the typical work life is just accepted as a way of life.

GETTING THE THINGS WE NEED (CONSUMER GOODS)

The basis for getting things we need is by working or receiving some sort of income, or being dependant on someone elses income.

Since each families needs or wants vary it may be necessary for more than one income per family. There are some families that can not get the things they need, there fore the city will help out with financial help (ie: food stamps) (this is for a family living in N.Y.) People who retire from their job may be receiving social security checks as well as a pension. If they become disabled some type of disability plan may be providing their sorce of income.

EDUCATION

The typical American education starts off with a young child (usually about 5 or 6) introduce to grammar school. There he learns the basics of education. The foundations for his future education are set in grammer school. He learns how to read, write, spell also basic math, history and general geography of the world. He stays in grammer school till he reaches his teenage years. Then he moves to his secondary education which is high school.

In high school he developes the basics he learned in grammer school. He choices weather to take academic or commercial coarses. Commericial courses prepare the student to go out into the bussiness world after graduating high school. Academic coarses prepare the student for college where he developes (usuallly in 1 or 2 spicific areas) what he learned in high school to an elevated degree. Up to this point the student is more or less forced to go to school it is not until he graduates high school till he makes his own desision on which way he will go.

Whatever one's decision a person must *realize* with his education that in order to obtain full fillness he must find contentment, a feeling of what he has done is what he is happy with.

HOUSING

The kind of house middle class America accepts would be a private unattached, 3 bedroom, 2 bath, Mod. kict. living & dining room, finished basement (party room) and garage. This typeof house would have to be located in a quiet, low crime convient neighborhood.

Americans feel the need to do this because of status. The American dream has influenced these people and expects this of them. Pride, feeling of acomplishment & self ownership also play a part.

The show middle class America puts on is very popular but, innersatisfaction is not allways there. The financial burden is some times greater than what they expected, & is questionable is the sacrafice these people made for middle class American housing is worth it.

VALUES/ASPIRATIONS/EXPECTATIONS

1. You deserve success if you work hard.
2. Double standard of sexual morality.
3. Desire to belong to religious organization.
4. Desire for social acceptance. (being considered "somebody"; "keeping up with Jonses")

5. Getting married & having children.
6. Desire for economic improvement
   —Own home, car, pension, insurance
   —bank account, summer vacation
   —Nice clothes, burial plot
7. Desire to see children married and to have grandchildren.
8. Desire to rise above present social-economic class.
   —send children to college
   —they might rise above your class.
9. Minority groups are considered inferior.
10. United States is the best country in the world.
11. Admiration for physical beauty, youth, wealth & success, & popularity.
12. People despise non-conformity, physical unattractiveness & anyone who reminds them how they themselves might fail.
13. People despise freeloaders.

ENTERTAINMENT

I think that entertainment falls into 2 different categorys. You can do something for entertainment or you can go somewhere to find entertainment. In Middle America, I believe that both of these are done fairly equally amongst us.

There are many different kinds of entertainment in American Life. One of the biggest is the television. It supplies the viewer with numerous forms of entertainment such as sports, gameshows, movies, soap operas and weekly series A sort of addictive form of entertainment.

There are those who get thier pleasures by going to bars, discotects, shows, movies and eating out. A way of breaking away from daily pressures and routines.

Entertainment also includes personal hobbies that pertains to the individuals own desires. This would includes such things as fishing, stamp collecting, bird watching, and numerous others.

POLITICAL ATTITUDES

Just the number of registered voter's and the turn out at the voting boots tells that many American's dont care about politics.

Durring the world war's the country was very concerned about what thier country did. Since the wide spread political corruption faith in the govt has dropped to a all time low mixed feeling in foriegn affairs has split the country even further (Viet Nam, secret grain sales to Russia) Ford's, Nixon pardon was a diaster to the credibility of the presidential decision making No new candidates have stimulated public interest in Govt. People are concerned with the amount of tax they pay,and feel their getting less for there tax.

Public opinion bares less influence on political outcome. Since it is Big Buisness that donates most of the fund's to run a campaine.

TRANSPORTATION

Most Individuals in Middle Class America must rely on mass transportation as a means of commuting. On the whole the experience ranges from mildly irritating to downright inciting. Large groups of people are compressed in a conparitively small area creating a atmosphere of hostility many times. Automobiles are the most used method of mass transit since mass numbers of people us them to get wherever they are going and there are large numbers of parkways—highways to get you there relatively quickly compared to subways and buses. However sometimes, it is more convenient to use subways and buses if you are going into a conjested area. Planes are a comparative luxery to those who can afford them. The atmosphere, if you can master the rising hysteria of a probable crash, is pleasent. Most people would rather not travel collectively when going on local trips, the experience usually being too rushed and inhibiting.

Mini-Text Two:

HOUSING

There are many types of housing open to those with money to pay for it. If you have enough money, you can live just about anywhere. There are luxury apartments in the city; there are private homes in the suburbs. Or you can choose a town house in Manhattan or a rambling colonial home upstate. Each of these options has its own advantages. An apartment or town house in the city is always near ready transportation (buses, subways, taxis) and it's usually easy to get to recreational and service facilities. A house in the suburbs can offer most of the same conveniences, but they are usually not as reliable. A house in the country comes complete with fresh air, a bit of land to call your own, and lots of peace and quiet. But it doesn't offer much in the way of services. The nearest store may be five miles to the east, and if they are out of what you need, the only other store may be 10 miles to the west.

Any type of housing has its disadvantages. The city is a dirty, crowded place, and the country is far from many modern conveniences. But, there are those who cannot even choose which of the disadvantages they would rather put up with. People with small incomes, or those on a fixed income, such as retired people, cannot pick and choose where they want to live. They must take housing that fits their income. This usually means high-rise, small apartments in a not-so-nice neighborhood. Services and facilities may also be lower-class. These people do not have much of a chance of moving away from their surroundings. For instance, on a fixed income, a person may move lower and lower in housing quality as rent and food prices go higher and higher.

As you can see, there are many different kinds of housing. Who you are and what yo do may be the deciding factor in where you live.

TRANSPORTATION

Transportation, in its broadest sense, can be defined as a means of moving persons or objects from one place to another. Walking, bicycles, ships, railroads, automobiles, and planes are all modes of transportation that are used every minute of every day.

In the United States, transportation is more than just a means of travel. Take cars for instance, at one time a car was a luxury that few people could afford but today it is practically a necessity. Usually a car is a way of displaying your social status and in many cases it is a sex symbol. For example, a person who drives a Volkswagen as compared to a Porsche.

The auto industry contributes approximately ten percent of our gross national product. This provides jobs for millions of people from the assymbly line to the gas jockey to the repair shop.

Even though transportation is necessary for all of us, there are also some problems created. We are subjected to over crowded roads, pollution, public hazzards,and criminal acts. The industry is a monopoly and it is a means of attaining political power.

RECREATION

In our everyday lives there are many varieties of recreation. For instance in sports there are participants in baseball, football, basketball, hockey etc. There are also spectators at these events who use these diversions as their form of recreation. Professionals in these sports earn their living and also use their particular skills as a form of recreation. Sex can also be defined as a form of recreation. Drinking with the boys can be a form of recreation. Hiking, boating, camping, cycling, montain climbing, swimming, bird watching, golf and bowling are good recreations. Recreation can be enjoyed by either yourself, or two persons, or in a group. Bowling is a good example.

Recreation can be broken down into two divisions. One is for the people who can afford the price to attend these sporting events. Then there are the people who can not afford these events so they have to stay at home and listen to them on the radio, or view them on T.V.

Large expenditures of money are being spent by the city for huge sporting complexes, while neighborhood parks and ballfields are deteriorating because of lack of funds. Due to the deterioration of the recreational facilities juvenile delinquincy is on the upswing.

Recreation in schools is good for the students, because it builds strong character and moral judgement. Also it is good for the student because he can relax from the rigors of study tension. For working people it is a good release of built-up tensions, which have been built-up during the work day.

HEALTH/DIET

In our society most people take care of their health problems by going to medical doctors, dentists or psychiatrist. They ususally have some sort of medical coverage plan. These plans cover all or part of the cost of a visit to the doctor and/or a hospital stay and testing. There are also free clinics for people who cannot afford to pay for medical care, however, people who are wealthy receive much better health care than the poor people in our society. Alot of people suffer physical and psychological problems due to the competitive society we live in. They also develop detrimental habits such as smoking, drinking, drugs, bad eating habits and lack of exercise. To combat the above problems rapid medical advancements are being made to enable us to combat or treat many serious medical problems.

In our society because of the fast pace in which we live and because food must be stored for purchase by the consumer much of our food contains preservatives. It also contains chemicals and artificial coloring to make it look nicer. Many of these chemicals and additives are cancer producing in animals and may be detrimental to our health. We also consume alot of sugar which has been proven to be bad for our health causing overweight problems and high cholestrol counts. We also eat alot of frozen food rather than fresh. Because of our technological advances adults and children do not get daily exercise. We drive our car around the corner rather than walk. Children spend many of their non school hours sitting in front of TV sets. Most people in our society pop a multiple vitamin and assume this will keep them healthy and make up for the lack of fresh foods and all other detrimental things we do to our body.

MARRIAGE

Marriage is an institution created by society, that is necessary for some people, but unimportant for others. When people get married they vow to love, honor, cherish and obey, til death. It is a legal contract of the vows they have taken.

Some people get married because they are afraid of growing old alone. This fear is mostly a subconscious one. The fear of being lonely is very prevalant in our society today, and some people, to counteract this, get married. Alot of early marriages are formed in order for young people to escape the pressures and restrictions put on them by their parents. They believe they are getting away from parental pressure but fail to realize the pressures of marriage.

The word and feeling of love is indescribable. For this abstract many and most people join together in matrimony. The first time is for love, the second is for money. This old saying proves true in some cases. Financial security is a whole different aspect of marriage. Some people have a twinge of love for someone, but a great deal of money is the deciding factor for this kind of marriage.

In our opinion, at this time in our lives, we feel that marriage is totally unnecessary. People should live together and ingore the legalities and traditions forced upon them by society.

RELIGION

Religion was a much stronger way of life in the days of our great great ancesters, as the years past religion grew weaker in belief for man. As the world grew more and more complex, the majority of the human race lives and needs concrete proof of what was, what has happened, and what will be for us. Religion is a combination of books old scrips and many hand me down storys of old that have changed to every human beings liking in the church and out. In todays complecated society peaple want more then storys and tales for them to live by book and by what other man reads them out of a book of what he believes what had happened once. For them to to put a side more then a hour a week, if that. Man demands more proof then he has for this demanding world of his, maybe evan a miricle or two would do it.

Our most celibrated holiday of the year Xmas, the time of the season that love an joy was spread threw out the world and land, with peace on earth, and not a thing expected in return. On todays market its the time of the season for industrys to boom and turn over ten to one to the other month. Its the gravy of the year. And for the retail what would Xmas be with out Macys. The truest feeling of Xmas is left only or the toddler, for the adult rush threw the stores and not to mention January bills and charges. That is part of what became of religion in todays world.

CHILD RAISING

Child raising is the center of a parent's life. Their first responsibility is to their children. This responsibility usually lasts throughout a parent's lifetime.

A good parent will of course, see that a child's physical needs are taken care of, however, a child's emotional development is based mainly on love and discipline. Discipline plays a strong part in every parent-child relationship. Discipline towards a child is another form of love. Children have to be guided by their parents and they have to be guided in their actions. This is how they learn.

Young children are great imitators of their parents. the child who sees his parents constantly bickering will be affected differently than the child who is brought up in an atmosphere where problems are discussed openly, and where what is preached is practised. Children learn love, trust and understanding early. If these are denied at an early stage of development a child can not recipricate these feelings to others. The child grown adult then denies his children the same and a viscious cycle is started.

RETIREMENT-WHAT TO DO?

Choices of how a person spends their retirement depends invariably upon their income. A person who has a comfortable income can retire in comfort in a retirement community of their choice. These communities consist of retired citizens who come together with a common goal, to find a way to spend their years of retirement. These communities consist of facilities for the enjoyment of its members; such as: golf courses, tennis courts, swimming pools, and theaters.

For those who are not as fortunate the cities provide Senior Citizen Clubs. These clubs are for people who don't have a generous income and want to have something to do in their spare time. These clubs provide group activities where a person can associate with their peers.

Many people who reach retirement feel learning isn't over and as a result continue their education. In many of today's institutions of higher learning you find the classrooms have their fair share of retired people.

Those retired people who can't make it in society for economical and social reasons seek refuge in old age homes. These people are well cared for and can socialize with people of their own peer group.

The final approach to the question of retirement is the responsibility taken on by the persons family. Due to the high cost of living this is becoming more and more popular, and as a result they can contribute to the household in various ways, giving then a sense of worth.

CHILDHOOD ADOLESENCE

The adverage child has a very simple role in society. They don't have much responsibility. Everything is usually done for them. The don't have to worry about where their food, clothing or shelter comes from. They just know its there and expect it to be there and they expect it to be there. For them life is fun and games. They feel that whatever is wrong Mommy or Daddy can and will make it all right. This way of thinking continues until they become school age. Gradually they learn more responsibility. They have homework to do. A set time to go to class and come home. Though recreation is a part of their day. It isn't the dominate function. As the aging process continues and they become adolence they are confronted with more complex problems. They experience bodily changes which confuse and sometimes frighten them. Girls begin to notice boys are differnt from them, and vice versa. They begin to experience the pressures of life, from parents, teachers and their peers. Parents expect them to contribute to the maintence of the household. Teachers expect them to excell in their studies and encourage competition by praising the "A" students and pressuring the other students. This is just the beginning of the long rat race ahead of them.

COMMITTEE PROJECT   SUBJECT: "WORK"

One of the most important decisions a person must make in his lifetime is the choice of a career. While no one will deny the basic dignity in all work, there are certain jobs which are very undesirable. What characteristics tend to make a job undesirable?

The prime incentive for working is to earn money. Some disagreeable jobs are compensated by a distortedly high salary. These salaries are kept inflated over supply and demand by union pressure. Two examples of this are the dull factory labor done by auto workers and the unglamorous job of garbage disposal done by city sanitation workers.

Many white-collar workers also feel unhappy in their jobs. They work in large, impersonal offices doing abstact and tedious jobs. these "tread-mill" jobs do not give the worker the satisfaction of accomplishing tangable goals and seeing the end result of his labor.

We can sum up by saying that the negative aspects of work are: (1) lack of interest in job, (2) inadequate salary, (3) feeling of alienation, and (4) lack of creativity and accomplishment. The positive aspects of work are: (1) personal interest in job, (2) adequate salary, (3) feeling of involvement, and (4) feelings of creativity and accomplishment.

One hopes that through automation and other measures, boring and menial jobs can be eliminated.

DRESS

Dress is a reflection of the culture of a period, and is a form of adornment, as well as an indicator of status. It is influenced by climate, and available material. In America today, clothes are worn for modesty, to enhance the appearance of the wearer, and to proclaim his or her specific place in society, including rank, occupation, age, sex, place of origin, marital status, and religion.

The current attitude in dress, is that "anything goes." Formal wear is gradually being replaced by sports wear. A more casual life style in clothing, is now emerging, although there are still some people, who are willing to pay exorbitant prices for "name brand" labels. Specific and concrete examples of different modes of dress are as follows:

(a) formal wear
(b) business wear
(c) casual wear
(d) sports wear
(e) uniforms—(those who attend, or work for establishments where uniforms are required.)

EDUCATION

The learning process is initiated at birth, and generally ends at death; but since our society invented schools, and their evaluation of our education is based on what we learn in school, that will be the basis of this analysis.

School systems in the U.S. are basically divided into three stages
1—Grade or Grammar School
2—Junior High Schools (Optional in some States or Towns)
3—High School

Grade school includes grades 1 through 6, and this is usually where basic reading, writing, and math skills are established. In grades 1 to 2 the alphabet is learned. Simple words, usually 3 to 4 letters, are formed and put together to form simple sentences. Basic concepts in math are also tackled at this point, and once the concepts are formed and accepted by the child they are worked on and reinforced throughout grades 1 to 6. Basic social values are also implanted in a child, but emphasis on this is light and the child rarely notices it. For instance, when the class reads a story it is usually about a boy, a girl, a dog and their friends. These characters never do anything against their parents' wishes, or against the law.

2—Junior High

In grades 7 through 9, (or 7-8) the same basic skills are elaborated on. The only difference is, the children are given definite schedules, times, and places to be. This is supposed to accustom them to the complexities of life, and instill a sense of responsibility in the childs' attitude toward work and school. Here again children are taught English, Social Studies, Science, and if reading scores are high enough, a second language (ie; Spanish, French or Italian). Two new subjects are also introduced; Shop for boys, and Home Economics for girls. The sex requirement has been recently revoked, and girls are allowed to take shop with the boys.

3—High School

Here again the same subjects are taught, and by this time the students are pulling at their hair and asking, "What good is all this?" The answer, "I don't know." In most cases, it doesn't prepare you for much in life at all. But the question is asked, not answered, and life in High School goes on.

At this stage of the game the students are expected to be able to write decent essays; solve simple algebraic equations; and face the adult world without difficulty. After all, we do know English, Math, Social Studies, and a language.

ASPIRATIONS

Some people develop aspirations from observations. They see something and want to imitate or change it. Some people have a sense of wanting to accomplish what he or she feels is fulfilling to their mental and physical being. Most people find it desirable to be successful in life; therefore it seems only natural for one to try and excell in whatever he or she choses to so and they set certain goals that they wish to achieve. Some of these goals might be to aspire towards fame, fortune, happiness or to all three. An example of this would be the professional athlete that strives to make the allstar team every year and usually does. Or the woman that went throughall the pressures and aspiried to become that doctor or that politician when they said it couldn't be done.

Some people have aspirations for happiness. Examples for this can be made in an individuals line of work or possibly marriage. The amount of success in work an individual aspires for can be measured in happiness rather than fame or fortune. Some peoples lives may be centered around a marital relationship; they may have aspirations to achieve a hormonous and happy family life. One outside factor of aspiration is how people can aspire for others in particular for their children. The feeling that prevails for the most part is to make it possible for your children to have mor and have it better than you did. One way seems to be is to accumulate money, other goods, to give their children a better start in life, and hopes that they will progress from there. These are the things that leads to a persons aspirations.

SEX ROLES

Although the present sex roles that we participate in have greatly changed in comparison to the past, I do believe that the sex roles today are an accurate reflection of the past.

Every individual in todays society has a variety of different roles to play. For example, a given female may play the role of the student, the daughter, the friend, the wife, the mother and the employee etc. Every one of these roles which she must play is greatly influenced by the sex role which she must also play.

For example in a typical marriage of today, most females are child raisers, cooks, house cleaners, food shoppers etc, while most husbands are breadwinners.

Sex roles determine the type of jobs which we have, who will pay the dinner bill, who will drive, who will prepare the meal, who will fix the car, who will change the diaper, who will mow the lawn, who will cry and who will hold the tears back, who will make the sexual advances, who will open the door, who will send flowers, who will be the first to ask a member of the opposite sex for a phone number and who will determine to the greatest extent our political values & laws etc.

Yes the list goes on and on, but I think that it is quite evident how great of a affect sex roles have on our entire society and how sex roles can easily become the basis for shaping an individuals life and future.

Sex roles can be a very convenient institution in today's society. It could be a method of avoiding chaos by deciding just who will perform the necessary functions in life.

Sex roles could also be viewed to some people as an obstacle or an invisible guardian who shapes their lives by directing the various decisions which they make in life.

POLITICAL BELIEFS

The majority of Americans have lost faith in their elected oficials. They feel the government has become corrupt and that the powerful lobbies in Washington D.C. representing business and industry are the ones truly running the show, e.g. Watergate; Nursing Home corruption in New York State; Oil industry tax evasion and manipulation. They feel that there is no point in voting because of dishonesty and broken promises on the part of the politicians.

The people feel we must fulfill our own needs at home before we engage in foreign aid programs. We should stop hunger, poverty and unemployment in this country before we worry about someone else (isolationism).

The people in this country do not want another Viet-Nam. They do not want to see our government send troops to suppc.t dictators and unpopular leaders because these futile efforts rob us of our youth, which is the single most important natural resource that any country can have.

In general the atmosphere of the country is politically conservative. The people seem to long for the past, which now seems less complex than the present.

CHAPTER SIX

SOCIAL INQUIRY:

Daily Life and Language Projects

Twelve Years After

Can you imagine studying something for twelve years and at the end you still haven't mastered it? Imagine my students sitting through long school years, through thousands of hours of instruction in reading and writing, math and history. All the autumns, winters, and springs of their youth are dominated by a schooling that refuses to sink in. At the end, they are on their way to college still needing more work in language, math and social studies, or else they are flung unceremoniously into the job-world that has little room for them. Whichever direction they go, their education has not permitted them to find out who they are and what's been happening to them, and what they need to be free and whole. A disorientation towards reality accompanies the students' weak possession of literacy and conceptual skills.

Up to this point, the liberatory pedagogy outlined in the prior chapters has addressed the dual need for literacy and for a critical orientation to reality. Structural perception enables students to see everyday life as a relational phenomenon. They learn how to discriminate social mediations interacting with each other. In the problem-themes of Work and Utopia, parts of daily existence were abstracted into discrete segments, so that the class could gain some detached reflection on its ordinary routines. In each course, language study was a vehicle for social inquiry, and the investigation of reality was the means to gain stronger literacy. This dialectical mode of learning took shape in some classes as a distinct "language project" whose social focus was more diverse than the themes of Work and Utopia, and whose conclusion was marked by the production of a document, a self-created medium. The learning mode I will refer to as a "language project" is an event lasting several weeks to several months, depending on the group of students and the thematic problem it is shaping through media. The document produced by the process represents their model reconstruction of a part of their reality.

In a language project, reading and writing are legitimized as human activities because the class study turns towards daily life in a critical and dialogic fashion. The students are not lectured about the meaning of their reality, but rather engage in a self-regulating project through which they discover and report that meaning to each other. The group nature of the inquiry supports peer relations for a student group largely alienated from each other. The project cannot reach completion without peer co-operation. The degree to which students assume responsibility for the thematic investigation serves again as an internal test of the learning process. I can initiate and animate the program along the way, but I cannot finish it without the class' participation, and I do not know in advance its eventual shape or endpoint.

Life in Language, Language in Life

A number of language projects have emerged in my classes. Some have developed as a prolonged orientation of students to a section of their reality. Other projects did not reach completion or did not become vehicles for critical perception. The successful ones include the re-writing of the Constitution of the United States (focusing on the practice of freedom in work and sexual life), the writing of non-sexist marriage contracts, and the design of democratic by-laws for the operation of the classroom. Another writing class took on the task of preparing a special issue of the school newspaper. The students managed to produce an edition far more critical than the routine copies. One of the projects which failed to mature was the writing of a "student survival hanbook." The handbook was meant to analyze and remediate a wide range of concrete student problems. It was too ambitious for that class. Another theme which lead to a rather uneventful project was a mock-radio show, "Ten Minutes of the Latest Bad and Good News." The students were able to systematize and mimic all the components of commercial radio, but did not transcend the form or ideology of the broadcasts they hear in daily life. In contrast, one of the more interesting projects involved correspondence with the steel mill mentioned earlier in the coordinated readings on Work. After one remedial class read about the mill where the union managed the plant better than its corporate executives, they agreed to write to the workers and find out if production was still high. Some other language projects include:

1. *The Sexual Abuse of Women.* This project evolved from a dialogue around sexist language. I asked the students to list all the words men use to refer to women. At the board, I made a composite of their lists. When the full lexicon of sexual language confronted the class, a heated exchange began between the men and the women. The female students became angry about the list—"broad," "cunt," "piece of ass," etc.—while the men thought the whole thing amusing. I asked the women if they would each write up an autobiography of their sexual harassments and share them with the class. They agreed and came back to the next sessions with incredible narratives of abuse. The men thought that these women kept running into perverts and sex maniacs. The women said it was an everyday thing. I next asked the class if they would agree to turn this autobiography into video scripts, so that we could re-enact them on TV and then tape a roundtable discussion of the material afterwards. They agreed, wrote scripts, rehearsed them, and following the dramatic section we had an impromptu and angry discussion between the men and women in the class about sexism. The video program was broadcast outside the college.

2. *New Liberal Arts Curriculum.* In a remedial class, I began raising questions about which courses are really needed

in college and which are useless requirements. The problem was to confront alienated feelings about being in a remedial writing class, and about the other courses students sit through with hostility. How do you determine what courses make for a good education? From this discussion the class embarked on revising the college curriculum. They called their program the "College of Human Awareness: Life Studies Curriculum." Their courses were self-help, oriented towards real needs in daily life, focused on handicrafts and arts, and interested in ecology and revolution. They prefaced each course with a description plus a rationale, and wrote their results into a long document.

3. *The Model Classroom.* A freshman composition class began a long study of traditional and experimental education, based in its own experience of school and its ideas for reconstruction. They wrote criticisms of their prior education, and then broke into work-teams to prepare video scripts which would dramatize their written analysis. They first dramatized the negative old way they were taught and then offered a model of the new classroom relations they wanted, based on egalitarian and critical modes for study. Blended into the longer segments on old and new education were shorter pieces in mime and dialogue which satirized their authoritarian schooling.

4. *Neighborhood Campaign.* Each student began a systematic analysis of her or his neighborhood: races, class and kinds of workers, housing, recreation, etc. They drew maps to accompany the descriptions. With an overview of their neighborhood's situation and development, I asked them to isolate the most important problem in the neighborhood and design a media campaign to mobilize people around that issue.

5. *College Re-design.* For its language project, one remedial class began to re-model the physical plant of the college. This direction for their study was facilitated by the architectural aspirations of some class members. We did a component breakdown of the layout of the college

and then drafted proposals for a new campus. The final document included a written text and a number of sketches. At the same time, the school administration was promoting its own new plan for the college, so this project was a timely chance to merge literacy development with the assertion of some grass-roots social policy making. We read the official plan as one "text" for the class, while we designed our own.

An Inquiry is Born: Shapes of the Process

As I learned more about liberatory teaching year by year, I began to use language projects as the pedagogical process of the class. I couldn't tell exactly what kind of project would shape up in any single class, but I began valuing the documents earlier classes had produced, and mentioning them as options to each new group. What became apparent was the absence of uniformity and predictability. Each class left its own stamp on a nominally similar process. Such diversity struck me as one way to characterize the subjective emergence of a student group. They emerged far enough to absorb the general idea of a language project while coloring it with their specific idiom.

The writing of the new U.S. Constitution was the very first project I shared with a class. It led not only to the production of an interesting document (published in the school newspaper), but it was followed by a television show, planned, written and acted by the same remedial class. They drew on their written document as a theme from which to design a video project. This semester-long event began from an unexpected place: writing and discussion on sex roles. I had asked the class to compose short compositions defining what they thought a man and a woman should be like. I wanted them to create a general type that would concretize their ideas about gender behavior. We read these writings out loud and compared thoughts. Student reports on homosexual encounters received a lot of snickering interest. So, I asked students if they would write accounts of all the times they crossed paths with a homosexual. Students wrote rather willingly—sex is an energizing theme—and read their narratives. Our discussion expanded outward from the issues of homosexual encounters and gay rights into the problem of sexual freedom in everyday life. What would sexual life be like in a free society? Each person then wrote up her and his agenda for a bill of sexual rights which every citizen deserves. I made a composite of all the items and then we debated them, and selected what we thought were the most valuable. I next asked the class if it would do the same kind of writing around the theme of labor. They agreed and produced a second statement about work in a democratic culture. From here, the development of a "Constitution" was natural. I asked the class to draft a preamble to both documents, which would set a general agenda of ideas in which to locate the specific demands on sex and work. They did so, and assembled all three pieces into a single document. Later, this document served as the base for video work in a variety of modes. We practiced campaign speeches—what kinds of proposals would a candidate make, if he or she believed in this new Constitution? Also, we convened the new governmental body in the United States—the neighborhood council—in a simulated session to hear charges brought against a homosexual teacher in the local school. One of the gay teachers at my college agreed to be interviewed by the class prior to the taping, while we were discussing sex and gay rights, and then was willing to be put "on trial" in the TV show. He was accused of distorting the healthy development of the schoolkids in the neighborhood. Members of the class chose sides in the debate and appealed to the new Constitution when making their arguments. Ultimately, the discussion abandoned the script and became a free-wheeling, boisterous and unpredictable confrontation between students, at the end of which the teacher won his right to continue working in the local school. I sighed in relief.

The class form for producing the new Constitution and other language projects is the component method. For each theme, we break down the larger idea into sub-themes, and either groups or individuals draft statements relevant to the smaller unit. Each piece is presented orally to the class, which debates the content. The project in which we wrote egalitarian by-laws for the operation of the class was organized in this fashion. It began with me entering the room on the first day of class and beginning a quiet discussion with some students on the uneasiness all of us feel when a semester begins. The dialogue evolved towards a question of power relations in the classroom, especially how everyone expects the teacher to enter and take charge. Others in class began to join the conversation as it grew. We began to analyze who sat where in the classroom, who was called by what name or title, who took the initiative, who spoke the most, etc. Eventually, we broke the reality of the classroom into its structural components: seating, speaking, grading, writing, reading, attendance, etc. For each item, one person drafted a model statement on how they would want this feature of education shaped. We discussed each, and began assembling the statements into a document which became by-laws for the class. The class adhered to these proposals fairly well, until we tried a second language project, the survival handbook which never emerged, and with that detour only parts of the self-designed rules for class operation remained operative. Even with regression, I thought that class made some significant break-throughs, in promoting a rotating chair for the class sessions and in deciding to use non-sexist pronouns when referring to students.

Writing the by-laws made the issue of power real, immediate and open to change. Power transferred from the teacher to the student because I was willing to surrender it, but my mere surrender doesn't guarantee that anyone else will rule instead. The important transformation involved the collective dialogue in which the students had to design for themselves what kind of governance they wanted. They needed to use language and conceptual skills to facilitate a political change in their reality. The document demanded clear writing, careful editing, reasoned thought. Ideologically, people in class were called upon to analyze how much power they lacked, how to shape power for them-selves in the class, and how to make this deliberation a mutual process. The discussion began from the theme of the classroom, but it drew analogies to the larger society. This project released a great deal of energy which made these remedial students capable of remarkable work during the semester.

Dark, Satanic Mills: The Union Makes Us Strong

Fuel for the fire can come from unlikely places, so it has amused me to find thought-provoking articles in the conser-vative daily paper published near my college. I cut out a report on a California steel mill that was going bankrupt until the union took over management and increased production an incredible 32% in only three months. The corporate executives ran a plant that was closing in the face of Japanese steel imports and in the face of a deep worker alienation that led to low productivity. The steel union, hardly a radical group, had its own back up against the wall. So, both trade union leaders and corporate managers found it necessary to animate the rank and file. The article, read through the dictation sequence described in the previous chapter on Work, provoked a lot of class discussion on the role of management in work organization. It showed rather concretely how a structural change in society can produce extraordinary results, validating a positive outlook in students towards cultural reconstruction. To focus attention on structures of power, I asked: Is management necessary? Are workers necessary? Can you run the plant without one or the other? What does management do that workers can't do? Why did production rise so sharply when the union began controlling the day-to-day work plans?

The prolonged dialogue on these issues encouraged me to ask further: What kinds of bosses have you had? Each student began to offer a torrent of work autobiography, in verbal and written form. They had tales of abuse they were glad to express at last. After sharing accounts of work lives, I asked if the class would want to write to the steel mill and find out how things were going eight months later. The students agreed and we made the letter into a language project. We began to analyze what kinds of questions were important to ask—productivity levels, absenteeism, morale, etc. We also had a discussion on whether we should write to the union or to the management, getting clear on the role each force plays in the plant. Three people chose to solicit management's opinion, while the rest decided to approach the union president. Each student drafted a letter and we read them to each other. Some were good, others poor. To get a deeper level of literacy, I suggested a systematic form for re-writing—who we are, our perspective on their experiment, inquiring how things were going. The students worked on a rewrite and produced uniformly improved letters.

I then asked students to divide into committees of four and discuss among themselves their rewrites and choose one letter or a synthesis of letters they thought we should send. Following this group caucusing, editing and rewriting, a delegate from each committee wrote her or his committee's letter on the board. The class reconvened as a whole, and we discussed each of the four letters, judging which best articulated our position. Eventually, we synthesized two letters on the board, and elected a recorder to transcribe the new letter. Meanwhile, the management committee was designing its own letter. Both were sent off and we received replies. One of the most encouraging moments of the process was when this group of remedial students examined the four letter-choices on the board. They very seriously criticized their own work, making corrections without my intervention. From this project, I next asked the class: If the management of the college were in your hands, how would you run it? The semester ended with a dialogue on that theme underway. Time ran out on our process before it reached an organic termination.

Taking Risks: The Highs and the Lows

The completion of a language project is inspiring. As we watch a document or a video program reach completion, we gain a sense of empowerment. In bringing a long event to fruition, students find their confidence restored. In our class, at least, they have proof of their competence. They can point to a document or bring outsiders to see their TV show. They know about the weeks and weeks it took to make this single project take shape. Their own conceptual and literate faculties emerge gradually in the process, through the constant exercise of verbal, compositional, editorial and analytic skills. Simultaneous to the evolution of cognitive abilities is their re-orientation to a rather familiar piece of their reality.

These developments are satisfying, and supportive of further studies. However, the other side of the coin can be as disturbing as the success is rewarding. When a project does not reach completion, it can magnify student alienation and cause a temporary regress in literacy. The failure to finish a project reminds students of their prior experiences in school, where they almost always wound up being incompetent. So, it is a mistake to rush ahead into a language project, before the class develops a working style. I have made the error of rushing, out of my enthusiasm to test new themes for a project, or new media forms to document the study. We paid a price for my impatience, in the meandering shapelessness of the semester's work afterwards. The gradient approach can help avoid raising expectations and demands prematurely. In the problem-themes of Work and Utopia, the learning process was experiential, integral and sequential. The difficulty of the literacy, conceptual analysis and ideology increased week by week, based on the prior development of the class. My own education into language projects involved knowing how to advance in a format and at a pace that was organic to the students' development. This has been key to the successful completion of a long thematic problem leading to a document.

Whether or not a project is finished, I learn a lot about my students in the attempt to orient all of us to their reality. I am able to continue assessing the possibilities and the problems of our learning situation, even if the specific project has to be abandoned. Their experiences are articulate to me in ways which teach me how to coordinate the study better next time. When it works, a language project is experiential and conceptual. It connects a field of particular experience to general meaning. In a structural re-perception of reality, the acts of writing and reading lose their awesome, arduous or plain irrelevant characters. As an exercise in critical literacy, the language project achieves the magic of orienting students towards their reality by detaching them from it. The purpose of school or learning finally becomes understandable to students. The meaning of study is to grasp the meaning of the lives we lead. This simple idea, so fundamental to a language project and so incredibly absent in the years of mass schooling, underlies the reconciliation of students to the teacher and to the learning process.

APPENDIX
A. Constitution Project
(from unedited student manuscripts)

CONSTITUTION FOR A SOCIETY
OF DEMOCRATIC NEIGHBORHOODS
PREAMBLE

We, the people of the neighborhood council, believe that the betterment of society begins with the individual's needs and wants. That we should have a common understanding in all areas and compromise wherever possible.

In our new society, one of the main concerns should be for equality for the individual. Each member of the society should have equal rights, and these rights should be protected. There should be a redistribution of the wealth in order to make this equality possible. As long as certain interest groups control the wealth they will always be in power. Once the power is removed from these interest groups, equality will be possible for all.

Each neighborhood will freely elect its own community council to make guidelines for the best interest of the people. The councils will by no means have the final say. If they do not function in a manner concerned mainly for the people, they will be removed.

People will share all materialistic things, helping each other out. Working for the common good and not just for themselves.

Races will become obsolete. People will judge other people the same way as they would want to be judged.

Gatherings would be held by the community every month to help improve the community and bring up beliefs and complaints against the community council. They would be able to replace council members by 2/3 majority vote if they feel fit.

Everybody who is able must pull his own weight in the society by working and by consistently making improvisions to improve relations and the society.

People will get rewarded by having anything materialistic when they need it. If they don't need it they should give it to somebody else who could use it.

Work will be distributed equally througout the community. The pay being not money, but equal amounts of food, clothing, depending on the size of each family. What we will do is eliminate money and recreate all men equal. All children will eat at dinner-time for sure instead of going days without food.

Money determines who's good or bad, richer or poorer, who has the potential and who hasn't the potential to prosper and the most important of all is who has the power to manipulate people's lives with the use of money.

The community will abolish the draft and make going into the armed forces voluntary for both men and women. The draft forces a man to join the armed forces, go to jail or flee the country, if he doesn't want to join. This would not fit into our society which is non-forceful.

The goal of each community council is to try to help the society be a better place to live, where equality, freedom and concern for others is to the highest degree.

Article on Sexuality

1. Sex will not be a commodity. You can't buy it and you can't use it to win favors.
2. Sex education will be taught along with all subjects in school. From first grade all forms of sexuality and sexual diseases will be treated, so as to make them understandable.
3. Sex will not be compulsory. No forced sexuality (rape) permitted. Neighbors cannot demand sex from each other. Free to choose, free to refuse.
4. All modes of sexuality will be socially acceptable as long as the people doing them voluntarily choose it.
5. Sections of community parks will be reserved for people who want to have sex out-of-doors. Other parts of the park will be used for non-sexual recreation in daylight hours, and for those neighbors offended by public display of sexuality. All neighbors are expected to exercise sexual freedom with taste, tact, and consideration for other people's activities.
6. A large community center will be built in each neighborhood, one floor or section of which shall be available for sexuality. Those using that section shall decide for themselves how to run it, with due respect to each person's sexuality.

Article on Labor

Labor is the backbone of our industry and our economy. The way controlling capitalists, executives and politicians misuse labor today in industry and business is not the way we the working class would like it. The evidence to back-up these two statements is unemployment, welfare, and poor working conditions, in the U.S.

In our new community a person should establish a quota of work credits per year. This would be their goal and motivation. This would prove their success to the community. When people work these hours they will be rewarded by being able to have anything materialistic in their society according to their needs. People who can't work or unable to work will receive disability credits provided they have reasonable proof they are unable to work.

Each individual should have the opportunity to become anything she or he wants. In order to make this possible education in different jobs should be available at all times. If one has learned to be a common laborer and feels she or he has the potential to better his or her educational and occupational states this should be available.

Children after completing junior high school should receive on the job training on every job in the community. On the job training would also give a child work credits. Classes would be held in factories, laboratories, and other places according to the job. Teaching of skills, humanities, arts, sciences, and technology would be open to everybody wherever people work, and not just to school children.

The way in which one should get her or his income should be according to her or his needs, regardless of that person's position in society. There should be a type of centralized store a place where one receives her or his needs. In other words you work for the community and the community cares for your needs. Each individual will have access to personal needs as well as community goods. This will be on a sharing basis and each individual will be responsible for the goods they use. People who have more dependents such as children under sixteen will receive a little more credit for their job. Equal distribution will be made according to the size and need of a person's household.

Jobs should be open to rotation so that individuals will not be stuck in menial labor or unpleasant conditions for a long period of time. This will also break up class distinctions and make for a more united community. People who are in menial labor or who are unhappy with their present jobs should contact special labor unions to see what jobs are open for rotation at that time. Upon mutual agreement and consent of the involved people rotation can be permitted. No individual will be in a higher position than anyone else. There will be a vertical division of labor where everyone works side by side, doing the total job, instead of over each other. Access to all administrative and technical levels will be achieved through education.

B. Letter to the Steel Mill
(from unedited student manuscript)

Dino Pappavero
United Steelworkers
Kaiser Steel Mill
Fontana, California

Dear Mr. Pappavero:

We are students at Staten Island Community College, a class of English, instructor Prof. Shor. Our class was recently reviewing an article in the Staten Island *Advance* newspaper, dated Feb. 4, 1973. Our professor brought in copies of this article and passed them among us. Our class has an age limit ranging from about 17 years old to 25. We all have different views and ideas in the class, but basically are all interested in this happening of your's. The class is somewhat like your steel mill, an experiment. For instance, here there is really no authority over you. By authority, I mean our prof. places himself on level grounds with us (the students). Henceforth, he can learn from us, as we can learn from him.

In our opinoin we feel that what you are doing and accomplishing is absolutely outstanding. It is an extremely unusual case where the employees turn around with the management and operate a factory without higher authority over their heads. We feel that all factories' operations should be like your's, and that it would be completely beneficial to employees' attitudes, work habits and production rates.

What we all seem to be wondering however is after months of operating like this, how the mill is keeping up pace and production, as well as quality steel, with your competitors over in Japan. Were any of the workers dissatisfied with your take-over of the mill? Also if production has increased, has the work week been lengthened or shortened? Is there any chance of the management returning to the mill now that the mill is back on its feet? Is the absentee or lateness rate better or worse than before? Have any pay raises been given? Is there a feeling of hostility between management and workers? And finally, are they keeping production rate better or as well?

A reply and brochure would be truly thankful, interesting and enjoyable.

Sincerely yours,

C. By-Laws Project
(from unedited student manuscript)

BY-LAWS FOR RUNNING OUR CLASS

Our class has written, debated and accepted the following rules:

1. People in class will not speak only at the teacher when they talk, but will speak to everyone, or to the person they want to respond to.

2. The teacher is not always the only one responsible for filling up silences, and for keeping the conversation going.

3. When the teacher is absent, all students will still be responsible to remain in class and do the 15 minutes free writing. After the free writing is finished any questions regarding the free writing should be directed to the tutor. After the assignment is done the class can pick someone to be chairperson of a discussion on any subject agreed upon by the students. The class meets twice a week and we can't afford to miss such a valuable lesson. And we should learn how to conduct the class when the teacher is absent because this shows us that we can conduct the class ourselves and we are intelligent and responsible enough to do our work.

4. Attendance will be voluntary and people will come if they feel the class is benefitting them. If the class is not benefitting the students, then the students will make the class into something which serves their needs.

5. The class being as informal as it is, has decided that it will be permissible for students or instructors to call each other on a first name basis. Calling each other by first names doesn't let one feel superior over someone else, as if Mr., Miss, Mrs., etc., were used.

6. No one is forced to say anything, except ta* should keep in mind ta duty as being part of the class to contribute to the class, by giving ta view, no matter how little it seems. Everyone should have an opportunity to talk at one time or another, not just letting the same person or persons talk and carry on discussion. But no one should be forced or called on to talk, if ta feels ta has nothing to say. Because forcing someone to talk might cause some differences between those persons trying to force ta to talk. This may cause ta to reject the class altogether.

7. Raising hands and interrupting people:
    a. The chairperson will be rotated each class session   for discussion.
    b. A person who hasn't spoken yet has priority to speak over someone who has spoken already.
    c. A person can use any symbol to interrupt the conversation, raising hand or politely interrupting.
    d. Male and female should be recognized equally, equal respect to all. Anytime someone speaks, there should be a feeling of donation to each other.

8. We can relate better if we sit in a circle. Everyone should sit where ta wants to. You should sit where you feel most comfortable and not in an assigned seat. The only time you should assign a seat is when ta can't give lesson because of continuous disruptions of people sitting next to each other or when ta doesn't trust someone taking an exam because ta thinks they are cheating. The decision of a chairperson to move a student has to be approved by the class.

*Note on ta: In this day and age of women trying to become equal to men, we think it is necessary to invent a word that refers to both men and women. The reason such a word is needed is because there are instances when it can be used. For lack of a better word we shall adopt the word ta which in the Chinese language means, he, she, him, her.

D. Re-Design of College Curriculum
(from unedited student manuscripts)

The Life Studies Curriculum was designed by the students, for the students. We put together this program, because we felt there's a lot more to learn, than what you're taught. There are courses in the arts, farming, sex hygiene, first aid, female and male anatomy and medical self help. The psychology course, will cover teenagers, children and parents. The History course will cover our government, women in history and other things that are interesting and good to know. Economics will cover shortages, inflation and consumer rip-offs.

This Life Studies Curriculum is interesting, fun and can really help you in life.

COLLEGE OF HUMAN AWARENESS:
LIFE STUDIES CURRICULUM SURVIVAL "75"

Take these new courses and you will be able to understand life today. These courses will help you in the outside world, to know what to expect out of life. Most of these courses will help you to understand how our government works and why we are in the state we are in. These courses are for you and you alone. Psychology will be giving you a chance to know yourself and those around you, helping you to deal with situations and to build a better you.

If you have your health, you have everything. Some of these will guide you to have better health, mentally and physically. They will help you deal with your surroundings and how not to get ripped-off by the dealers. It may help you in the long run to save money. So I say to you, take this new curriculum and you will be happier.

NEW LIBERAL ARTS CURRICULUM

This new curriculum was designed by students who were interested in learning different subjects which they can really use in the future. This is a very important curriculum because of the way it's arranged. It's not forced upon the students to take, which can make it more interesting for the students who plan on taking this new program. The student has a choice in picking various course which might interest him or her and can be very valuable later on in life.

This curriculum also gets the students aware and closer to the outside world of today, not of yesterday. It might possibly bring change or solutions to help with today's problems.

I. SOCIAL SCIENCES

1. *Women In History*—This course is designed for all women who want to know more about their sexual backround. We will study all the forgotten woman of the past. We will center on the important roles woman play or have played in the making of Western Civilization. We know enough of Lincoln, Washington, and other great men, but What

about the great women? We will study women poets: Sylvia Plath, May Swenson, Erica Jong and Dilyis Laing. We will go back in time and study the sufferjets and how they paved the way for the now, "Women's Lib." This course is good for women who are in search of self-satisfaction and a more complete outlook on women. This course wil benefit you by giving you the facts about women. Women will be discussed as people, not as objects for use and disposal.

2. *Economic Shortages*—Today there are problems of inflation and recession which are brought about by high prices. We have shortages in almost every conceivable human need. And nobody knows why? Well, this course is designed to find out. We will discuss how companies are ripping us off and how to prevent them from doing so.
The earth can give only so much. In ten to twenty years the shortages will ruin the planet we live on. If that time comes we must be ready! This course will prepare you for such a day. So much material is wasted, when it is that same material that can be used for another useful purpose. This course will teach you how to get the most use out of all your everyday items. "Waste not, want not."

3. *Surviving Urban Life*—To survive urban life, one of the most essential things is to fully understand it, and what it means. This course has been designed to do just that. We will focus on such issues as, budget basis, dealing with bills, dealing with mass transportaion, community law enforcements, and use of policemen as a means of survival not someone to be afraid or against.
Life in itself is a very complex entity. We cannot grasp it all at once we must take it step by step until we are capable to understand. After we have understood, we will incorporate our knowledge into our every-day lives. We will deal with each problem as they arise and in their entirty. We will read such books as, Housing and Development, Urban Aesthetics, and Urban Renewal. Living is a wonderful way to live and this course will prove it.

4. *Consumer Rip-Off*—Are you tired of being ripped-off? You prbably are! People today are being ripped-off and most of them don't even know it. This course was developed by students who have realized that they were being ripped-off and would like to spread the news of how it is happening.
After taking this course you will understand why taxes are so high and where the money is really going. You will learn also why food and housing prices are so high.
You are being ripped-off constanly! Find out how and why, and what you can do about it!

5. *Conservation of Water and Air*—This course will cover topics on how to improve the enviroment. We will discuss ways in which an individual can help clean up, water and air pollution before the situation gets out of hand.

The course will include the discussion of major rivers and oceans that are polluted and how they affect our enviroment. We will also discuss ways to clean up. We will also discuss chemicals and substances which pollute air and water. We will get into some of the effects that this pollution has on people and wild life. Areas of garbage disposal and sewage will also be dealt with in this course. This course will help you understand how everything came to tbe polluted and how we can stop it.

6. *Revolution 3rd World*—This course is offering the knowledge of various changes in past and present events. It will also detail possible future conditions as a result of revolution. It will not deal with personal desires rather it will cover group or identity of statehood in various peoples. Actually it will look at conditions both social and economic, and change. It is sincerely wished that each student will be able to justify the supposed betterment of society.
Not to be excluded in a comparison of democracy and communism in relation to a revolution.
The discussion of the importance of young and old taboos will be discussed. Finall we will discuss the opposing forces which constitute a revolt.

7. *Inflation and Recession*—Inflation plays a big part in today's living. It's happening today! Sugar, milk, and soda prices have skyrocketed. Approximately a year ago, five pounds of sugar sold for 58¢, then it went to 90¢ and in 1975, up to $3.00 in most stores. And no one knows why! The sugar companies probably reasoned that if the gas can go up and get away with it, why not them too. Also, there are many products which have gone down and then all of a sudden they go up twice as high.
In this course we would like to find out why and how these companies can raise prices and get away with it. We will also discuss how inflation and recession begin and end. This course will be ver useful to learn, so that you will have information on the economic situation and what can be done to improve it.

8. *Unemployment*—Unemployment has always been a problem. Though it was bad in the twenties and thirties, I feel it will be much worse this time around. There are so many people out of work, collecting unemployment checks. What we would like to know is how can we help? To study this subject we can come up with ideas that will help the solution. We will also study unemployment throughout history and see what caused unemployment. We can learn some of the causes, such as automation, not enough jobs and population with the economy. We will study how a family is affected by it and what should a person do about being unemployed.
We will study this system of unemployment and see if we can stop it or make some improvements. Also another very important aspect will be to study how the system operates.

II. ARTS

1. *Pottery*—If you are interested in being creative with our hands and mind, and at the same time learn a good skill that pays off well in the business world, this course is for you!

This course will teach you to make various things that you never thought you could make. You will be taught how to use clay properly and how to bake it and later paint it. Yo will also be taught how to varnish it and other products in your home.

This course will be alot of fun and at the same time you will be learning a skill from it. You will be able to use your skill effectivly, either for a business venture or for your own enjoyment.

2. *Sculpture*—Sculpture is the art of human ability to apply mind into hand and produce a creation. In this course we will use instruction books in an attempt to learn by doing. Museum observations will enrich creativity within us. These exhibits play a major role in the art world.

Man is an interesting and amazing species. Throughout the centuries human beings have contributed fascinating art pieces to society, some of which are pre-historic. To some, art is classified as rubbish and disregarded. To an art master it would be considered a fantastic creation. Through analyzing and investigation, art pieces will be interesting to many people once they are familiarized with this field.

3. *Coming to Cope with Reality*—This course is considered an art primarily because the topics that will be discussed are about developing our artistic talents. We will begin with American Poets and their veiws on reality. Is reality real? Or is it something humans cannot percieve? We then will view some paintings on realism at the Metropolitan Museum of Art. Afterward we will begin to write our own journals and in conclusion we will come to understand what reality really is and how to cope with it.

4. *Furniture Building*—This course will consist of basic furniture building for the home. We will explore the ways of making chairs, the cheapest most sturdiest way possible. We will try to put to use all the materials we receive including scraps.

Our major aim will focus on building furniture for our homes, economically and comfortably, without being ripped-off by man-ufacturers.

5. *Arts.*—This course is designed for students who are interested in taking the different kinds of Art courses available, such as painting, drawing, sculpture, photography, music, theatre and dance.

Each one of these are an introductory course to get YOU aquainted with the kind of work involved in each individual course of art. You will learn the basic methods, techniques, materials & style used in each course.

There are also advanced courses which cover more detailed and more involved work which can be taken after the completion of the introductory course.

6. *Photography*—This course is offered to students interested in photography as career. Also for those who would like to learn it for fun. This course will teach you basic and fundamental steps. You will learn the uses of different types of cameras, lens, tripod, darkrooms, chemicals, and the making of enlargements.

After this course is completed you will be expected to show ability to perform in this feild. Therefore, there will always be jobs open for you in newspapers, magizines, and related pictorial fields.

7. *Painting*—For painting the tools to use are brushes, paper, water, and canvas. In this course you will learn how to use them and how to sketch. Later we will go into the fundamentals of painting and matching colors. To match them you blend them so that each color will balance. Mixing colors will be our next venture, to mix them you take two colors which will make another color on the same basic scheme. We then will go into the forms of painting like, perspective and the proper visual eye contact with the painting.

This course would be good to know because of the many varied uses that art plays in our world. For example you will be able to know what colors go good with what colors. You will learn the sequence of matching colors and how to use them in either decor or on canvas. Another very good advantage of this course would be when you buy a painting. You would have a good knowledge about what it is your buying. You could also design a painting yourself.

You can even use this art in your own nieghborhood designing or painting such things as fences, buildings, homes or walls in homes. This course is a MUST becuase of its many varied uses and its aesthetic value.

III. BIOLOGY, HYGIENE AND SEX EDUCATION

1. *Body Cleanliness*—This course will instruct the student inthe proper method of caring for the body. The importance of cleanliness of teeth, body nails, hair, ears, and eyes will be explored. We will discuss at great length menstrual cleanliness. A subject important to caring for children, keeping them free from infection and caring for new borns.

Participation in this class will benefit all people dealing with everyday life. If we learn to become free from infection through cleanliness, we will become a human race free from disease.

2. *First Aid*—If you would like to save on doctor bills, or learn what to do in case of an emergency, this course is for you! You will learn to mend broken bones and to help someone who has had an overdose or even someone with epilepsy. You will also learn about minor abraisions such as, sunburn, poison ivy and common cuts and scratches.

You will be prepared to cope with heart attacks and also learn mouth to mouth resuscitation. This course is a good course to help accident prone people.

3. *Hygiene and Sex Education*—This course will emphasize as it's basis, the fundamentals in names and descriptions and in the functions of both men and women's sexual organs. It may be added that certain slang usage may be briefly mentioned for familiarity to the individual. This couse will prove very essential for personal body knowledge of yourself. To learn how to take better care of yourself is one way to goodliving. It will give an adult and mature people more information for the younger generation besides the "birds and the bees" idea. As parents you will be able to teach your children better.

4. *Puberty and Maturity*—This course plans to study the stages of human development. We will concentrate on sex and hygiene. We will also learn how to cope with different stages in a human life span such as, menopause and puberty. The psychological effects that occur will also be discussed in great detail. This course will give you a better outlook and a better understanding of how to cope with your body's changes and maturation. There is alot to know about yourself...Why not start now?

5. *Money and Health Care*—This topic will cover and examine the high costs of perscriptions. Where drugs are made and how? What the real costs of perscriptions are before the drugest adds his fees. This course will bring out why doctor's charges are so much for visits and operations. Also why they do not make house calls anymore.
This course will also answer questions on medicare and meducade for young and old. We discuss the facts behind why some people aren't eligible for these services and why more doctors don't accept some of these services. And also how good are the doctor's that do accept these services. Questions will be answered on where to go for free good health care.
By taking this course you will learn where to go for good medical care and how not to be ripped-off by bad M.D.'s. You will even know how to deal with bad M.D.'s and how to get them prosecuted.

6. *Birth Control*—Birth control is used to prevent unwanted pregnancy. In today's world, it is very important to use birth control. Why? To prevent children from going on in life unwanted and neglected. There is a great responsibility in raising children. Some parents or couples might not be able to handle such a resposibility, therfore the child might either be aborted or given to a adoption agency. These agencies can affect the child's mental state and leave he or she with a complex that they will carry on in their life.
In this course we will study the different methods of birth conrols available today. We will learn how to use them and what efects each of them have on the body. We will discuss the advantages and disadvantages in their use. This course will give you a broader outlook on what birth control really is.

7. *Drugs and Your Body*—There are so many questions as to why people use drugs, none of which have been truly looked at. This course plans to study the pro's and con's of drug abuse. We will learn about each kind of drug. Where you can get them? How they are administered? What affects they have on the body? And what they do to the human mind?

There is another drug we will study in depth and that is alcohol. Most people don't even know or consider this a drug, but it is. Too much drinking causes damage to the liver. It also kills brain cells. We will study how to prevent drinking and how to cope with problem drinkers. Another drug that we will study is marijuana. We will study its effects and after effects. This course will benfit you by teaching you that drugs misused are no good to you and to the people around you.

8. *Biology*—In this course students will be able to learn the different functions of the body and the role they play. It will also cover: The digestive system, respiratory system, circulatory system, and the excretory system. This course will break up each of these catagories and describe the different activities of each.

It will also deal with the chemicals, nutrients, and protiens that each of the different organs use. You will learn what vitamins to take and why. You will learn how to take care of your skin and it's tissues. This course will also study arteries, nerves, and bloodcells and their vessels. The topic of heredity and genes will also be discussed.

9. *Nutrition*—Nutrition is the most important subject to be talked about. In this course you will get a better understanding of the four basic food groups: meat, fish, poultry, vegtables, and dairy products. Most people have been conditioned to eating in a certain way that can be harmful to them. Whatever mama served us we ate.

As youngsters we ate many foods without having any idea what we were really eating. The food tasted good so we ate it. But they were not really nutritious. Some of the ingredients that will be looked at are: starches, protiens, acids and chemicals. We will also see how much of these ingredients your body needs a day. Another group that will be discussed is the vitamins. The lack of them and the excessive use of them.

You will get a better understanding of soul, organic, and health related foods. But mainly the course is designed to help you create a properly balanced diet and to feel good all over. You can even create your own special diet to suit your own needs. Last but not least you will learn that being in good physical shape will be the best road to good health.

CHAPTER SEVEN

QUESTIONING SEXISM:

Poetry and Marriage Contracts

The turn in liberatory pedagogy towards daily life provides the classroom with a limitless supply of themes. The previous chapters on Work, Utopia and the critique of social relations, and the document-language projects, suggested a number of modes through which everyday concerns become the objects for critical scrutiny. A reflective learning process will be an eventful addition to mass experience. It can offer popular consciousness exactly the development it now lacks. My students have not been encouraged to practice systematic thought on their reality. This has left them mystified, but hardly pacified. They agree that social life is riddled with problems. Yet, they can't transcend the outstanding issues in their social field without knowing the reasons for their daily blues. Without a critical appreciation of reality, they are condemned to individual maneuvers to feather their nests, repeating patterns in the circle of routines which traps them.

The absence of critical options in everyday life makes it ruthlessly hard to practice transcendence. When people are pretty much doing and thinking the same things, where do you go to find some choices, some reconstructive models? Of course, no one is a carbon-copy of anyone else, but behavior in daily life is highly norm-setting. In this limited context, liberatory learning builds on those transformative resources in mass life which have not yet coalesced into self-conscious models. The classroom critique and redesign of concrete experience offers students practice in transcendent activity. A wide variety of daily themes needs to be absorbed into this kind of process. One experiential issue particularly stimulating in several of my classes is the question of sexism. In a number of writing courses, we began studying a woman's poem and developed towards the production of egalitarian marriage contracts. A literary form, speaking to a tangible issue in life, offered us exercise in literacy and conceptual thought, aimed at the reconstruction of sex roles in marriage.

Here Comes the Bride: An Extraordinary Wedding

Marriage is an obvious subject around which to design problematic study in virtually any academic discipline. It is such a familiar part of daily life. It is rooted in so much history. Enormous bodies of law pertain to it. Most students grow up in nuclear families and are still living at home or are beginning their own families. Unmarrieds are playing a waiting game full of parental pressure towards matrimony. So many illusory expectations punctuate the linkage—finding the "girl of my dreams" or "Mr. Wonderful," or "giving my kids everything I never had." The difficulty of sustaining family life is also visible, a fact which causes a good deal of confusion in a culture which ideologically promotes family life while economically sabotaging it. The high tension between the ideal images of family life and the rough realities makes the theme of marriage a rich resource of contradictions.

Students come to class with a multitude of opinions and expectations concerning marriage. They bring to this problem-theme a special form of false consciousness: their conditioned sexist behavior. Sexist attitudes are deeply imbedded in the social interstice of marriage. Predominant in my male students is a fairly solid notion of the roles they and their mates will perform. They want a "little woman" who will complement their being the "breadwinner." Accompanying this typical male expectation are feelings which taper away from narrow sexism. Many of my men students want their wives to hold wage-earning jobs. They see how hard it is for a family to make it on a single income. The simple fact of tight money will require them to loosen the limits on their wives. They know that a working wife will have to be out of the house and not attending to domestic chores and child-raising as much as a full-time housewife. So, they accept the need to give their wives a hand with the kids and with cleaning. Throughout, these household tasks are always conceived as "the women's work," which the men graciously assent to take part in. In addition to the expectation that a working wife will perform "the double shift"—earning money outside and doing housework/childcare inside—is the persistence of the double standard vis á vis sex. The men think it ordinary for husbands to have affairs but find it unacceptable for wives to do the same. Competing with this predominant sexism among my male students are two low-profile developments. Some men seem to blandly react to women as their equals, while a handful espouse the women's right to equality. These voices, when present in a classroom, have had an effect disproportionate to their small numbers, because the position they present runs counter to sexist conditioning in mass life.

The women's consciousness is not uniform either. There is a solid contingent who expect to be the kind of home-makers wanted by the breadwinners. Their non-assertiveness carries into all areas of life, including the classroom. So, their presence is felt by their silence. They make their position clear in their writings. Another woman's voice in class shapes itself around the mature experiences of married females. They have had a chance to see what goes on after the days of wine and roses, so they have some illuminating messages for the younger men and women in class. Their sense of the rigors of family life and the excess burden placed on women is a sobering moment for romantic skywalkers. From this voice, there emerges a sense of the problems, of the unresolved and unhealthy reality lying behind the routine experience of family life.

The older women deepen the inquiry into marriage by reporting troubles and complaints. These mature female students have an emerging feminism in their assertions. They are often joined on this score by some militant young women in class. The number of younger women expressing feminist ideas has been increasing each year, so it has become familiar for almost every class to have voices that the other students characterize as "women's lib." The women's movement itself has a mostly negative image because of the media hype done on it. The most feminist women in class have not had their conscious- ness raised through their working in women's organizations, but rather from the permeation of society by women's issues. The prolonged evolution of feminist politics in the culture as a whole has exerted an ideological pull on the men as well as the women, even in the absence of their organizational activity. Year by year, as more women turn sympathetically towards feminism, more of my men students are having to take the woman question seriously.

What is most apparent in this state of thought is the underdevelopment of consciousness. Whether the issue is fem- inism, racism, or socialism, there is virtually no mature thought on the problem in any class. However, if the ideological profile of my students is low and dominated by regressive thought, the profile of social problems is high. Family life is a nexus of problems easy to point out, readily acknowledged by even the most conservative of students. Joining social problems as a propellant to consciousness-raising is the students' ability to begin critical thought on reality. Their real social needs and their residual intelligence are the twin pillars for an examination of marriage.

Wives and Lovers

Beginning in a milieu that is largely sexist, anti-women's movement, and confused about feminism, I introduced a poem by Anne Sexton, "For My Lover, Returning to His Wife." In the long-evolving work which grew out of our study of the poem, the atmosphere gradually changed. The sexist men failed to dominate the women in the debate. Female students, who had been suspicious of feminist demands to change their life styles, gained a more assertive stance on their rights as women. The men too were called upon to reassess their positions. Some hardened their breadwinner ideology. Other men found their assumed superiority called into question, and began contributing to a project which redefined roles for both sexes. The poem which provoked this development goes like this:

She is all there.

She was melted carefully down for you
and cast up from your childhood,
cast up from your one hundred favorite aggies.

She has always been there, my darling.
She is, in fact, exquisite.
Fireworks in the dull middle of February, and
as real as a cast-iron pot.

Let's face it, I have been momentary.
A luxury. A bright red sloop in the harbor.
My hair rising like smoke from the car window.
Littleneck clams out of season.

She is more than that. She is your have to have,
has grown you practical your tropical growth.
This is not an experiment. She is all harmony.
She sees to oars and oarlocks for the dinghy,

has placed wild flowers at the window at breakfast,
sat by the potter's wheel at midday,
set forth three children under the moon,
three cherubs drawn by Michelangelo,

done this with her legs spread out
in the terrible months in the chapel.
If you glance up, the children are there
like delicate balloons resting on the ceiling.

She has also carried each one down the hall
after supper, their heads privately bent,
two legs protesting, person to person,
her face flushed with a song and their little sleep.

I give you back your heart.
I give you permission—

For the fuse inside her, throbbing
angrily in the dirt, for the bitch in her
and the burying of her wound—
for the burying of her small red wound alive—

For the pale flickering flare under her ribs,
for the drunken sailor who waits in her left pulse,
for the mother's knee, for the stockings,
for the garter belt, for the call—

the curious call
when you will burrow in arms and breasts
and tug at the orange ribbons in her hair
and answer the call, the curious call.

She is so naked and singular.
She is the sum of yourself and your dream.
Climb her like a monument, step after step.
She is solid.

As for me, I am a watercolor.
I wash off.[1]

This beautifully crafted poem began our deliberation on sexual politics. Not only did we gain some command in a literary genre, but we also began to structure and re-structure reality from a feminist point of view.

One of the simplest formal devices of poetry is diction, so the language of the poem is an obvious place to begin. The thematic distinction between "wife" and "lover" is realized through different images used to characterize each. I asked the class to make two lists, one for all the words referring to the wife and another for the ones referring to the lover-poetess. Acting as recorder, I placed the inventories on the board:

WIFE	LOVER
melted down	red sloop
marble	luxury
cast-iron pot	smoke in
fireworks in	car window
dull February	littleneck clams out
wild flowers	of season
placed at window	experiment
exquisite	watercolor
harmony	
monument	
naked and singular	
flickering flare	

The act of making image inventories encourages close reading of the text. The poem is a printed puzzle, whose meaning is metaphorical and referential. The language creates a dramatic distinction between the two women, which can be structurally represented by opposing word-lists. In essence, the two women are negations of each other, because they play such different roles in the life of the man. The wife in the poem is characterized by heavy, metallic and dark images; her weighty domestic life is only touched with color. In contrast, the lover presents herself in bright, lively, and romantic terms. The drama of this characterization rests in the sad, angry farewell the lover makes to the man. She is romantic but unrooted in his life. Meanwhile, the wife is substantial, rooted, but unromantically buried in family chores. We spent a good deal of time in class discussing the meaning of the two characterizations. To go deeper into the consequences of the situation, we developed the love "triangle" as a controlling principle.

I drew a triangle at the board and placed one character at each point:

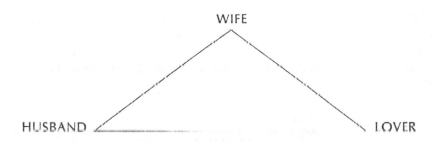

The theme of a love triangle is one of the most common subjects for mass culture. Countless movies, TV shows, magazines and books have used the triangle affair as a formula for melodrama. This makes it an ideal entry point for critical reflection. Its familiarity permits the study of marriage to begin from a point of mass recognition. The triangle theme not only validates the study of marriage but it also supports the legitimacy of poetry as a vehicle for learning about reality. The deep cultural roots of the triangle thus point to a mass situation rich in possibilities.

I handed out sheets with the triangle on it, with each point indicating one of the three characters in the poem, and asked people to write down on each side of the figure the name of the relationship connecting those two people. The results were easy enough to predict:

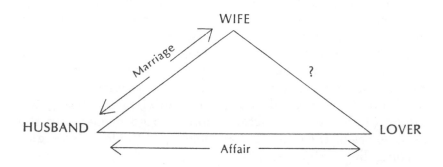

It became apparent that the man was the only person with two relationships. Our discussion lingered on this fact. The two women took part in only one dimension while the man had access to both worlds. The women were locked into either side of the image inventory, while the husband had both available to him. To work on the question-mark which defined the side connecting the women, I asked the class to come up with more roles to describe the people named at each point in the triangle. Here is what emerged:

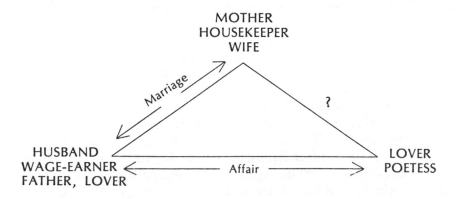

Once again it became apparent that the man had more going for him than did the women. His four roles and his life in two sexual worlds compare to the one sexual dimension and fewer roles for both women. This systematic analysis of a melodramatic love triangle begins to transform the problem-theme from a soap-opera subject to a critical encounter with the structure of sexism. According to the class's own analysis, the man quite literally has the best of both worlds. Laid out before them, in their own terms, is the concrete notion that men can enjoy career and family life without choosing between them, while the women are relegated to one or the other. The husband can be a sexual person, a working person and a family person. The sex-bias in culture makes this much harder for women.

To make the social structure of sexism more apparent through the developing triangular paradigm, I next asked the class to place on each side of the triangle words they find appropriate to describe the relationship between the connected people. They came up with this elaboration:

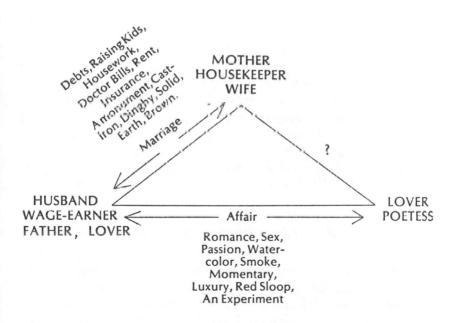

To contrast marriage with the affair, the students drew some words directly from the poem and other words from their reflection on family life versus romance. Our discussion focused on the social responsibilities of marriage which interfere with romance. The husband could go looking elsewhere for what his domestic life lacked. His affair with the poetess did not include debts, laundry and diapers, so it offered him an emotional extra that the women needed.

From the class discussion and from the study of the triangles, it became apparent what sex discrimination means. Concretely, discrimination of one kind or another divides a population into the privileged and the unprivileged. In the case of racism, the segregation is done by skin color. In the case of ageism, the distinction is based on how old you are. Here, in the case of the love triangle, the abstract idea of sexism or sex discrimination assumes tangible meaning. The man is simply able to have things that the women can't. There is a security and a harmony to domestic life, which coexists with its demands. The man can return home and bury himself in the reassuring comfort of his wife and children. And there is an excitement in the passionate affair, which the wandering husband can experiment with. The man had two times and spaces to get his needs met, while the women were separated into single dimensions which fulfilled only one part of their humanity. In moving from the poem to the triangle, and from the triangle to social life, we discovered that the great marital preoccupation with children is at the poem's structural center (lines 19-28). The mother's relation to children receives more attention than any other part of the situation. The center of the poem is also the center of the wife-mother's life in the family home. The husband has his erotic experiment someplace else. When it ends, he goes home to a full family life, while his female lover falls into the loneliness which makes the poem so poignant.

Why is she sad? She cannot neatly detach from him in the way he leaves her, and she has no family to retreat into. For her, the roles of wife and mother would be so time-consuming as to preclude being lover and poetess. Once again, we ran into the facts of sexual politics and daily life—women have a hard time merging domestic life and work life. For the man to have the best of both worlds the women have to give up a full life. His privileges are supported by their lack of freedom. Why can't they do what he does? If it's right, why don't we all do it? If it's wrong, why should anybody have the right to do it? These questions are intended to develop relational thinking from this problem-theme. Somebody's privileges exist at somebody else's expense. What would have to happen for the women to be as free as the man? Well, he'd have to spend more time at home doing childcare and housework, so that his mate could be outside pursuing a work life and erotic experiments. Not only would he have to give up his free time and freedom of motion, but he'd need a change in attitude to allow his mate to do what he does in the world, and to allow himself to do more of what she does, at home. The less privileged women in their separate spheres kept home-fires and love-fires burning, so that he could warm himself at both.

Fires of Reconciliation

The extra privileges of the man not only result in less freedom for the women, but they also separate the women from each other. The side of the triangle connecting the two women has a question-mark on it, suggesting that the women are divided by their roles. In the first classes where I used this poem and triangle problem-theme, I wanted to draw attention to disunity in the less privileged group, caused by the way in which the male exercised his privilege. I was preoccupied with a lesson in solidarity which I thought the triangle made manifest. So, I tested a mode of illuminating this awareness, and came out with some dismal results. I was searching for a model reconciliation between the women, and asked the class what kind of relationship could they invent for the two females in the poem. I asked them to write letters from one to the other. Later, we taped impromptu dialogues between two women students who played the wife and the mistress. My own imagination thought of their reconciliation as a paradigm for the emergence of the women's movement; they might be "sisters" instead of sexual competitors for the man. I didn't mention my expectations in advance, so the women students began their invention of the two characters without being cued by a teacher's lecture on what they should come up with. What they did create made a whole lot of sense, far more than my own abstract conclusions. First in letter form, and then in dialogue, the women expressed anger, bitterness, sarcasm and contempt for each other. There was no model of solidarity or of working through the problem. They leveled hurting blasts at one another. In writing and in speech, they were surprisingly articulate and imaginative. Their characters rang true. I was very taken with their aggressive use of language. In these early experiments, I began to feel closer to the real language skills of my students, displayed in a learning milieu they approved of. I was all set to promote a fast consciousness leap, but instead I got educated about some of their unexpected hidden resources. It supported my own pedagogical testing to discover that they possessed far more skill with words than they will use in ordinary classes. As I sat there in class, listening to the women harangue each other, I had a strange moment of frustration and illumination. A detour around this divisive female reality became necessary.

One Step Back, Two Steps Forward

At first, I thought of inviting some advanced feminists to class, to enact the encounter between the two women in a solidary fashion. The presence of alternate female role models would have been a problematizing form of theater. I approached several women for this but could not get a commitment from them. So, I then backtracked and asked the class to invent confrontations between the husband and the wife, and the husband with the lover. Let's suppose the wife found out about the affair and the man was saying farewell to his mistress. The students took readily to creating these encounters in letters and on tape. They created meek, guilt-ridden husbands, who apologized to their wives for "losing their heads" and asked to be taken back. The wives emerged as tough, angry and hurt. They always took the man back, but on their terms, usually involving the punishment of more housework for the husband and the reward for the wife of more free time outside the home. It was encouraging to see the women negotiating for equality. They were practicing the reconstruction of traditional marriage, as they had defined it on the triangle.

In successive husband-wife exchanges, the female students grew more and more militant. Once the opposing figure was the man who abused them, they grew in assurance. When the man accused the wife of driving him into the arms of the other woman because their home-sex was not vigorous enough, the women responded in terms of the rigors of housework and childcare. They lashed out at the man for expecting the wife to be both a domestic servant and a sexpot. The exchanges on this score became highly emotional moments in class. The women in class laughed and applauded whenever one of them playing the wife gave the husband hell for carrying on behind her back. The women's responses to the men, in the tapes, proved far more articulate and assertive than the men's self-defenses. Male students weakly apologized for being infatuated with the lover. None of the men perceived a social contradiction between monogamy and the aggressive sexuality conditioned in growing boys. How could family life contain their sexuality when they were permitted to have affairs outside and when their upbringing made philandering basic to their validation? These unanswered questions remained in my mind for other class projects. Within the evolving terms of the poem-process, the breakthrough was the spontaneous re-negotiation of domestic life which the women imposed on the men as the condition for their return to the family. As an expression of the students' development, the self-discovery of demanding marital equality was the best place to deepen the discussion. I didn't understand this right away. Before I eventually introduced the writing of marriage contracts, I tested some other ways to examine the problem-theme. The comic irony here is that the class had already embarked on the reconstruction of marriage before I saw it as a key to their development. Neither of us had a conscious grasp of the actual transcendence emerging in front of us.

My attempts to systematize the learning went off in abstract directions. I thought of questioning the alienation of romance from marriage. With a feminist friend, I taped a conversation we had about group living, as a counter-model to the isolated nuclear family. I had an idea that collective family life would ease the economic burdens on parents and would also offer them more free time. The class patiently listened to this tape and firmly rejected it. They were right; it was an unconvincing argument laid out in a teacherly way. From this dead-end I found means to push on to still another *cul-de-sac*. I thought of asking: What did men have to gain from equal rights for women? Specifically, what could a husband gain from an egalitarian marriage? This problem was a whole lot more concrete, so it did provoke more debate. We had been sharing a lot of writing, speaking and analysis which primarily focused on the women's anger, hurt and unmet needs. It seemed obvious to the class that the husband in the poem had had affairs previously and would have them again. However, what emerged as the predominant concern of the men in class were the many bills that had to be paid. Family life was expensive. They were the self-proclaimed breadwinners taking care of the kids and the little woman. They confessed that the burden was heavy to think about. The traditional sexist role models offered the husbands a privilege at a price. Their extra freedom meant having the wife remain as a full-time home-maker and non-wage-earner. This places extra pressure on the men to earn money. They admit the need to have both spouses become wage-workers. The implication of this is a challenge to their image and an invitation to the women to grow more independent, once on the outside bringing home the bacon also. In addition to the need for income contradicting the male need for the breadwinner image, there is also the fact of stress-related diseases afflicting men especially. I raised these questions with poor results. These problems sunk in only slowly, partly because men are defensive about admitting themselves wrong and partly because physical illness is remote from young people.

While the men's development through this evolving poem-theme was slow, the women's growth was accelerating. Their sense of exploitation was clarified by the discussion of male privilege. Confronted with a systematic exposure to their lesser place in marriage, some of the women responded by forming a women's liberation group. It met for an independent study of feminism and then took over the class for several sessions. The women organized a militant discussion of female oppression, to which some men responded by forming an anti-women's liberation committee. The men's group also met privately and then led a class discussion around their ideas. The solidarity of the women students during the men's negative report was startling. The women rose in a body, tore down each of the men's arguments, and nearly hooted them out of the room. Their articulate relation of feminism to their lives was astonishing, as was their self-assurance. They had come very far in a surprisingly short time, and I was not clear how to account for their development. Their change occurred despite my mistakes and detours, and reached an expression far more advanced than I expected. The growth was partly gradual, but there was something *not* incremental in the leap that occurred under the pressure of a direct sexist assault from the men's committee. In these last sessions, I had one of my first experiences of the teacher withering away. The students had emerged subjectively to take command of their learning process. In the heat of the last debates, I had to do and say very little. They fought out the sexist issues on their own while I watched in awed and grateful silence.

Conscious Reconstruction

My first experiment in questioning sexism was satisfying enough to encourage me to try more. In subsequent classes, I introduced the Sexton poem again, and noticed that our dialogues evolved in different directions from the same problem-theme. From the class discussions on sexism and the triangle we flowed naturally into the re-negotiation of marital life. I suggested formalizing the wife's demands on her returning husband through the writing of marriage contracts. My classes readily agreed to this, and we began a component breakdown of the theme of marriage. Eventually, the documents we produced were interesting enough to publish in the school paper, and students took them home to discuss them with their lovers and mates.

With "marriage" broken down into sub-components such as "housework," "childcare," "finances," etc., we formed a work team to draft a model provision for each item. These teams met separately in class, and then reported their results when we reconvened. The class as a whole vigorously examined each proposed section of the contract. Students drew on their own experience for discussing the shape of options. They shared reflections on their own family lives and on the marriages they have seen, as negative models against which they were designing a better example in the contract. The writing of the contracts thus served the dialectical function of orienting students towards their reality in such a way that they were transforming it as they understood it. Each of the clauses in the contracts was accepted by majority vote in class, only after prolonged debate and several revisions. The discussion on "housework" clarified sexist male attitudes towards "women's work." The section on "sexuality" structured for us a deliberate analysis of the mystified question of birth control and abortion. My students come from predominantly Catholic backgrounds, so it was fortunate to discover an organic mode to examine these issues. Further, the item referring to "childcare" brought us into an unexpected discussion of racism. Should couples adopt a child from another race? We considered our attitudes and the projected responses of friends, family and neighbors to a mixed-race adoption. Generally, in class, there emerged a critique of the prejudice they know of in daily life.

In each familiar area of life, unfamiliar analysis propelled close attention to the routine phenomena of marriage and family. It would have been most likely for my students to flow uncritically into matrimony and child-raising, without reflecting on the structure or values involved in such habitually momentous decisions. The poem and the writing of marriage contracts developed in them a critical scrutiny of these life activities. As people became thoughtful, they tended to ask what is the meaning of what I do and what would it look like if I acted on different principles. The questioning of sexism in one area of everyday life led to a democratic remodeling of sex roles in marriage.

Our prolonged attention to marriage raised consciousness about reality and its options, while developing stronger literacy and conceptual habits of mind. The final contracts not only expressed the literate and ideological progress of my students, but they also showed attitudinal biases and cognitive limits. All the classes focused on the single predominant form of mating in society—heterosexual monogamy. Either you get married to a mate of the opposite sex or you stay single. This is a truth in daily culture, so it made sense for the class to ignore collective family life, the single-parent family and homosexual coupling. Another issue left slightly considered is the fact of manipulated consumption in mass culture. Each family is absorbed into a consumer world where it is driven to buy more and more. This places great strain on parents. Consumer-awareness is only briefly problematized as a structural feature of family needs. While the contract-dialogues made good progress in the area of non-sexist childraising, they did not entertain the question of public daycare, to ease the responsibilities on each parent.

Some of these deeper questions emerged naturally in a later course, the one on Utopia, which took a panoramic view towards social reconstruction. The Sexton poem and marriage contracts took shape in first-term writing classes. As the first encounter of my students with liberatory pedagogy and a critical orientation towards their reality, they produced a substantial base on which to deepen social inquiry. From the question of sexual politics, the contracts idea can be applied to other unequal power relationships—parent-child, boss-worker, teacher-student, and doctor-patient—as a mode through which to systematically critique the full range of undemocratic social relations. The imposing nature of daily life liquidates options to mass culture, so it matters for a transcendent class to begin the self-design of alternate models. Critical consciousness is so absent from everyday living precisely because it is a threat to the routine behavior which supports the present society. The process of reconstructive learning fulfills a prophetic cliché—big things can grow from small beginings, extraordinary changes can be provoked from scrutiny of the ordinary features of mass life. Using mass culture against itself is the comic irony of liberatory education.

Note

1. "For My Lover, Returning to His Wife," from *Love Poem* by Anne Sexton (Boston, Houghton Mifflin, 1969). Reprinted with permission of publisher.

APPENDIX
Sample Contracts
(from unedited student manuscripts)

MARRIAGE CONTRACT

I. Raising Children

In order for children to grow to be happy, stable, individuals, they must be reared in an atmosphere of peace and security.

1. Children should not be frightened of their parents. For example, when parents are having an argument or important discussion, it should not take place in the presence of the children, The effects of such an experience is shattering to children. This must be avoided.

2. To encourage children's abilities and talents, give them confidence by consistent praise, build trust, insure love, be patient and understanding. These factors will enhance their self-image.

3. Be a protector in a favorable manner. Do not neglect the children.

4. Children should be disciplined in such a way that they should not lose love or respect for their parents. For example, they must realize their wrong-doing and take their punishment as fair, reasonable, judgement. Of, course, in this action, we must assume that parents will use appropriate tactics. One thing not allowed is cruel beatings by parents towards their children.

5. Sex should not be tabooed. Parents should realize this is a natural drive in humans. Therefore, children should be as free and open about it as seems possible. Parents should have discussions with their children about sex without feeling embarrassed or ashamed.

6. Do not stereotype the child by prohibiting any activity that you feel is not appropriate for their sex .For instance, girls will be allowed to play with trucks and boys will be able to have dolls without any hassle or intimidation by their parents or friends. Children will be able to express themselves, thus giving more room for creative abilities to develop. Parents will let their children pursue what they feel they'll be happy with.

7. In teaching children about other children, parents should not be biased in their opinions. They should encourage their children to have friends in all denominations, but should not pressure the children into it. Parents should point out that there are good and bad types of people in every group. They should not lead the children to believe that because one person from a group is bad that all members of that group are bad.

8. When helping children with problems, parents should remember that they were once kids, themselves.

II. Sexuality

1. Birth Control: People about to enter into marriage should seek professional help from a counsellor or organization in the planned parenthood field, so that they may decide upon how many children they want. The couple should be fully informed of all methods of birth contol. Alternating periods of time should be decided upon for each partner when he or she will choose a method of birth control, during the planned parenthood cycle. Sexual problems after marriage can be solved through help of people who aided the couple in the planned parenthood counseling.

2. Abortion: Abortion must be decided by both parents, since it is a part of both of them. Both parents should know the advantages and dangers of abortion before coming to a decision. There must be a good reason why they want the abortion (either financially, emotionally, or physically). If there is a good reason for the abortion and both parents agree, it should be free and easy for it to be done.

3. Adoption: Coming parents should have time for bringing up children. Parents should be financially stable, could afford at least 20-40 dollars per week to sustain food and clothing per child. The couple should adopt when they feel they are ready to accept the responsibilities of raising a child. The couple must be physically able, and will treat the adopted child the same as the natural children. Race, religion or color should not be instrumental in the adoption of a child. The parents, however, should be informed on the advantages and dangers of such a situation. In some cases, the situation may be delicate and the parents should be advised on what to look out for. Also, if a problem does arise, the parents should consult the agency, and should receive from the agency information of the child's background, so that when the child gets to be mature, they can tell him or her of their past.

III. Family Budgeting

There are many things to do in working to support a marriage and family. If the man works and the woman stays home to take care of the family, this puts a lot of pressure on the man. He has to take care of all the expenses and bills. Both mates should be encouraged to work, outside the home. When a husband and wife each work to make ends meet, the have more love and support for each other. Today's cost of living makes it necessary for both to work to survive and pay their bills and expenses.

1. Before marriage, a couple should decide where and how they want to live, in terms of apartment, house, furnishings, etc, basing their decision on mutual preference and what they can afford.

2. The American Way has been to buy it new, use and destroy it, throw it out and buy it new again. Even early American farmers did this with their soil, using it up and moving west. Old items should be either sold to people who can use them, or they should be refurbished, recycled and reclaimed for further use.

3. People should not have to keep up with the consumerism of other families, because that would only give them a feeling of being an outcast. Whatever a family can afford and is able to manage for its necessities, should be all that matters. Happiness is the place they can consider themselves equal with all other families.

4. Here is a recommended budget: Percentages of monthly income:

Rent....20%	Clothing....5%	Entertainment....6%
Food....15%	Children's needs..4%	Pocket Money...14%
		(carfare, lunch, papers)
Utilities....10%	Car....6%	Medical....5%
Savings....15%		

5. Children's allowance will be given in payment for household chores.

6. The one who should have final responsibility for management of family money is the one with the best head for money. Every family member's wants and needs will receive serious attention.

IV. Coping With Problems

1. Dealing with problems:
a. Discuss the problem like mature human beings.
b. The result must benefit both parties as completely as possible.
c. A decision must not be for the benefit of one's personal gains.
d. The answer must be that which will benefit the relationship only.
e. The mates must be understanding and as considerate as possible.

2. Wrong decisions:
a. Keep cool. Don't get uptight.
b. Re-evaluate the subject.
c. Try the best possible way to understand a new answer.

3. Spur of the moment decisions:
a. When one mate doesn't have time to consult the other, then he or she must make a decision which will benefit their marriage, not only one of them.
b. If the wrong decision is made, refer to section 2, a, b, c.

4. If problems keep occuring, then seek legal help.

V. Housework

Housework is something few people like to do, but which women usually wind up doing. Because of the way sexes are stereotyped in our society, women and men are raised thinking that females should do the housework, while men pitch in sometimes to help the 'little woman'. Its 'racism' whenever you think any special group is better fit than any other group to do menial work. When women, a whole sex, is considered better at low work, that's sexism. Human beings are just human beings, needing and wanting and capable of pretty much the same thing, no matter what age, sex, religion, race or ethnic origin.

1. Housework should be shared between husband and wife, especially if they both hold jobs.

2. The couple should take turns on deciding on who should do the work which has to be done. Neither partner should be told what to do.

3. In case of illness, one mate should take on the responsibilities of the other.

4. Cooking can be done by the mate who enjoys it more, or whose schedule makes it more convenient for him or her to do it. Each mate should teach the other how to cook. Whoever doesn't cook, does the dishes, on any night.

5. In fixing minor and major repairs, the man is more likely to know how to do it, but he should teach his wife how to do them also.

6. Dusting, washing, waxing, vaccuuming, bed-making and laundry and shopping can be shared mutually. Shopping should be done by either but not by both, because if both go they are likey to spend a lot more money than expected, and if the family is very budget-minded, this can be a disaster.

7. If one mate is working and the other is not, the mate working outside the home will be responsible only for weekend cooking, heavy housework, and sharing shopping and laundry duties.

MARRIAGE CONTRACT

I. Housework

Housework should be divided according to who has free time.

Cleaning: Consists of vacuuming, washing floors, doing beds, dusting, etc. The cleaning should be divided between both partners. One should do the floors while the other is doing the beds. This only applies if both people are working. This does not apply if one does not work. The one that stays home should clean.

Cooking: This should be done by the person who is free at that time. And, if both are free they should take turns. Both should do the dishes.

Laundry: Should be decided upon by the couple, according to who has the free time to do it.

Shopping: Food shopping should be done by the one who drives the car or who has time.

Fixing the house: should be done by the one who is capable of doing the job. If both are not capable, hire a professional to do the job.

Car maintenance: is usually done by the man. Gas should be paid by whoever has the car. In doing repairs and in cooking, the partner who is capable of doing either should teach the other.

II. Sexuality

1. Both mates cannot think of only their own satisfaction in sex. They will seek to satisfy their partner.

2. Sex should be an unplanned, private and spontaneous affair between the couple.

3. The couple will acquaint themselves with contraceptive methods. They will decide together which to use and who should use them.

4. Abortion should be decided upon by both the man and the woman.

5. If the couple want children but cannot have them, they will decide on whether or not to adopt.

6. When a child asks about sex, both parents should explain things truthfully to him or her about sexual needs and protection, no matter how young the child. Sex is a natural, beautiful thing, and the parents will treat it as such when answering their children's questions.

III. Raising Children

1. Number of children: the parents should decide on how many they want and can afford, employing birth control as joint effort. They will seek to have adopted children accepted by their parents and friends and other children.

2. Care and Guidance: is the responsibility of the mother and the father. In a household where the father goes out to work, the mother will be the one who gives the most care and guidance. However, when the father is not at work, he should spend his free time with the children. On non-working days, the parents should spend time doing things with the chldren as a family. If both mates work, they should spend equal time with the children.

3. Discipline: The child has to be taught to learn to love himself or herself, because that's where loving has to start, that's what its all about. The parents are responsible for their child's peace of mind. When parents discipline their child, they ought to ask themselves if the punishment is just, and not just means of relieving their anger. A child should be taught to act the same way to others as he or she would want someone to act toward himself or herself. They should not be taught prejudice, but should learn about people for themselves.

4. Allowances: In order to deserve an allowance, the child should work for ː, by doing little chores such as: doing the garbage, straightening their own room, going to the store, and so on.

5. Schooling: The child should be encouraged to pursue his or her own interests. He or she should be sent to a school that will help him to enjoy learning. To help make the child into a good citizen, parents must set an example. Children look up to their parents for direction and want their parents' approval of themselves.

IV. Budget and Finance

If not planned correctly, use of money can bring heart-ache and head-ache. The husband and wife should work and pool their money equally. They should share everything. Here is a recommended budget:
Percentages of monthly income:

Rent....25%   Non-car transport..4%Phone....3%
Food....20%   Electric bill...3%   Clothes....8%
Car....6%   Gas bill....3%   Entertainment...6%
Medical, Dental...3% Insurance....2%   Children's $....3%
Community Fund (Neighborhood Donations)....2%
Savings.........12% (for large purchases and emergencies)

1. If both mates work, earnings should be pooled and all the bills paid. The remainder should go to savings, children's allowances, and the community fund. The family budget should be made up by both the husband and the wife. The finances themselves should be left up to the person best able to handle them.

2. A community fund should be established for the neighborhood from contributions given by each family. In rotation, one family should act as secretary-treasurer for the money. It should be decided as a whole in the community where the money is to be distributed, for community development, entertainment and aid. Such contributions from the family budget are part of being a good citizen.

3. The couple should not have to buy items that are unnecessary for them. They should not have to keep up with the Jones. There are certain items which are luxuries and they should not buy things they can't afford. They should not put themselves into a hole with expenses. If possible, the couple should try to re-use, reclaim and recycle things for their needs.

4. When children reach an age where they have a sense of the value of money, they should be given an allowance, in return for chores. When they reach the age of employment, they should be encouraged to get a job.

V. Leisure Time

1. Vacations: should be taken twice a year, if the couple earn a sizeable income, preferably one in January and one in the summer, all providing they do not have more than two children. The more kids the less chance there is of going on vacations. Split vacations can be permitted, with the wife going one place and the husband another, if both mates agree.

2. Visiting Friends: When visiting friends and relatives, visit those you get along well with. Visit the wife's family as much as the husband's. When either mate goes out alone, he or she should give the other a decent time when the mate expects to return. Also, when visiting friends or relatives, bring something to their house.

3. Daily Entertainment: should be something the both of them will enjoy together. For example, he may play the piano and she may sing for fun. Or if there is a pool table in the house you can use that. Or do what is common, watch TV. When the couple has free time, they should be devoting much of it to playing with their children. Family entertainment can be built around reclaiming, reusing and refurbishing things for the house.

VI. Religion

1. Let the children choose the religion they would like best. Teach them the religion of each of the mates if the mates have different religions, but let them choose.

2. If the mates are of different religions, each should get to know the holidays and holy days of the other mate's religion. When these religious occasions roll around, each mate could be expected to visit family, and eat certain foods. This knowledge of the other mate's religion will help them both know how to celebrate the event, what clothes to wear and what to bring when visiting. The couple can choose to celebrate all the holidays.

3. The couple will decide what church or synagogue they want to be married in, or if they want the ceremony performed by the state.

CHAPTER EIGHT

CULTURE AGAINST ITSELF:

Reflection Through Drama

Solutions in the Problem

Because mass culture is the largest interference to critical thought, it makes sense for liberatory learning to use that culture against itself. This contradictory notion amounts to turning the problem into a source of solutions by studying the things which interfere with study. The critical orientation towards daily life does just that. It abstracts false consciousness so that students can reflect on and transcend the ideas, language, behavior and institutions which limit them. A learning process which translates skill-development through the many themes of everyday living can take countless shapes. The last four chapters reported a number of concrete forms developed in my classroom teaching. In this section, I want to describe a creative writing class where both mass culture and high culture were assimilated for an exercise in conceptual learning.

I taught a basic playwriting course which led to video productions of short student scripts. My students had never written creatively or acted before. Yet, they are literally surrounded by theatrical illusions in mass culture. They watch television, go to movies, and receive information from corporations and politicians through dramatized advertisements. As an enormous audience for video, radio, magazine and billboard commercials, they have been socialized into spectating theatrical persuasions. The information flow goes one way, from the medium to the person. Each student is not trained to analyze critically the messages thrown at her or him or to be a creator of the media filling daily life. A course in dramatic arts and video production can help reverse this domination. My students wind up being inside and outside the medium at the same time. By creating their own video shows, they dissolve the alienation of producers from receivers. For the first time, they experience themselves as artists and as an audience which has shaped the language and images of the medium.

CBS, Eat Your Heart Out

In successive stages, we studied the techniques which underlie fine drama, and used this demystified knowledge to create scenes from student experience. This study not only merged the elements of high culture with the mass video form, but it also served as a means to gain conceptual detachment on daily life. Such a course became a vehicle to critical literacy by orienting creative skills to the flow of mass reality. This process was rich in an empowering *esprit*. Students who began shy or guarded emerged with surprising assurance. They entered doubting their ability to act or to write, and ended with a relaxed confidence. This development was inspiring to all of us. It supports further intellectual growth. They not only gained self-validating skills, but they also shared in a bonding experience with their peers. In the design of self-created media, the class was a communal workshop.

The relation of ego-restoration to intellectual development assumed a high profile in this course because a number of students were in my remedial classes the previous year. As they reappeared to study Utopia or playwriting, I saw that our learning process was achieving a broad impact on their characters. They were writing, reading, speaking and thinking with more care and authority. The limits on their behavior were being gradually shed. In the playwriting class, the containment of their voices and bodies received special attention. They practiced using words and motions to create conscious effects. Mastering literary form was not a mere academic exercise, because it offered them development of nascent resources while it provoked a confrontation with reality. These are daring tasks for students who are largely alienated from school and each other. Their access to creative activity, and their distancing from daily life and commercial media, were eased by the sequential, experiential and integral shapes of the process.

Reflecting on daily existence through self-created media seems like an obvious way to expel mass culture. What is less obvious is the means to evaluate development. I noticed my students' literacy, conceptualization and self-assurance growing week by week and term by term. This growth is hard to measure mechanically, but it is striking when you compare their activity in liberatory and traditional classrooms. From another evaluative perspective, I examined how much of our class dialogues carried over into the scripts. This reflection on my part uncovered for me the different levels of development happening in the process. Our verbal exchanges remained more probing than their dramatic writings. Critical modes emerged rather quickly in thought and speech, and then gradually in writing. To be able to read authentic development in amateur work, I needed to learn evaluation from the bottom up, instead of from the top down. If I could understand the actual pace and structure of the learning underway, then I could design sequential exercises appropriate for my students' emergence.

World of Words

As in the other liberatory courses, I wanted the study of a concrete subject—creative writing—to promote structural perception in my students. Literary technique is a structure for knowing reality. It can organize experience into meaningful shapes. To begin provoking a conceptual habit of mind in the playwriting course, I asked the class to casually systematize the world of words. Systematic scrutiny enables students to decelerate from mass culture. The developmental base for learning in any of these classes is the examination of a body of experience with unaccustomed care. I begin the deliberation by asking: What are all the ways words are used in society? Students list the verbal and written forms of language, on their own at their seats, and then read off their items so that I can record a composite agenda at the board. I next ask them to divide the list into written and spoken categories. They structure the list into opposing groups, and I again hear their distinctions and make a new list at the board. I next ask for the "art" and "non-art" uses of words. They then divide their items into aesthetic and non-aesthetic categories Following this analysis, I go on to question which uses of artistic works belong to the area of drama and which are in art fields different from drama. From here, I ask if they can think up kinds of artistic presentations which do not use words at all. Eventually, we develop the following structural paradigm:

USE OF WORDS
newspapers
magazines
conversations
lectures/speeches
books
advertising
TV/radio

WRITTEN	SPOKEN
newspapers	lectures/speeches
magazines	radio
books	spoken ads
printed ads	

ART	NON-ART
Literary:	journalism
novels	essays in
poems	books & magazines
plays	talking
movies	lectures/speeches
short stories in	textbooks
books & magazines	

Non-Literary:
sculpture
painting
crafts
music

The above layout is simplistic, but it is a useful place to begin orienting students to words in reality. It encourages students to go on to more complex exercises because one part of social life takes meaningful shape from their own structural reflection. Another simple means to demystify art is to present the printed conventions of literature as a visual puzzle. To do this, I draw three models on the board and ask students to identify which is the conventional form of poetry, which for fiction and which for drama:

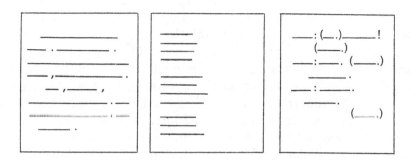

The students readily identify the first as the form for fiction, the second for poetry and the third for drama. As with their itemizing the use of words in society, they discover that they possess some knowledge about the structure and conventions of the thing we will study. This is an encouraging start. Their verbal, written and informational resources serve as the base for more complicated exercises. One of the first problems I pose to evoke more demanding reflection involves the conventional form of drama. Why is a play written out like this? Why does it look like it does on paper? There is a lesson to be learned by simply examining the visual impact of a drama's printed text. Our discussion here has been interesting. We converse on how drama tries to dramatize something. It offers us action and words, onstage and on paper, about a problem or idea. There is abstract meaning behind concrete dialogue and motion. This exploration of specific and general content in drama is a fertile place to study conceptual thought through the study of literary form. It focuses attention on the ideological dimension of single gestures or situations, in plays and in daily life.

The Play's The Thing

To develop abstract thinking, I next offer the class a sequence of exercises based in the simple distinction between the general and the specific. I usually walk over to one student and place a hand on her or his shoulder, and tell the class "Danny is a hero." They stare curiously at both of us. I say, "He really is. I know something he did to prove it." They want to know what. I ask them to imagine my answer. Can they gain a good mental picture of something Danny did, to justify calling him a hero? They sit and think for a few minutes, and then I ask some people to share with us the narratives they thought up. Each person tells a different story, and through their speaking voices, we get a rich assortment of possible situations. They have begun practicing conceptual thought by inventing existential details to validate a general assertion. They connect an abstraction to concrete circumstances. From this start in mental images and verbal story-telling, I next say, "Maria is a good friend." This time I ask people to gain a mental image of the situation and then write it down on paper. I say it's good to try to prove she's a good friend without even using the word "friend" in their stories. Try to convince us just by letting us know what she did. The action should speak for itself. The students focus their attention on the concept and begin writing. After a time, we read our short narratives to each other, and again hear a wide variety of options for realizing a general idea.

Following these first conceptual problems using words, I introduce similar exercises in mime and tableaux. I ask the class to break into groups of two or three, and attempt first in silent motion and then in a frozen scene, to express an idea or feeling, like Fear. Each group practices on its own, and then we perform for each other, discussing the expressive shape of the motion and the frozen bodies. Once again, we get familiar with a variety of ways to express a larger concept. After each group has presented, I next ask them to return to their caucusing and prepare a mime and a tableaux based on whatever idea or emotion they choose. This time, keep the general theme secret from the others in class. As the rest of us watch each team perform, we write down on paper what abstraction is being played out for us. Following each performance, we go around the room and read off the things we wrote down. When we disagree on the general meaning of the action or tableaux, we then have a dialogue on what features of the show could justify reaching that general conclusion. The most interesting moments are when the class disagrees with the group performing on the content of the display. This dramatic and conceptual exercise develops powers of abstraction. In a simple way, it demonstrates the general meaning behind particular impressions.

First Characters: Me and My Shadow

After several weeks systematizing social word-usage, and then creating more demanding expression in general-specific narratives, mime and tableaux, we move on to first efforts in characterization. To make this an exercise in self-awareness as well as in creative writing, I ask students to focus on someone directly opposite to themselves, maybe even someone they don't like. Can they write a description of this person? Each student spends some time thinking and then produces a short composition on his or her opposite. We read these pieces to each other and discuss the range of types we get. Then I ask people to prepare a monologue where their character talks to us about her or his feelings and ideas. What would he or she sound like if we heard them speaking to us? Once again, students compose their speeches and we read them aloud. For this exercise, I bring a tape recorder to class. I record their monologues and play them back, several times. As students hear themselves creating another person, the levels of language and reality become more complex. They hear their own voices creating their self-designed opposites. With growing fascination, they listen attentively to their own work.

It becomes obvious which are the strongest creations. The best characters are models invented by the students themselves, so we initiate aesthetic awareness from their self-generated material instead of turning first to literary masters alien to their culture. Their activity becomes the focus for their further activity. When we re-play the most expressive characterizations, we analyze what contributes to its impact on us. This discussion turns to the choice of words, the kinds of detail, and the quality of the voice reading the narration. As they practice aesthetic criticism, their evaluation calls for making abstract statements on a specific material.

From this early exercise in character-creation, it is easy to attempt a first effort in scene-setting. I next ask students to imagine the bedroom or living room of the person they created. This writing calls upon them to transfer their general appreciation of a personality into a milieu that physically expresses that character. A persona realized in speech now has to be realized through concrete objects. The conceptual dynamic is the same, even as the exercise changes. Reality has several dimensions of meaning. Beneath the surface impression of words, actions or objects there is an abstract content, a more general meaning. To make an ensemble of objects express a personality demands thoughtful and selective scrutiny of details.

We read these writings to each other, again focusing on which environments most successfully conveyed the person's character. From this exchange the next step is fairly natural. We have already created a character in a setting. I ask students to introduce a second person into the scene and invent a dialogue encounter between the two people. The second character can be themselves or it can be another type who they think is opposite to the figure they already developed. As a preparation for further character-invention, I offer to the class an exercise in "point of view." This is a rather simple technique: You are witness to an incident—a young secretary has an altercation with her boss at the water-cooler in the office. He fires her on the spot. Write up a report as if you were a 20 year old office boy or a 50 year old bookkeeper who saw the incident. I ask the women in class to write a monologue for the boy, and the men for the older woman. This challenges students to produce an idiom appropriate for characters very different than themselves. It also calls upon them to imagine the entire scene and decide where their person was at the time. These monologues have been remarkably authentic. The women invent a sexist stock-boy who has lusted after the secretary, and envied the power of the boss to abuse the younger woman. He comes off sounding juvenile and repulsive. The men in class produce an angry bookkeeper who is jealous of the young woman's attractiveness but who also thinks the boss is a tom-catting fool. Each narrative offers special features on the same theme of the young woman finally slugging the boss for all his sexual harassment. We tape these insightful and entertaining monologues. At this point in the sequence of exercises, the class is becoming more confident. An awareness is emerging of its own creative resources. As they read out loud, write, think to themselves and in groups, and hear their voiced creations on tape, they find themselves immersed in their own uses of creative words. Hour after hour of this immersion leads them to value their work, and what comes next.

Two Directions

The class interaction so far has created the conditions for more complicated writing. Following the successful completion of the water-cooler scene, we have moved in two directions at once. On one hand, I begin introducing exercises in dramatic techniques, using themes from daily life as the subject matter. On the other hand, I ask students to take the character they invented as their opposite and compose an encounter between her or him and a second person. The writing of these dialogue confrontations is continued at home as well as in class, and the scenes eventually become the material for our video productions in the school studio.

The kinds of scenes which emerged involved the "generation gap." Inter-generational conflicts in families, at work and on the street, have been the initial focus of the students, who feel oppressed by immediate authorities in their lives—parents, bosses, teachers, cops, etc. The older students wrote this theme from the point of view of a person burdened with too many adult responsibilities. The generational frictions are over money, sex, abortion, birth control, marijuana, clothes, noise and school-work. A second theme which developed portrayed husbands and wives arguing over money and the absence of good times. The working man in each story is pictured as tired, under-appreciated, over-worked, accountable to too many people, short on cash, and stiffly unable to love or to have fun. They developed these themes spontaneously.

Using dramatic form to explore their experience, the students began composing two-character scenes of older working-class men who are disapproving of a young person or a female spouse. After finishing these encounters, we read them to each other, broke into teams of two to dramatize them, and discussed the theme in each as well as its dramatic quality. The social confrontation stirred serious interest, so I asked the class to attempt another scene, using the two original characters, but introducing a third figure. I wanted them to explore a transcendence of the conflict they depicted, through a third person who attempts in the scene to bring the other two together. In the class discussion, I raised questions about how to reconcile the conflicting characters. What did each have to know about the other to hear his or her problem? Why has each become what he or she is? What does each of them need, to change her or him from a character involved in conflict with the other? From this problematic consideration of a social theme they chose for themselves, they transformed their scenes from a two-person confrontation to an encounter involving a third element mediating the divided people.

In this task, their writing skills continued to improve, while their search for transcendence went in many directions. In some scripts, the third person only makes things worse. In other cases, the new character has no impact. In further instances, the bridge-figure manages an unreal reconciliation between the conflicting pair. Some scenes present critical and possible resolutions. By examining the shape of the new scripts, the students did socio-drama. They tested models of social relations. The creative milieu allowed them to explore real conflicts and test some answers. Our analysis of the creative vehicles used to demonstrate a social theme facilitated their development in both writing and the critique of daily life.

While using class time to read, discuss and rehearse the video scripts, we also undertook a formal study of literary technique. I introduced a dramatic exercise for half the session and then we used the remaining time to dialogue on the scripts in progress. Two levels of study offer a refreshing change in the class gestalt.

Formal Technique

The students have been emerging as the subjective actors in this learning process. As they experience their own powers in writing, speaking, thinking and creating, they become ready to absorb and use the range of techniques the teacher knows about. This moment in their development, when they are prepared to receive a formal body of knowledge, turns me into a resource person, one who has studied a specific subject they want to master more fully. Because of their emergence, I am supported in systematically presenting a wide range of dramatic methods, in the form of exercises. The scheme we worked through presents Verbal and Non-Verbal techniques:

VERBAL: imagery, metaphor, simile, intensifiers
        references
        description
        lexicon
        styles of language
        levels of diction
        written motifs
        tone and rhythm
        control

NON-VERBAL:
        mime, tableaux, gesture
        pause, entrance, exit
        noise
        objects
        processes
        scene-setting
        visual motifs

Some of these elements have already been studied in the class process, so this scheme has started its assimilation into our work. The familiar appearance of "mime" and "tableaux" allows students to feel that this agenda is not a new or alien thing but is rather the systematic shape of what we have already been doing. In addition to drawing on our previous work for examples, I also bring sample plays to class, such as Brecht's *Galileo*, because it is a rich example of dramatic methods. Several key distinctions we work on are the absence of the narrator so familiar to fiction, and the dual use of words and actions, language and motion, to create effect. The Verbal dimension involves the creation of expressive speech, while the Non-Verbal modes employ non-speech effects—bodies, objects, motions, sounds, lighting, etc.

    In a workshop format, we practice these basic elements. For "gesture," I ask the class to try body-sculpting. I divide the group in two, and the first half practices shaping its face and body around an emotion, while the other section watches. Then we switch roles. They practice communicating such things as pain, confusion, depression, joy, love, and so on, for each other. I blend into the student audience, withering my presence as much as I can. The half that watches has helped me wither by being actively critical and supportive of the ones who are doing the sculpting. The students' attention naturally drifts away from me because the people who are shaping themselves dramatically are far more interesting to look at than I am. This not only builds conceptual thought, in adjusting your body so that it expresses an abstract idea, but it also builds peer relations. Body-work of this sort releases a lot of energy in class, and has been good fun as well. From here, we go on to do improvisations around an object and a process. Breaking into teams, the class chooses a variety of objects in the room, and then each unit invents a scene around a single thing. Following this, we choose everyday processes like cleaning, cooking, eating, waiting for a bus, and then focus an improvisation around them, performing for each other.

Using the Verbal/Non-Verbal scheme in a supportive learning process, students who had never written or understood drama before suddenly become able to pick up a play or selected scene from a master-work and dissect its technical components. They can then practice these techniques for themselves, in writing and in action. Once they emerge subjectively, they can penetrate the structure of drama with surprising ease. Because it's so much easier to criticize art than to create it, the transition from seeing structure in another's work to using structure in your own work takes more time than the term allows. We make a beginning that is rewarding enough to support fairly intricate exercises. One such exercise offers practice in creating idiom for characterization. I introduce it as the "style grid."

Grid Stars

One of the most difficult tasks of creative writing is to invent an authentic language for every character. Each of us is immersed in the immediate language milieu of our class, race, sex, region, age group and job title. We know who sounds like we do and who doesn't, but rarely do we ever put our own lexicon down on paper, let alone that of others. We do have more familiarity verbally mimicking other classes, races, sexes and regions. If we can gain some detachment on our own speech, we can extract from it a written code for a character like us and not like us. When we perform for each other in class, this is exactly what we are doing—detached listening. Hearing another person attempt an idiom of characterization is a whole lot easier than trying to hear yourself. For this reason, the peer-performance method and the use of tape recorders are aids to the detachment needed for critical judgement. Rarely have students paid such careful attention to their language. Such scrutiny not only decelerates their perception but it also rehabilitates language from the debased communication of mass culture.

As we do dramatic exercises or apply some of the methods to master-works, the class becomes a self-regulating workshop of peers. They correct each other when they detect a deviation from careful practice or from authentic characterization. One exercise which promotes the emergence of self-education uses the traditional division of language into four styles and three levels. The words "hyperbole," "praise," "criticism," "abuse," "formal," "colloquial," and "slang" have already crossed swords with the students, in their prior English classes. It's fair to say that these close encounters of the rhetorical kind have not sunk in. Once a liberatory process is underway, it has the power to assimilate many kinds of learning that never worked before, so I was encouraged to test a grid which might exercise language skills for the creation of authentic characters. What I call the "style grid" is located on the next page.

I offer students a brief explanation of each of the seven title words. There is both a transparent clarity to this grid and an invitation to test it through group study. It also uses one means of simple perception to develop another more difficult one—it moves from vision to writing. I mention simple examples of what a statement would sound like in each of the boxes, and then ask the class to pick something they want to use the grid on, and then divide into twelve groups, one for each square, to write up a sentence talking about their chosen object in the linguistic style appropriate to their section of the grid. The class chose to develop my shirt in the grid, and busily divided into groups to write up statements. After each committee was finished, I drew a large grid on the board and asked a delegate from each group to write grid sentences in their boxes on the board. What they came up with for my shirt is on the page after next.

	HYPERBOLE	PRAISE	CRITICISM	ABUSE
FORMAL	1. Formal Hyperbole	2. Formal Praise	3. Formal Criticism	4. Formal Abuse
COLLOQUIAL	5. Colloquial Hyperbole	6. Colloquial Praise	7. Colloquial Criticism	8. Colloquial Abuse
SLANG	9. Slang Hyperbole	10. Slang Praise	11. Slang Criticism	12. Slang Abuse

The least precise part of this exercise has been the formal statements, which is the language level least familiar to students. The slang variations are the most colorful. They offer us some comic moments, as my shirt gets so much negative attention that I want to never wear it again. We practice rendering other items through this grid, but it is not offered as a rigid formula or as a judgemental scheme. What it achieves in practice is the exercise of linguistic creativity. Students use it as one more means to experience themselves as masters of words. The levels are not ascribed social value; formal is not better than slang. In fact, the slang level is appreciated for a richness of expression missing in the other two. Students gain a re-perception of a language mode uniquely theirs. They begin to see their language as a creative resource, whereas they used to apologize in school for talking wrong. Through the grid they not only master a structural knowledge which has eluded them, but they also address the self-doubt which surrounds their own speech.

Your shirt has a truly beautiful color.	I do very much like that shirt.	That shirt is attractive, but it fits badly.	Your shirt is much too large and in bad taste.
That shirt's really pretty.	It's a nice shirt.	Too bad that shirt's too big for you.	Why'd you pick such a big shirt?
Man, your shirt is dynamite.	I dig your shirt.	Two of you could squeeze into that shirt.	I wouldn't touch that shitty shirt.

Working-Class Heroes

While we practice using the verbal and non-verbal techniques of literary form, we are also developing the scenes for video-taping. In these scripts, two noteworthy, loud characters have emerged. The class chose to name them the Working-Class Hero and the Superstar. These predominant types generally follow the characters of Archie Bunker and Tony Manero (played by John Travolta in the movie *Saturday Night Fever*). The Hero can be young as well as middle-aged. He has a crusty appeal to him, but he is angry, over-worked, irritable, needing money. As a graduate of the School of Hard Knocks, he is worn out from dealing with life's demands. Contrasted to the earthy and rigid Hero, is the funky, hip Superstar. This second character is usually male, sexy, loose, but flaky and phoney. He wears flashy clothes and considers himself sexually irresistible. He is laying his own ego-trip on the people around him. Both the Hero and the Star are portrayed as imposing themselves on others. They are two aggressive male types.

These two characters emerged gradually through the two-stage writing of scripts. First we took the opposite-characters we invented and put them in a dialogue confrontation with another person. Then, we expanded this scene to include the third figure, who attempts to bridge the conflict between the other two. The Hero and the Star sometimes resolve their differences and sometimes don't. There is a realistic stubbornness to their male polarity. Around them, the students create the wives, daughters, sons, lovers and friends who are oppressed by the macho men. The deep roots of these conflicts make their remedies hard to portray. Two sample scenes are included in an appendix to this chapter. The first shows an unresolved confrontation between the Hero and a young woman Star, while the second uses an artificial crisis to bring Hero and Star to an understanding. There are no single or simple answers to the reconciliation of working-class peers, whether divided by age, race or sex.

I did not know that the theme of conflict and reconciliation would play such a prominent role in our work. I was also surprised at the critical view students had of their Hero and Star—they did not glorify Archie Bunker or the disco Superstar (The writing class occurred before *Saturday Night Fever* appeared, so their imagination was not cued by Travolta-itis). I was impatient for their scripts to come up with transcendent models, but what was a legitimate answer? The evolution of consciousness is uneven and unpredictable. So many forces interfere with critical thought. With liberatory classes here and there, change-agents are unevenly sprinkled through mass life—rank-and-file union caucuses, ecology groups, special sectors needing equality, like women and non-whites. The low profile of transcendent options in daily life makes the role of critical education all the more important. Imagination needs transcendent exercise. The one-semester playwriting course cleared some time and space for literary skills and social reflection. The grand finale of this event took place under lights and in front of cameras.

The Last Round-Up

In the college's small studio, we produced the scripts, which varied in length from a few minutes to a half hour. We had to design our own sets, make-up, costumes, props and graphics. The school provided little support and a bare minimum of time in the studio. The students' own commitment to the project served as an in-process test of their emergence. They weathered the obstacles, and devoted hours to rewriting and rehearsing, after class. Some of them played several roles in the scenes. The material and the acting were of uneven quality, but the impact on the class was extraordinary. They became awe-struck with themselves, when they viewed their completed tapes. They brought friends, mates and relatives to share their fascination. They demanded to have the tapes played again and again. When the last tape ended, they wanted to start writing another show; was I teaching a follow-up course?, they asked. They clapped and laughed at the good moments, and acknowledged the unsuccessful pieces. I asked what would we change if we could do another production; they shared reflections on improving the writing and the acting.

This course promoted the long de-conditioning from mass culture. In its reconstructive effect, it influenced some students more than others. The duration was only four months or less, and each class hour was snatched jealously from the students' over-crowded lives and school schedules. The best thing would be to have more time to work together, and to have other liberatory classes for students to enter each term, so that their development is continuous. Unfortunately, only a minority of teachers in the school can continue the process of critical emergence. A non-academic form would also be supportive—like a political theater club. Within these limits, a surprising amount of development was possible. It was rewarding for me to discover how to use all my years of university training in literary form, for an exercise in popular awareness.

APPENDIX
Student Scenes
(from unedited student manuscripts)

"NO SALE"

Setting—Fashionable women's clothes store. Late afternoon. Counters and shelves full of goods—account books and sales slips piled up. Telephone on one counter along with various sized cartons and boxes for clothes.

Characters—Adele—superstar salesgirl (20)
                Harry—working-class hero (50)
                Max—store manager (30)

As scene opens Adele is working hard and fast. She is answering the phone, finishing a sale, folding sweaters, arranging shirts on a counter, unpacking clothes. Now and then she takes time out to puff on a cigarette, but then goes back to work. There is an issue of *Cosmopolitan* on the counter, and Adele holds it up to the light, and arranges her makeup in a mirror, to fit the cosmo look.

Harry enters, sees Adele fixing her face, and frowns at her vanity, Adele takes a while to notice him. Harry is there to buy his daughter a birthday gift.

HARRY: Excuse me, miss but do you work here?

ADELE: (carelessly drops cosmo) Yeah, I do.

HARRY: Can you help me pick out a birthday gift for my daughter?

ADELE: How old is she?

HARRY: Eighteen

ADELE: Oh, old enough to get in trouble.

HARRY: She don't get in no trouble.

ADELE: Oh, she's *that* type.

HARRY: Now, whadaya mean by that?

ADELE: Nothing. Why don't you buy her a nice dress? Something like I'm wearing. (She models her dress for him.) (Harry looks her up and down, half angry, half lecherous.)

HARRY: I wouldn't want my daughter to run around like that. People'll get the wrong impression.

ADELE: About what? You don't like the way I look? Whatsamatter with my dress?

HARRY: Don't get so upset. When I see a young woman walking down the street in a dress with hardly anything to it, and wearing those elephant shoes, and all that jewelry, and makeup, I take it for granted she's a _____, a loose woman.

ADELE: A loose woman? Yer crazy.

HARRY: I'm what?

ADELE: These dresses are the latest fashion.

HARRY: The latest filth. It all pours out of the TV, the movies—a river of filth.

ADELE: That's just like your generation, always complaining. Years ago women had to hide themselves when they dressed. It was a crime to expose your body. Working girls were poorer when you were young and you were all afraid of sex. Now, women can look as beautiful as we are. We're works of art, not creatures of darkness.

HARRY: You call all that makeup and jewelry art? What so art about it? Shoes a foot high? That's art? That's beauty? God help me. If you had to work hard all day you wouldn't run around in elephant shoes and you wouldn't wear a paper-thin dress. You're too young to know how hard it is, *still*, to keep a family fed. You're too busy wearing the latest fashion.

ADELE: I hear that same bullshit from my old man every night.

HARRY: Yeah, well the old man probably gives you too much. That's what's wrong with you young people. You're spoiled.

ADELE: Hold on there, mac. I work my ass off in this store. Life ain't no bowl of cherries. You have some nerve. You old people think you're the only ones who work hard. All of you got no class at all.

HARRY: Yer a little snot-nose. If you were my kid I'd make yer ears ring.

ADELE: Son-of-a-bitch, just try it.

(Max enters. 30 year old manager. He intervenes.)

MAX: What's all the commotion about?

HARRY: Who the hell are you, buddy?

MAX: I manage this joint.

HARRY: At your age? I bet yer losing plenty of dough.

MAX: Listen, buddy, you wanna buy something, or you here to cause trouble?

ADELE: He said I was a whore.

HARRY: She is. Look at the way she dresses. I came here to buy my daughter a birthday gift and the bitch wants me to make my kid look like she does, a ten-cent whore.

ADELE: (to Max) See what I mean?

MAX: Get with it, pop, times have changed. Women are liberated now. They don't hide what they got.

HARRY: You make a lot of dough selling these kind of duds? How much you guys bring in by having the women walk around with their skin hangin' out?

MAX: This is a new age, old man.

ADELE: Right. We show what we got.

HARRY: Yer all cheap. (To Adele) You should be home raisin' the kids and (to Max) you should be diggin' ditches.

ADELE: You should be in a museum.

MAX: Why don't you get your ass out of here and go back to the cave?

HARRY: Be glad to. If this is the new age, you can have it. No respect for work. No respect for morals. Only one big party. I'm goin' home and take a shower. (He spits on the floor and leaves. They shout after him.)

MAX: Use plenty of soap.

ADELE: And scrub hard.

END

SECOND SCRIPT

SETTING: *Joe's place: a neighborhood cocktail lounge, during the interval between the departure of the regular day patrons and the arrival of the younger night set. Joe is behind the bar washing glasses. He turns as Smittie enters. Smittie walks slowly to one end of the bar. He wears a worn black leather jacket, a brown cap covers his graying hair. His crouched shuffle makes him appear shorter than he actually is.*

JOE: Smittie, how are you? What will you have?

SMITTIE: I'm no better than yesterday. *(Cough)* Gimmie a double.

(As Joe pours drink, Smittie squints in the dim light and looks at Joe.)

SMITTIE: You feel all right?

JOE: Yeah. Why?

SMITTIE: You don't look so good.

JOE: Ya know Smittie, that's what I like about you. You always have a kind word for everybody.

SMITTIE: Hey Joe, listen, you really don't look good! You got bags on both eyes and your hands are shaking.

JOE: *(Slightly annoyed)* I had a bad day that's all. *(Pauses, then in a calmed tone)* How's the job? You working any overtime?

SMITTIE: Overtime? I just about get through the day. That God damn shop's so hot...and that foreman, pretty soon if you take a break he'll make us punch the clock. I'm only surprised he don't chain us to the damn machines. Put on some lights will ya. Looks like a morgue in here.

(Joe turns and flicks a light switch and a multi-colored reflector begins to turn around in front of a series of blinking bulbs. The lights, rather than add more illumination, create a psychedelic effect.)

SMITTIE: *(Pointing to the lights)* What the hell's that?

JOE: *(Turning and looking in the direction Smittie points)* Oh, the lights. They're new. I got a young crowd at night. The kids like them.

SMITTIE: Kids, don't talk to me about kids. Whata they know.

JOE: Well...you can't be too hard on them.

SMITTIE: Hard on them? I can't even understand 'em. Your six are killing you. I got two strangers home. I'm not sure if I even got a son. Looks like two daughters. Asked that clown to get a haircut. Ya know what he said, "Pop, you don't dig the style. You don't know where it's at." If I dug a hole and put him in it he'd know where it was at.

JOE: I don't know Smittie, he seems all right to me. At least he ain't like my Bobby.

SMITTIE: Yea, but a father should be able to tell his son from his daughter. Took a couple a days off last month. Thought we'd go huntin. Ya know, up in the woods, figured together...maybe it a been good...we could talk...and what did he say? "He couldn't kill an animal." What aya think a that?

JOE: Well, I'd rather not hunt. *(Shakes head and wipes sweat from his brow with towel.)*

SMITTIE: We're too good to 'em that's why. And these God damn commie, jew, teachers. It's their fault. Puttin all these weird ideas in their heads. Nothin' sacred anymore. They don't believe in nothin' anymore. All they think about is music and free love.

JOE: Ya know, some of that musics not all that bad. It takes my mind off of things. With the juke box, I hear it all. I even bought a few records myself.

SMITTIE: Can't talk to him. Tried to give him some advice...about ya know, be careful, use protection. And what does he say. He doesn't need it. "All the chicks he knows use the pill." The pill! If I ever catch my daughter with them I'll break her ass. Hit me again Joe. *(Smittie shakes his head, rubs his eyes with thumb and forefinger of right hand.)* And shut off that God damn light. All that winking and blinking, I'm goin' blind.

(The front door opens and both men turn to look. Scottie enters; his long blond hair extends below the collar of a colorful, printed shirt. Bell bottomed jeans hide the platform shoes that make him appear taller than his actual six feet. He walks toward the opposite end of the bar. He is casual, relaxed.)

SMITTIE: *(Pointing with his finger and speaking in a tone he does not think Scottie can hear)* Hey Joe, look at that willya. His hair's so long he looks like a broad. Giv'er a drink on me. Ha Ha Ha.

SCOTTIE: You talkin about me old man?

SMITTIE: Ya, your hairs so long you look like a broad.

JOE: *(Interrupting)* Smittie, shhh, leave the kid alone.

SCOTTIE: *(Runs his hand over his hair and says in a barely detectable effeminate tone)* Yes, it is nice isn't it? *(Continues in a more normal tone)* I like to keep it this way so the chicks can run their fingers through it when I'm balling them.

SMITTIE: Balling them? What does that mean? *(Motioning to Joe with both hands, pleading)* Ya see, ya can't talk to them. *(Turns back to Scottie)* Tell me, where do ya get the money to take 'em out. I'll bet you never worked a day in your life.

SCOTTIE: Money! *(Steps away from bar to present a full view of himself to Smittie)* Man look at me. Look at these threads. You think I need money? *(Steps back)*

SMITTIE: You got a name?

SCOTTIE: Scottie.

SMITTIE: Sure fits. Ha Ha Ha.

SCOTTIE: And yours?

SMITTIE: Mr. Smith to you.

SCOTTIE: Like a glove. Like a glove.

SMITTIE: What?

SCOTTIE: Nothing. Never mind.

SMITTIE: I thought all you hippies had beards. How come you don't?

SCOTTIE: *(Motioning with his hand toward his face)* And hide this?

SMITTIE: Ya, we saw guys that looked like you in France. Ya kow what somebody finally did to them.

SCOTTIE: Did you enjoy it?

JOE: *(Turns towards Scottie and speaks in a fatherly tone)* Now son, take it easy. Take it easy.

SMITTIE: What?

SCOTTIE: It's not important. Forget it. *(Turns to Joe)* Joe, have you got the paper?

JOE: *(Takes paper from under bar and hands to Scottie)* You want anything to drink?

SCOTTIE: *(Pauses)* It's a little early. Give me a Seven Up. *(Begins to read paper) Joe pours drink as he turns he drops drink and breaks glass. Both men look up.*

JOE: Damn it.

SMITTIE: There go the profits.

JOE: Yea. That's the third one today. Maybe I'm comin' down with something.

SMITTIE: You ever in the Army?

SCOTTIE: *(No Response, continues to read paper)*

SMITTIE: *(Louder than before)* You!

SCOTTIE: *(Looks up)*

SMITTIE: You ever in the Army?

SCOTTIE: No.

SMITTIE: Why not? Afraid to act like a man. Afraid to leave all the dope and other shit you clowns take.

SCOTTIE: *(Beginning to get annoyed)* Just couldn't get loose from all the chicks.

SMITTIE: Sure all you shits are just the same, let somebody else do your fighting for ya. Hey Joe, I thought you only served men in here.

JOE: *(Annoyed)* Look Smittie take it easy. I had a bad day and I've got a long night ahead.

SCOTTIE: *(A little more anger)* You have a daughter old man?

SMITTIE: Yea. Why?

SCOTTIE: Bring her around. I'll...

SMITTIE: You keep on talking like that and you'll leave here in a basket. I'll rip that ring out of your ear and wrap it around your balls. *(Pointing menacingly at Scottie with finger)* Understand?

SCOTTIE: Hey man, keep it cool. You don't even know what I was going to say. Don't get up tight. I don't want to hassle you. You're old enough to be my old man.

SMITTIE: Old man! Listen, if I was your father I'd cut my throat before I'd admit it. As a matter of fact...*(Gets up and starts toward the other ind of the bar and Scottie)*

JOE: *(Both hands on bar, leaning forward and looking back and forth at both men. His tone is now forceful and demanding)* O.K., now! That's it! Cut it out!

SCOTTIE: *(Putting up his hands palms out as if to hold Smittie off)* Hey wait. Look, forget it. I apologize, O.K. Have a drink. Joe, give my man a drink on me.

SMITTIE: I'm not your man. *(Pounds on bar with right fist in frustration)* And Joe, if you pour that drink I'll never come in this place again *(Pushes money toward Joe)* Take out what I owe you.

SCOTTIE: Cool man cool, you stay at your end and I'll stay at mine.

(Joe takes Smittie's money and puts the change back on the bar. As Smittie reaches for the change he looks up at Joe's face. Joe has become pale and beads of perspiration appear on his brow.)

SMITTIE: Joe, you feel O.K.?

JOE: Yea, why?

SMITTIE: Ya look pale and you're sweating, and look at your hands.

(Joe looks at his hands, they are trembling, takes bar towel ad wipes them. Turns around and looks in mirror, wipes brow.)

JOE: Yea. Maybe I'm coming down with the flu or something.

SMITTIE: *(Doubtfully)* Yea, maybe that's it.

(A brief pause, Smittie is about to leave when Joe utters a low gasp and grabs for his throat. He falls down behind the bar. Scottie runs behind the bar and kneels down beside Joe. He checks his pulse and checks his pupils for dilation. Smittie remains frozen at the bar.)

SCOTTIE: Call an ambulance. He's had a heart attack. *(Smittie does not move)* Call an ambulance!

(Smittie runs for the phone and dials)

SMITTIE: Yea, an ambulance. A guy passed out. We think it's a heart attack. 516 State Street. A bar. *(Hangs up phone returns to bar)*

SCOTTIE: Come here and give me a hand. He's had a heart attack.

SMITTIE: How do you know?

SCOTTIE: Never mind how.

(Smittie goes behind bar)

SCOTTIE: Pick him up and put him on the table. You know anything about CPR?

SMITTIE: No.

SCOTTIE: O.K. don't ask any questions; just do what I tell you.

(Scottie loosens his tie and opens his shirt. They place him with his head hanging over the edge of the table. Scottie takes three quick breaths and breathes into Joe's mouth he then stops and punches Joe's chest hard three times.)

SCOTTIE: Now watch!

(He places both hands together, arms straight, and leans down on Joe's chest compressing it.)

SCOTTIE: You see what I'm doing?

SMITTIE: Yea.

SCOTTIE: O.K. When I stop, you start. Slowly, about one a second.

(Scottie stops and returns to Joe's mouth.)

SCOTTIE: O.K. Start

(*Smittie begins cardiac massage and Scottie begins mouth to mouth breathing. Between breaths he says:*)

SCOTTIE: Slowly, you are going too fast.

(*For a very long pause the only sound heard is Scottie's forceful breathing. Smittie slows they continue this way for about five minutes. Suddenly Scottie stops and checks Joe's chest. Joe shows signs of life.*)

SMITTIE: Jesus, he's breathin. He's breathin.

(*Joe begins to become fully awake. They move him from the table and seat him in a chair.*)

SMITTIE: (*Slowly, softly.*) O.K. Joe, you're all right. Relax, the ambulance will be here soon. Try not to breathe too fast.

SMITTIE: Shouldn't we give him something? A shot maybe?

SCOTTIE: No, nothing.

SMITTIE: You sure?

SCOTTIE: Yes I'm sure.

(*The ambulance arrives and a doctor and an attendant enter. They both act in a quick professional manner. The doctor's dialogue is sharp and concise.*)

DOCTOR: (*Walking to and looking at Joe*) Is this the patient?

SMITTIE: Yea...he's...aa

DOCTOR: What happened?

SMITTIE: He...he...

(*As Scottie speaks Smittie stares at him in awe and nods his head slowly*)

SCOTTIE: He collapsed behind the bar. I checked the carotid artery and his pupils. I got no pulse and his pupils were dilated. He wasn't breathing. We moved him to the table and gave him CPR. After about five minutes he came around.

SMITTIE: That's right the kid told me how.

(*The doctor and attendant move to examine Joe but the camera follows Smittie and Scottie as they return to the bar.*)

SMITTIE: Jesus Christ! We saved his life. Where'd ya learn all that stuff.

SCOTTIE: I was a life guard last summer. I did it a couple of times before, but you know this is the first time it actually worked.

SMITTIE: I can't get over it. We saved his life.

SCOTTIE: Yea. It makes you feel good doesn't it?

SMITTIE: (*As he answers he puts his arm around Scottie and the camera fades to black.*) Feel good. I haven't felt like this in years.

CONCLUSION

CRITICAL TEACHING
AND
A LIBERATORY FUTURE

He does more than treat them when they are ill; he is the objective witness of their lives. He represents them, becomes their objective (as opposed to subjective) memory, because he represents their lost possibility of understanding and relating to the outside world, and because he also represents some of what they know but cannot think.

John Berger, *A Fortunate Man*

The new man and the new woman will not be constructed in the heads of educators but in a new social practice, which will take the place of the old that has proven itself incapable of creating new persons.

Paulo Freire, *Pedagogy-in-Process*

I did more experimenting than usual in the last few years, but I don't know if I collected more anecdotes about exceptional students than other teachers have. Those who make startling progress in my classes have been a lifeline during the tough days. Their stunning growth supported me to find ways of generalizing their development to the rest of the class. My most advancing students rise as models of what even the most resistant can achieve. About resistance, I'm reminded of what I said in the book's Introduction: there are failures accompanying successes in a process where nothing can be taken for granted and nothing is automatic.

In a pervasive mass culture like ours, it makes sense for liberatory learning (de-socialization) to be an unpredictable experience. The transcendent process goes backward and forward, up and down, ahead in an unexpected leap and back in an unanticipated problem. I find it surprising and frustrating, illuminating and rewarding. Clarifying the issues raised in this book has armed me with a knowledge I sorely need in the early years of teaching. For certain, the liberatory enterprise demands a tolerance for anxiety and a disposition to experiment. Teachers who come out of traditional graduate schools are hardly prepared to trust alienated students and an unpredictable process. Learning how to wither, how to problematize daily life, when to intervene, takes patience and humor. When I was able to let myself go into the learning flow, I discovered what I needed to know to do my work. The classroom studies taught me things I did not know in advance of experiencing them. In joining my students' exodus from alienation, I became one more pilgrim soul, in an inquiry that pushed beyond confusion for a break with the past.

Like every other teacher I've met, I had an inappropriate training for all of this. Even after twenty-five years of community college growth, the academy has made little pedagogical concession to the presence of millions of worker-students. Attendance at traditional graduate schools and *the research doctorate* are still the tickets of admission to the professoriat. My story is typical. I was to become a literary scholar as rigorous as the New Critics who trained me in the university. I later found my hundreds and hundreds of literary books to be of small application in the Open Admissions setting sprouting up everywhere in academe. Instead, I experimented with learning strategies and studied my students' reality. I read labor history, political economy, phenomenology of daily life, philosophy of consciousness, sociology of work, social policy, teaching methods, and the history of mass education. As pieces of the puzzle fell into place year by year, I shared spoken and written reports with interested teachers.

It all came together in a moment of grand irony, like finishing a fresco in Pompeii just as Vesuvius heaved. Open Admissions was decimated as we made breakthroughs into cogent liberatory methods. This book is one public record of what was accomplished under some of the most trying conditions. I see this report as a means to resist the erasure of memory; the Open Admissions years in New York were a creative and exciting frontier for cultural democracy. The opening of the colleges to non-elite students was achieved by popular action in some of the most determined protests of the 60s. It is easy in a culture of debased mass communications for memory of the breakthroughs to dissolve. I have recorded my teaching experiments and have related a theory and a social-history underlying them as one means to prevent the forces which ended Open Admissions from ending our appreciation of an episode in social reconstruction. Education and memory are two fronts in the battle for the future.

The shape of memory and knowledge in this book—a joint social history and pedagogy—reflects the Freirian tradition in teaching. As a dialogic educator, I do with myself what I do with my students. I organize for critical study what I learn from my students in a disorganized and uncritical way. In this book, I've presented systematically and critically what I learned unpredictably. Further, I have characterized learning as a broad social problem rather than as a narrow pedagogical or personal one. In considering the contradictions of community college development, the shape of consciousness in daily life, the interferences to critical thought, and a general theory for liberatory process, I was taking a holistic and historical approach to the problems of my work.

We have little choice but to situate liberatory teaching in the anti-liberatory field conditioning the classroom. This kind of project is no different from other exercises in social change, which begin from the concrete reality they are destined to negate. The hegemony of mass culture and false consciousness prevents my students from realizing their transcendent possibilities. This is the reality we confront, for the making of a future which meets our articulate needs. Teaching in this mode is a Utopian challenge to social limits on thought and feeling.

I can't imagine a more optimistic way to go about education. The grand conception of teaching as preparing students for their history-making roles defines our work as the restoration of our full humanity. Perhaps the most breathlessly Utopian aspect is the conviction that critical thought and the practice of freedom are foundations for exorcising mass culture, purging sexism and racism, evoking class solidarity, and initiating social reconstruction. These are the nascent eventualities of dialogic pedagogy, whose model of social relations prefigures a liberatory society. Autonomy, critical thought, and egalitarian solidarity are incompatible with corporate culture.

Critical teaching is one of many politicizing and polarizing forces in the culture as a whole. It plays a contributory and non-measurable role in the process of social change. In a time of insurgent movements, the impact of critical classrooms is visible and immediate. In periods of diffused radicalism or of conservative reaction, the influence of critical learning is low-profile and long-term. The consciousness developed in a liberatory course lays a base for transcendent change which will have to be fought for and won in multiple social arenas. Rejecting domination, such a learning process resists the social transition to barbarism, the final, grotesque possibility of false consciousness. While I find the results of liberatory teaching supportive, I am troubled by the barbaric potential of mass culture and by the uneven development of popular awareness. We need to go farther than the experiments reported in this book.

Behind every alienated face is a compelling story. I have tried to see reality from the eyes of my students. For years, I have studied, written, spoken and thought about my work in teaching. I will go on reflecting for years more and will learn about a thousand new ripples in the sea, but there will always be a thousand more I passed by. I feel pleased to have been at the right place at the right time to become grounded in a transformative social moment, to have shared some change and reconciliation with my students. I encountered things I never knew existed and designed projects I never conceived before. This has been for me one of the inspiring ironies of history.